空间法评论 第5卷
Space Law Review Vol.5
(第2版)

赵海峰 主编

哈尔滨工业大学出版社

图书在版编目(CIP)数据

空间法评论 第 5 卷/赵海峰主编. —2 版. —哈尔滨：哈尔滨工业大学出版社,2016.8(2018.10 重印)
ISBN 978 - 7 - 5603 - 6166 - 6

Ⅰ.①空… Ⅱ.①赵… Ⅲ.①空间法 - 文集 Ⅳ.①D.999.1 - 53

中国版本图书馆 CIP 数据核字(2016)第 191741 号

责任编辑	田新华
封面设计	卞秉利
出版发行	哈尔滨工业大学出版社
社　　址	哈尔滨市南岗区复华四道街 10 号　邮编 150006
传　　真	0451 - 86414749
网　　址	http://hitpress.hit.edu.cn
印　　刷	哈尔滨圣铂印刷有限公司
开　　本	880mm×1230mm　1/32　印张 8.25　字数 255 千字
版　　次	2016 年 8 月第 2 版　2018 年 10 月第 2 次印刷
书　　号	ISBN 978 - 7 - 5603 - 6166 - 6
定　　价	45.00 元

(如因印装质量问题影响阅读,我社负责调换)

编委会

顾　问
  李　巍　工业和信息化部政策法规司司长
  赵宏瑞　哈尔滨工业大学人文社科与法学院院长、教授、博导

主　编
  赵海峰　国家法官学院教授，哈尔滨工业大学空间法研究所原所长

副主编
  李　滨　北京师范大学法学院教授，哈尔滨工业大学空间法研究所副所长
  Fabio Tronchetti　哈尔滨工业大学空间法研究所副所长

编　委
  马新民　外交部条法司副司长
  张振军　中国空间法学会秘书长
  王冀莲　中国长城工业集团有限公司总法律顾问
  Armel Kerrest　法国西布列塔尼大学航空与空间法研究中心主任、教授
  Marco Pedrazzi　意大利米兰大学国际研究系副主任、教授
  Stephan Hobe　德国科隆大学法学院教授，科隆大学航空与空间法研究所所长
  Joanne Irene Gabrynowicz　美国密西西比大学法学院荣誉教授，密西西比大学国家遥感、航空与空间法研究中心前主任
  Frans von der Dunk　美国内布拉斯加大学法学院空间法教授
  Setsuko AOKI　日本庆应义塾大学教授
  Sang‑Myon Rhee　韩国首尔大学法学院教授
  Ram Jakhu　加拿大麦吉尔大学航空与空间法研究所教授、所长
  Tanja Masson‑Zwaan　国际空间法学会主席、荷兰莱顿大学航空与空间法研究所副所长
  V.S. Mani　印度斋浦尔（Jaipur）国立大学法律和治理学院院长、教授

Lesley Jane Smith　德国吕内堡(Luneburg)大学教授
Steven Freeland　澳大利亚西悉尼大学教授
Stephen Barnes　中国政法大学法学院客座教授
李寿平　北京理工大学法学院副院长、教授、博导,北京理工大学空间法研究所所长
张会庭　中国航天系统科学与工程研究院航天信息中心研究员、副所长
龙卫球　北京航空航天大学法学院院长、教授、博导
凌　岩　中国政法大学国际法学院教授、博导,中国政法大学航空法与空间法研究中心副主任
尹玉海　深圳大学法学院教授,深圳大学空间政策与空间法研究中心主任
赵　云　香港大学法律学院教授
高国柱　北京航空航天大学法学院副教授、北京航空航天大学空间法研究所执行所长
李居迁　中国政法大学国际法学院教授、中国政法大学航空法与空间法研究中心副主任
侯瑞雪　哈尔滨工业大学法学院副教授、哈尔滨工业大学空间法研究所副所长
荣吉平　哈尔滨工业大学法学院副教授、哈尔滨工业大学空间法研究所副所长
吴晓丹　中央财经大学法学院副教授,哈尔滨工业大学空间法研究所研究员
高立忠　哈尔滨工业大学法学院副院长、副教授
李晶珠　哈尔滨工业大学法学院讲师
左晓宇　中国航天员训练中心助理研究员
蔡高强　湘潭大学法学院教授、博导
王国语　北京理工大学副教授
主编助理:张　宇　哈尔滨工业大学法学院教学秘书

主　办:哈尔滨工业大学空间法研究所

Editor in Chief
Prof. Haifeng Zhao, Director of Space Law Insitute of Harbin Institute of Technology (H. I. T.), School of Law, H. I. T.

前　　言

《空间法评论》第 5 卷即将付梓。我很高兴，一些名家贡献了他们的大作。首先，各位可以看到空间法学的大家———郑斌先生的译著《月球条约：关于各国在月球和太阳系内地球以外的其他天体上活动的协定》。该文是郑斌先生的名作，现又经常景龙老师的翻译和郑斌先生的校译，其可靠性当然不言而喻。其次，Stephan Hobe 教授的《联合国空间碎片减缓指南》经联合国和平利用外层空间委员会通过又获得联合国大会认可，而 Hobe 教授是外空法方面的名家，其研究深度和权威性难以置疑。同时，本卷还刊登了法国著名空间法学家 Amel Kerrest 的论文。Kerrest 教授在文章中探讨了海洋发射及其对商业的一些思考，尤其对我国载人航天相关法学问题的规制，可以起到启发的作用。

本书作为中英文的发表平台，正在不断增加英文来稿的数量，本卷发表的中国民航大学聂晶晶的作品就属于这种情况。其论文对国际航空和空间法中全球卫星导航系统信号提供者在飞行导航中的责任进行了探讨。

李杜和赵海峰的论文《世界各主要空间法中心硕士点课程体系和考核情况分析》，则是两位作者对国际各大空间法中心硕士点课程体系的详细研究。本卷《空间法评论》为了丰富我们的研究，特别推出了《加拿大政府、欧洲航天局成员国政府、日本政府、俄罗斯政府和美国政府签署的关于民用国际空间站合作的政府间协议》(中、英文)。该协议虽然出台于 1998 年，但意义仍然非常重大。同时，本卷还推出了 2010 年空间法领域的大事记。

鉴于美国的国家航天政策在美国和世界都具有非常大的影响

力，本卷刊登了美国2006年和2010年国家航天政策，突出了文献的中英文特点。

《空间法评论》是哈尔滨工业大学空间法研究所主办的连续性文集。《空间法评论》的出版，得到了中国空间法学会、国防科工局、外交部、中国国际法学会、各兄弟院校、国外空间法研究机构和各位名家学者的大力支持，我们表示衷心的感谢！

赵海峰

国家法官学院教授

哈尔滨工业大学空间法研究所原所长、

人文社科与法学院特聘教授

注：本书在第2次印刷中对部分内容进行了补充及删减，原作者单位、职称和个人简介等，除主编更新外，其他仍保留第1次印刷时的信息。

目 录

□论文

月球条约:关于各国在月球和太阳系内地球以外的其他天体上活动的协定　　　Bin Cheng 著　常景龙 译　Bin Cheng 校
　　……………………………………………………………（1）

联合国空间碎片减缓指南
　　　　　　　　Stephan Hobe 著　侯瑞雪 译　李滨 校
　　……………………………………………………………（31）

海洋发射:对于商业努力的一些思考
　　　　　　Amel Kerrest 著　曹永根 译　张宇　李滨 校
　　……………………………………………………………（50）

Responsibility and Liability of GNSS Provider States in Air Navigation under International Air and Space Law
　　　　　　　　　　　　　　　　　　　　Nie Jingjing
　　……………………………………………………………（61）

世界各主要空间法中心硕士点课程体系和考核情况分析
　　　　　　　　　　　　　　　　　李　杜　赵海峰
　　……………………………………………………………（105）

□学术信息

国际法与外层空间的和平利用研讨会在哈尔滨召开
　　……………………………………………………………（117）

国际空间站政策与法律问题研讨会在北京举行 ……… （120）
亚太空间合作组织国际研讨会在泰国举行 ………… （122）
第51届国际空间法年会在英国格拉斯哥召开 ……… （123）
第53届国际空间法年会在捷克布拉格召开 ………… （124）

□ 法律文件

加拿大政府、欧洲航天局成员方政府、日本政府、俄罗斯政府和美国政府签署的关于民用国际空间站合作的政府间协定（中、英文） 　　　　　　　　　　王　晶译
………………………………………………（125）

美国国家航天政策（2006）（中、英文）
　　　　　　　　　　　　　　　　　　晓　宇译
………………………………………………（185）

美国国家航天政策（2010）（中、英文）
………………………………………………（211）

□ 大事记

外层空间法大事记（2010）　　陈丽君　马闻羲　李　红
………………………………………………（247）

Contents

☐Thesis

Moon Treaties: the Agreements about Activities on the other Celestial Bodies besides the Earth among the Moon and the Solar System
  by Bin Cheng, translated by Chang Jinglong, revised by Bin Cheng ·· (1)
Space Debris Mitigation Guide of United Nation
  by Stephan Hobe, translated by Hou Ruixue ········ (31)
Marine emission: some Considerations for Business Efforts
  by Amel Kerrest, translated by Cao Yonggen, revised by Zhang Yu&Li Bin ································· (50)
Responsibility and Liability of GNSS Provider States in Air Navigation under International Air and Space Law
  by Nie Jingjing ······································ (61)
The Analysis on the Course Structure and its Evaluation of the Master Degree in the World's Major Space Law Centers
  by Li Du & Zhao Haifeng ························· (105)

☐Academic Information

The Conference on International Law and the Peaceful Use of Outer Space held in Harbin ························· (117)

The Conference on the Policy and Legal Issues of
International Space Station held in Beijing ·················· (120)
The Conference on Space Law of Asian-Pacific Region
held in Thailand ·· (122)
The 51th Annual Meeting of International Space Law
held in Glasgow, UK ·· (123)
The 53th Annual Meeting of International Space Law
held in Prague, Czech ·· (124)

☐Documents

Agreement among the Government of Canada, Governments of the Member States of the European Space Agency, the Government of Japan, the Government of the Russian Federation, and the Government of the United States of America concerning the cooperation on the Civil International Space Station (Chinese & English) translated ································ by Wang Jing(125)
U.S. National Space Policy(2006)(Chinese & English)
································ translated by Xiao Yu(185)
U.S. National Space Policy(2010)(Chinese & English)
·· (211)

☐Major Events

Major Events of Outer Space Law(2010)
························ by Chen Lijun Ma Wenxi LI Hong(247)

月球条约:关于各国在月球和太阳系内地球以外的其他天体上活动的协定[①②]

Bin Cheng 著[③] 常景龙 译[④] Bin Cheng 校[⑤]

---

① 译者注:本文(The Moon Treaty: Agreement Goveming the Activities of States on the Moon and other Celestial Bodies with in the Solar System other than the Farth)首次发表于1980年的 Current Legal Problems(第33卷),后收录于 Bin Cheng, Studies in International Space Law, Clarendon Press, Oxford, 1997,根据1997年再版原作译出。

② 首次发表于33 CLP(1980),第213~237页和勘误表。Studies in on Space Law 的再版承蒙 Sweet & Maxwell 的许可。

③ 译者注:Bin Cheng(1921—),中文姓名郑斌,英籍华人,海牙常设国际法院法官郑天锡之子。郑斌先生系日内瓦大学法学学士(Lic.-en-dr.);伦敦大学法律系哲学博士(Ph. D.);伦敦大学法学博士(L L. D.);英国皇家航空学会院士(FRAeS)。郑斌先生以国际法院和法庭适用之一般法律原则(General Principles of Law as applied by International Courts and Tribunals)论文获伦敦大学法律系哲学博士(Ph. D.)学位,导师系乔治·施瓦曾伯格(Georg Schwarzenberger)。郑斌先生系国际法、航空法和外层空间法领域的最重要的权威之一。郑斌先生现任英国伦敦大学航空和空间法荣誉退休教授等职务,曾任伦敦大学大学学院法学院院长和国际法协会航空法委员会主席等职务。

④ 译者注:常景龙(1969-),厦门大学国际法学博士,现任河南科技大学法学院副教授。

⑤ 同注③。

一、序言

《关于各国在月球和其他天体上活动的协定》是正式名称,在其长期的创制过程中,通常称《月球条约》①。即使没有其他因素,由于《月球条约》这一名称的简短,在实践中,它无疑会成为该条约的普遍称谓。该协定于1979年12月18日在纽约开放供各国签署,其具有使国际法中的"全体人类的共同财产"概念生效的第一个条约的盛名。实际上,起草《月球条约》的联合国和平利用外层空间委员会(COPUOS)出其不意地抢先于像拉奥孔②一样的正纠缠于这一概念之中的第三次联合国海洋法会议(UNCLOS Ⅲ)③。迄今为止,国际法把世界三分为:(1)国家领土;(2)无主地:指可以被获得为国家领土的区域;(3)不可占有地:指法律不容国家占有的区域④。现在有了第四类:(4)全体人类的共同财产:此类区域,国家不仅不得占为领土,而且其收益和资源被认为是全人类的财产。因此,尽管仓促及由此带来的简陋成形,《月球条约》仍值得最全面

---

① 如参见,就在委员会第22次会议议程第4(g)项(UN Doc. A/34/20,第ⅲ和第2页)的措辞以后,就《协定》最终达成协议的联合国和平利用外层空间委员会(COPUOS)第22次会议(1979年6月18日至7月3日)报告目录,继续在Ⅱ.A.7中称为"有关月球条约草案"。

② 译者注:Laocoon(拉奥孔)源自希腊神话中的特洛伊战争故事,是特洛伊的太阳神祭师,因警告特洛伊人不要中战争对方希腊人的木马计而连同其两个儿子一起被两条海蟒缠咬而死。现收藏于罗马梵蒂冈美术馆的《拉奥孔和他的儿子们》("the Laocoon and his sons")大理石群雕,又名拉奥孔,由阿格桑德罗斯等创作于约公元前一世纪。雕像中,拉奥孔位于中间,神情处于极度的恐怖和痛苦之中,正在极力想使自己和他的孩子从两条蛇的缠绕中挣脱出来。

③ 参见,第三届联合国海洋法会议(UNCLOS Ⅲ),1979年出版的第8次会议《修订的非正式综合谈判文本》(RICNT), UN Doc. A/CONF. 62/WP. 10/Rev.1;再版于18ILM(1979),第686页。

④ 译者注:就译者所见中文文献,res extra commercium指不可流转物、非交易物;res extra nostrum patrimonium 或 res extra patrimonium 指不可占有物。

地关注。

二、起草历史

(一) 背景

为理解《月球条约》的历史,回顾空间法发展的初期阶段是必要的。最初,非空间强国,除了期望禁止外层空间及天体的殖民主义和军事化以外,还想分享以科学知识、技术和适当时候的其他物质或金钱上的利益为形式的空间探索和开发的一份成果。然而,其所成功地得到的一切,即空间强国在十分重要的 1967 年《外空条约》所授予的,是包括月球和其他天体在内的整个外层空间为不可占有物;当它排除空间强国占有外层空间、月球和天体为领土的同时,尽管存在反对的意见,仍然使其资源可以自由占有①。根据 1967 年《外空条约》,尽管月球和天体被保留完全的和平利用,但外层空间仅被部分地非军事化②。1967 年《外空条约》留给了非空间强国诸多不满。外层空间的利用问题一直保留在外层空间委员会法律小组委员会的议程中。在 1967 年以后,与在月球与天体上活动和来源于其资源有关的建议继续被提出③。

---

① 详见,B. Cheng,'Le Traité de 1967 sur l'espace/The 1967 Space Treaty', 95 *JDI* (1968),第 532 页,第 564~568 页,和第 576~582 页(Studies in International Space Law)第 9 章,V. B:不可占有地,V. E:为所有国家的开发和利用;但,如参见,M G. Marcoff, Traité de droit international public de l'espace (1973),第 665 页及其下。

② 见本页注释①,Cheng 引文,V 以下 [Studies in International Space Law 第 9 章,VI:外层空间的部分非军事化]。

③ 如见,法律小组委员会第 8 次会议 (1969) 上以下各国提议:波兰,A/AC. 105/C. 2/L. 53;阿根廷,A/AC. 105/C. 2/L. 54;法国,A/AC. 105/C. 2/L. 64;阿根廷和波兰,A/AC. 105/C. 2/L. 66(替代 A/AC. 105/C. 2/L. 53 and L. 54);阿根廷、法国和波兰 A/AC. 105/C. 2/L. 69;全部重印于《法律小组委员会第 8 次会议报告》(9.6-4.7.69),A/AC. 105/58,附录 I,第 4~7 页。

(二)阿根廷的倡议

1969年,人类登上月球。第二年,阿根廷向法律小组委员会提出《关于利用月球和其他天体自然资源活动的协定草案》[①]。其第一条明确地宣布"月球和其他天体自然资源为全体人类的共同财产",为促进较高的生活标准和经济社会的发展,所有的人应能够得到对其利用所获利益。该草案进一步区分了原地使用的资源和带回地球的资源[②]。

(三)苏联的建议

在只可以被看作是阻止阿根廷倡议的行动中,苏联于1971年5月27日提议在联合国大会即将召开的一次会议的议程中增加一项新的议题,即"关于月球国际条约的准备"。1971年6月5日,苏联提交其本国的月球条约草案[③]。与阿根廷的草案相比,苏联的建议:(1)仅适用于月球而不包括其他天体;(2)不涉及资源问题。这是使条约达成协议拖延了7年的争议中的两项。事实上,苏联的草案几乎没有超越对1967年《外空条约》的一些条款的详细阐述。1971年11月29日,联合国大会通过2779号决议,除其他事项之外,注意到苏联的草案,要求外层空间委员会及其法律小组委员会把月球条约问题作为优先考虑事项。

(四)初期热情不久遭遇僵局

作为程序性策略的结果,当法律小组委员会在下一年春季开会时,苏联的草案优先于阿根廷的倡议,成为法律小组委员会及其

---

① A/AC.105/L.71 和勘误1。
② 见第3、4、5条。另进一步见阿根廷代表 Mr Cocoa, A/AC.105/C.2/SR.154 (9.6.71),第19~21页;同上/SR.168 (30.6.71),第144~145页;另进一步见阿根廷代表 Mr Delpech, A/AC.105/C.2/SR.190(4.5.72),第41~43页。
③ A/8391、勘误1及附录。

设立的工作组讨论该事项的基础①。工作组兴致勃勃地从事其工作。除了苏联和阿根廷的建议,工作组从美国收到不少于16份的建议,从其他国家(或地区)收到9份建议②。不足一个月,法律小组委员会就已经能够通过一个包括21条内容的初步草案,该草案至少在形式上与21条的最终条约大体相符③。然而,许多条款中包含着方括号括起来的部分,这样的标记意味着其中的内容仍然未能达成一致协议。

当法律小组委员会1973年会议(第12次)继续改进初步草案中一些条款中的措辞时④,不久就发现有三个基本问题不易解决:(1)条约的范围;(2)关于提供向月球飞行的任务情报的时间先后问题;(3)月球的自然资源问题。简言之,主要以解决问题的时机未成熟为借口。在有些国家代表的支持下,苏联反对:(1)把条约扩展到月球以外的天体⑤;(2)在条约中包括涉及月球自然资源的条款⑥。而且,无意接受提供向月球飞行任务的预先情报的要求,该要求与提供"已完成任务"情报是对立的。

---

① 见《法律小组委员会第11次会议报告》(10.4 – 5.5.72),A/AC. 105/101,第18段及附录1。苏联的建议之所以处于比阿根廷建议优先的地位,因为它是提交给联合国大会的,并且是大会的主题,而阿根廷的建议仅是提交给法律小组委员会的。

② 同上。

③ 同上第21段。

④ 见《法律小组委员会第11次会议报告》(26.3 – 20.4.73),A/AC. 105/115,第17段。

⑤ 如,日本,A/AC.105/C.2/SR.187(2.5.72),第3~4页;苏联,同上,第8页;匈牙利,同上,第148页;波兰,同上,第15页;埃及,同上/SR.188(3.5.72),第19页;保加利亚,同上,第29页;捷克斯洛伐克,同上第30页。

⑥ 如,USSR,A/AC.105/C.2/SR.187(2.5.72),第8页;匈牙利,同上第14页;波兰,同上第16页;法国,同上/SR.188(3.5.72),第26页;比利时,同上第29页;捷克斯洛伐克,同上第31页;蒙古,同上/SR.190(4.5.72),第42页。

当非正式的和幕后的讨论无疑继续进行的时候①,官方层面上,尽管联合国大会不断地号召以及一些紧急状态②,虽然,包括由主持过一系列非正式磋商③的奥地利代表详尽阐述的尝试性协定草案在内的被普遍认为具有良好前景的"工作文书"④被提交到法律小组委员会的17次会议(1978年),但在从1973年到包括1979年在内的各种各样的会议中,法律小组委员会取得的进展微乎其微。因此,在广泛的信息交流后,苏联政府在1979年夏季向联合国提出关于1967年《外空条约》的重要性的文件,声称:一些国家完全非情愿地放弃在新条约中引入"共同财产"这一概念会产生威胁,使条约不可能缔结。然而,在法律小组委员会的1978年会议上,奥地利代表提出的建设性建议,为达成妥协打下了良好的基础……⑤

然而,在从1979年3月12日到4月6日召开的法律小组委员会对奥地利代表的"工作文书"花了相当多的时间情况下,似乎难以达成进一步的协议⑥。到这样的程度,以致对该事项的进一步考虑几乎无济于事。

---

① 如参见,N. M. Matte,'Legal Principles Relating to the Moon', 载 Jasentuliyana and Lee (eds.),1 Manual,第253页,又见第267~268页。

② 决议:1972年11月9日2915号;1973年12月18日3182号;1974年11月12日3234号;1975年11月18日3388号;1976年11月8日31/8号;1977年12月20日32/196A和1977年11月10日33/16号。

③ A/AC.105/C.2/WG1(1978)/WP.2 (3.4.78);见 A/AC.105/218,附录I,第2页。

④ 见《法律小组委员会第18次会议报告》(13.3-7.4.78),附录I,第4段。

⑤ 《为有效利用空间技术发展国际合作而指导各国探索和利用外层空间原则条约的重要性》,A/AC.105/219 (15.5.78),第35页。

⑥ 见《法律小组委员会第18次会议报告》(12.3-6.4.79),附录Ⅲ。

(五) 诞生的神秘与奇迹

后来,当外层空间委员会在 1979 年 6 月 18 日召开其第 22 次会议时,其主席在他的开幕词中谈及当年早些时候在法律小组委员会所发生的一切,异常坦率地说:

的确,最终的结果不是十分令人鼓舞,我们必须平静地面对这一事实……只有在成员国(或地区)表现出一种积极的热切期望,让我说,是一种争取必要妥协的更加强烈的政治愿望,小组委员会在突出的问题上才能取得进展……有鉴于此,为了看看是否我们真的不能消除这一分歧,要求我们重新评估各自立场的时间也许已经到来。而且,尽我们所有的真诚,如果我们发现自己不能做到,时间还可能会要求我们把我们的力量献给——至少是目前——其他值得我们关注的有关领域[①]。

正是这样的建议回荡在他们的耳旁,"委员会"建立了一个完全在 Gyula K. Selei 先生(匈牙利)领导下的非正式工作组考虑这一事项。该"工作组"在 1979 年 6 月 26 日和 7 月 3 日之间举行了四次会议。在把大部分论题分流给各小组的新体制下,小组的议题以节约的名义不被公布。事实上,当时的公众被排除获悉发生的事情[②]。后来任何人见到的外层空间委员会的有关月球条约的逐字记录的参考资料是一种含义隐晦的六行(cryptic six-line)报告。在委员会草案报告(A/AC.105/L.113/Add.1)中被冠名"关于月球条约草案"的"第 2 章 A 节第 7 小节"未经投票被全体一致通过[③]。只有在任何人翻开委员会的实际报告时才会发现记录是以一种最真实的方式进行的:

---

① A/AC.105/PV.190 (18.6.79),第 7~8 页。

② 详见 B. Cheng, Convention on International Liability for Damage Caused by Space Objects,载 Jasentuliyana and Lee (eds.), 1 Manual,第 83 页,又见第 89~90 页[Studies in International Space Law 第 11 章,III F.3:报告讨论趋弱]。

③ A/AC.105/PV.203 (3.7.79),第 6 页。

委员会已经以此种方式完成这一事项的工作,并决定向大会第 34 次会议提交关于各国在月球和其他天体上活动的协定草案,以供考虑、最终通过和开放签署……①

由 38 个代表团发起的协定草案,在 1979 年 11 月 2 日由大会特别政治委员会通过②,同时,在 1979 年 12 月 5 日大会本身的 34/68 号决议中通过③,这两个决议均未经投票而协商一致通过。《协定》由联合国秘书长在 1979 年 12 月 18 日开放签署。

由于缺乏官方记录,导致似乎毫无结果和令人丧气的 7 年劳动突然在 15 天的一段时间内开花结果的 1979 年 6 月 18 日外层空间委员会主席所指的政治愿望是怎么产生的,只能是一件推测的事情。答案可以在第二个《战略军备控制条约》(SALT-Ⅱ)中找到,出于巧合,该条约也是在 1979 年 6 月 18 日签署的。在月球条约草案被通过后的外层空间委员会 1979 年会议上,民主德国代表在闭幕会议致辞中所说的话不是没有意义的。他说:

我的代表团希望强调这一思想……SALT-Ⅱ 协定的实施……及它的精神在和平利用外层空间上将会有积极的意义④。

的确,在后来的政治特别委员会上,在提到月球条约草案时,当其他大多数代表团赞扬采用人类共同财产的概念时,那些来自苏联集团的代表最喜欢强调第 3 条中再次确认月球和天体的非军事化⑤。事实上,对于超级大国来说,外层空间规则的政治和军事方面比经济方面重要得多。因此,当 1967 年《外空条约》缔结的时候,L. B. Johnson 总统选择强调的是"它是自 1963 年有限的禁止试

---

① 《外空委员会第 22 次会议(1979)报告》,A/34/20,第 66 段。
② 见 A/SPC/34/SR. 20 (2.11.79),第 9 和 10 段;《特别政治委员会报告》,A/34/664,第 8 和 9 段。
③ A/34/PV. 89 (条文),第 7~10 页。
④ A/AC. 105/PV. 203 (3.7.79),第 19~20 页。
⑤ 如见,民主德国,A/SPC/34/SR. 15 (29.10.79),第 47 段;乌克兰,ibid./SR. 18 (1.11.79),第 49 段;另参见,苏联,见 5 页注释⑤。

验条约以来军备控制方面最重要的发展"①。

三、协定的范围

(一)宇宙的范围

1. 扩展至"太阳系内地球以外的其他天体"

月球条约确切的宇宙范围直到最后一刻还没有得到实质性解决。因而,条约中所有的实质性规定指的仅限于月球。在最终文本里,它们的适用已经由第1条第1项扩展至所有的"太阳系内地球以外的其他天体,但如任何此类天体已有现已生效的特别法律规则,则不在此限"。其很可能意味着约束有关成员国(或地区)的国际法规则。

为了把这种扩展考虑在内,条约序言就在其各段提及"月球及其他天体",然而,也有例外,其第2段和第4段仅提及月球。在第2段省去"其他天体"无疑是有意的,因为它把月球称为"地球的天然卫星"。但是,表示各缔约方切望"不使月球成为国际冲突的场所"第4段的省略,可能引发各种各样的猜测。

无论如何,这种起草方式显然不能让外层空间委员会所有的代表团完全满意,当通过协定文本的时候,外层空间委员会决定通过以下解释性谅解:

由于第1条第1款,委员会同意,包含在第11条第1款中的原则也适用于太阳系内地球以外的其他天体及其自然资源②。

对于协定中单个条款的过度谨慎所带来的问题是,它将把疑问带入所有其他条款中。除了序言的第4段,应当认为这样的疑

---

① 见第3页注释①引文,第534页[Studies in International Space Law 第9章注4及相应正文]。

② 《和平利用外空委员会第22次会议(1979)报告》,A/34/20,第62段。应注意,在大会最后通过时《协定》中的条文编号由罗马数字改为阿拉伯数字。

问是没有理由的。在第1条中写入定义之后,除非另有所指,协定下文所有的对月球的提及将具有第1条所赋予的含义。

2. 包括环绕月球的轨道和其他飞向或飞绕月球的轨道

第1条第2项规定:

为了本协定的目的,"月球"一词包括环绕月球的轨道或其他飞向或飞绕月球的轨道。

在通过协定草案文本时,外层空间委员会对其协议做出如下记录:

第1条第2款提及的飞向或飞绕月球和环绕月球的轨道,不包括仅在地球的环绕轨道上的空间物体的环绕轨道和飞向或飞绕它的轨道,也不包括飞向或飞绕在地球和这些轨道之间的空间物体的轨道[①]。

紧跟协定草案文本的通过,外层空间委员会的美国代表 S. Neil Hosenball 先生就此补充说:

考虑到"仅地球的环绕轨道"这一用语,地球的环绕轨道上的空间物体也是在太阳的环绕轨道上的事实,不会把条约范围内的仅地球的环绕轨道上的空间物体纳入条约范围内;而且,环绕月球的空间物体,当月球环绕地球和太阳运转时,事实上也在条约范围内[②]。

当时未见有异议。美国的表态显然认为太阳在协定范围以内。

3. 不包括循自然方式到达地球表面的地球外物质

在1972年英国提出建议后[③],协定的第1条第3款规定其"不适用于循自然方式到达地球表面的地球外物质"。

---

① 同第9页注释②,第63段。

② A/AC. 105/PV. 203 (3.7.79),第26页。美国代表向特别政治委员会重申,A/SPC/34/SR. 19 (1.11.79),第22段。

③ A/AC. 105/C. 2(XI)/WP. 24 (20.4.72)。

（二）属人范围

根据第 19 条,《月球条约》"对所有国家"开放签署、批准和加入。1975 年《关于登记射入外层空间物体的公约》规定先例之后①,联合国秘书长成为交存当局。

如同联合国在外层空间领域缔结的前 4 个条约,除最后条款外,《月球条约》的规定适用于进行外空活动的任何政府间国际组织,但该组织须声明接受本协定内所规定的权利和义务,并且该组织的多数会员须为本条约及 1967 年《外空条约》的缔约方②。

（三）时间范围

《月球条约》的缔结没有限定时间。据条约第 20 条,任何缔约方有权通知退出本协定,这种退出应在接得通知后一年生效。如果本协定多数缔约方希望修改本条约,条约可被修改。然而,只有在缔约方接受修正案的条件下才对其发生效力（第 17 条）。本协定生效 10 年后联合国大会应将是否需要修订本协定的问题列入临时议程。但在本协定生效 5 年后的任何时候,作为协定保存人的联合国秘书长,经本协定三分之一的缔约方提出要求,并经多数缔约方同意即应召开缔约方会议以审查本协定。基于对有关技术发展的考虑,审查会议还应考虑第 11 条第 5 款规定的开发月球自

---

① 联合国大会第 3235（XXIX）号决议附录。
② 第 16 条;详见第 3 页注释①,Cheng 引文第 588 页及其以下 [Studies in International Space Law 第 9 章, V. G:国际组织]；B. Cheng. 'The 1968 Astronauts Agreement', 23 YBWA (1969), 第 185 页, 又见第 204~205 页 [Studies in International Space Law 第 9 章, VIII. A:人与时间范围]; B. Cheng, 'Convention on International Liability for Damage Caused by Space Objects', 载 Jasentuliyana and Lee（eds.）, I Mamual (1979), 第 83 页 [Studies in International Space Law 第 11 章, V. A. 6:国际组织]。详见 1975 年 1 月 14 日《关于登记射入外层空间物体的公约》第 7 条。

然资源国际制度的实施问题①以及适当的责任规则问题②。

四、全体人类的共同财产

(一)协定的中心

对很多国家来说,焦点和事实上协定的真正存在理由,是协定第 11 条第 1 款所宣告的内容:

月球及其自然资源均为全体人类的共同财产,这将在本协定的有关条款,尤其是本条第 5 款中表现出来。

这一宣告是最初 1970 年阿根廷的倡议所追求的目标。另一方面,直到第二个《战略军备控制条约》协议的达成,全体人类的共同财产这一概念激起苏联的反对,是《月球条约》的缔结被拖延到 1979 年的主要原因之一。

为了理解这一规定,回顾条约的背景是必要的③。在太空时代的黎明,很多人希望外层空间应仅用于和平目的和全人类利益。如上所述,1967 年 1 有 17 日的《外空条约》所给予他们的相当有限④。碰巧,稍后的当年,1967 年 8 月 17 日,马耳他常驻联合国使团代表 Arvid Pardo 大使提出联合国大会第 22 届会议应列入这样一项议程,其题目为:"排他性地保留现有的国家管辖范围以外的海床和洋底用于和平目的及其资源用于全人类福利的宣言和条约"。一件附随的备忘录解释了宣布海床和洋底为"全体人类的共同财产"⑤,以及为实施这一理念起草一项条约的必要性。不管直接由于其自身还是间接由于其国民,对于这些兴趣在于实际地开

---

① 第 18 条;详见以下 IV.L:国际体制。
② 第 14 条第 2 款;详见以下 IV.M:导致损害的责任。
③ 见以上 II.A:背景。
④ 见第 3 页注释②。
⑤ 联合国文献 A/6695 (18.8.67)。详见 G. Weissberg, "International Law Meets the Short-Term National Interest: The Maltese Proposal on the Sea-bed and Ocean Floor", 19 ICLQ(1969)第 41 页。

发洋底资源的国家,潘多拉的盒子才刚刚打开。对于发展中国家而言,这一概念似乎是天赐甘露(manna)①。

因此,联合国大会于1969年12月15日以62票赞同(主要是发展中国家)、28票反对(工业化国家)和28票弃权通过了2574D号决议,决议宣布暂停海床开发活动②。第二年,在1970年12月17日,在2749号决议中,联合国大会"庄严宣布":

国家管辖范围以外的海床和洋底及其底土(以下称区域),包括区域的资源,属于全体人类的共同财产③。

然而,联合国大会决议仅仅是建议,不具有法律拘束力④。起草一项条约以把这一概念转化为条约性法律,建立"当局"以"组织和控制区域内的活动"要留给第三次联合国海洋法会议(UNCLOS Ⅲ)。UNCLOS Ⅲ,于1973年12月在纽约召开了其组织性会议;从1974年6月20日到8月29日,在加拉加斯举行了第一次实体性会议⑤。同时,阿根廷的倡议已经发起了把这一概念适用于月球及其以外的其他天体的一场运动。不管这一用语意味着什么,空间法律人终于被证明其第一次成功地把宇宙的一角在法律上转变为全体人类的共同财产⑥。

---

① 译者注:manna,吗哪——《圣经》故事所述,古以色列人经过荒野所得的天赐食物。

② 联合国文献 A/RES/2574D (XXIV), 9 ILM (1970), 第422页。

③ 联合国文献 A/RES.2749 (XXV), 10 ILM(1971), 第220页。

④ 见 B. Cheng, 'United Nations Resolutions on Outer Space: "Instant" International Customary Law?', 5 Indian JIL (1965)第23页,尤其第33~35页[Studies in International Space Law 第7章,尤其 Ⅷ:联合国大会决议的影响]。

⑤ 参见 A. O. Adede, 'The System for Exploitation of the "Common Heritage of Mankind" at the Caracas Conference', 69 AJIL (1975),第31页。

⑥ 那时在海洋法上的立场,见第三次联合国海洋法会议,《修订的非正式综合性谈判》(RICNT), A/CONF. 62/WP. 10/Rev. 1 (28.4.79), 18 ILM (1979),第686页。

从纯粹技术和法律的观点来看,苏联反对通过这一概念的理由之一,是这一概念缺乏法律定义,以及随之发生的或在将来演绎出所谓的规则和义务的危险性。在提交给有关该问题的法律小组委员会1973年会议的"工作文书"中,苏联做了解释:"这一问题与其说是术语问题还不如说是实质问题"①。在此意义上,1978年奥地利"工作文书"的优点在于通过详细地说明这一概念而固定其内容,从而完全地限制了《协定》中的这一概念。事实上,它是说这一概念在于它不多也不少于《协定》本身所规定的全部实质性义务。奥地利草案的第11条第1款规定:

为了本协定的目的,月球及其自然资源应当被认为是全体人类的共同财产,这将在本协定的有关条款尤其是本条第5款中表现出来②。

在《月球条约》文本的第11条第1款中,通过删除句首的介词短语——为了本协定的目的——以及更换主句中的动词——应当——为现在的陈述式——是,"协定各成员国(或地区)"大概有意将第11条第1款当作是对现行法律原则的宣告。但是,因为限定这一概念的定语从句,无论如何,将依然能防止它们将这一概念理解为,包括没有"在本协定的有关条款尤其是本条(第11条)第5款中表现出来"的条约权利或义务在内。在此意义上,《月球条约》使用的全体人类的共同财产这一概念,并非国际法上现成的一揽子权利责任,更不是创立了一个具有新法律特征区域的协定中许多规定的标签。现在将对这些规定做简要的分析。

(二)国际、和平、安全、合作、谅解、福利、进步和发展

第2条和第4条规定,月球上的一切活动,尤其是包括其探索和利用在内,应按照国际法予以进行。这是一大堆陈腐并且在法

---

① 《法律小组委员会第12次会议报告》(26.3-20.4.73),A/AC.105/115,附录I,第24页。

② A/AC.105/C.2/WG.I(1978)WP.2(3.4.78),重印于A/AC.105/218,附录I,第2页。

律上不具可执行性的劝告,在很大程度上是对 1967 年《外空条约》第 1 条和第 9 条的重复①。其意图是促进国际和平、安全、合作、谅解、福利、进步和发展。

(三)非军事化

第 3 条重复了 1967 年《外空条约》的第 4 条第 2 款,规定"月球应供全体缔约方专为和平目的而加以利用",并且因此应与其从属的 1967 年《外空条约》有相同的法律效果,这意味着全面非军事化和禁止一切军事活动。但是,美国坚持要把"和平的"解释为"非侵略的"以代替"非军事的"②。

第 15 条或多或少地重复了 1967 年《外空条约》第 12 条所规定的相互检查的权利。但是,明确了该权利是为了保证与条约相符合。而且,第 15 条放弃了对等的前提条件③。

第 3 条第 2 款规定:"在月球上使用武力或以武力相威胁或从事任何其他敌对行为或以敌对行为相威胁概在禁止之列"。关于此规定,英国代表在特别政治委员会上做了令人迷惑的声明,说英国已经同意,提到"任何其他敌对行为或以敌对行为相威胁",在理解条约——和因此的禁止——仅仅与月球有关而与地球无关④。根据《联合国宪章》第 2 条第 4 款的规定,在国际关系中,以与《宪章》目的和原则不相符合的任何方式使用武力或以武力相威胁已

---

① 详见第 3 页注释①Cheng 引文,尤其 IV. 1,2 ,5 和 VI. I [Studies in International Space Law 第 9 章 V. A,V. B,V. E 和 VII. A];详见 6(3)条。

② 在《协定》通过后,美国在外空委员会的代表 Mr Hosenball 对此做了澄清,A/AC. 105/PV. 203 (3.7.79),第 22 页。关于 1967 年《外空条约》IV(2) 详见第 3 页注释① Cheng 引文 V. 3;关于美国的态度,详见同上第 606 页 [Studies in International Space Law 第 9 章 VI. C;天体的非军事化]。

③ 关于《外空条约》第 XII 条详见第 3 页注释① Cheng 引文 V. 4 [Studies in International Space Law 第 9 章 VI. D:自由进入];关于《月球条约》下的相互监督,详见以下 K 部分。

④ A/SPC/34/SR. 19 (1.11.79),第 42 段。

经是非法的。那么,这些敌对行为或以敌对行为相威胁是什么行为?因此,根据英国政府的声明,它们似乎在地球上是合法的,而在月球上是非法的。所以,发现法国在签署《月球条约》时,附随的对其签署所做的以下解释是有趣的:

法国的观点是:为了《月球条约》范围内所尽力的领域的目的,其第 3 条第 2 款有关使用武力或以武力相威胁的规定,不能被解释为是对《联合国宪章》所规定的国家有义务遵守在国际关系中禁止使用武力和以武力相威胁原则的再度确认以外的任何含义"①。

(四)不得占有

1. 国家不得据为己有

第 11 条第 2 款重申 1967 年《外空条约》第 2 条所规定的国家不得将月球的任何部分据为己有,就其本身而言,笔者主张,这并不禁止占有月球的资源②。

2. 不得对其表面或表面下层或其中的自然资源享有所有权

第 11 条第 3 款规定:

月球的表面或表面下层或其任何部分或其中的自然资源均不应成为任何国家、政府之间或非政府国际组织、国家组织或非政府实体或任何自然人的财产。在月球表面或表面下层包括与月球表面或表面下层相连接的构造物在内,安置人员、外空运载器、装备设施、站所和装置,不应视为对月球或其任何领域的表面或表面下层取得所有权。上述条款不影响本条第 5 款所述的国际制度。

应当指出,关于自然资源的禁止性规定,仅仅适用于"其中"的自然资源。

---

① 随后被援引于 Nandasiri Jasentuliyana,'The Moon Treaty',载同一作者(ed.),Maintaining Outer Space For Peaceful Uses(1984),第 121 页,第 131 页。

② 见第 15 页注释③Cheng 引文,IV. 2 [Studies in International Space Law 第 9 章 V. B:不可占有地]。

(五)科学调查的自由

尽管1967年《外空条约》在其第1条第3款中主张在外层空间普遍的科学调查自由,而宣称月球为全体人类的共同财产的《月球条约》第6条第1款却反而仅仅提及"所有缔约各国"的自由。无论如何,《月球条约》至少为其本身解决了1967年《外空条约》第2条关于不得据为己有的正确解释所引发的争论。第6条第2款规定,在实施协定或科学调查过程中,缔约方享有以下权利:

1. 采集标本

它们"有权在月球上采集并移走矿物和其他物质的标本"。尽管条约避免使用该术语,事实上它们成了有关缔约方的财产,"它们可为科学目的而使用"。无论如何,《月球条约》赞同为科学目的将标本的一部分提供给其他缔约方和国际科学界的愿望。

2. 使用月球物质以支援任务

缔约方还可以"使用适当数量的月球矿物和其他物质以支援它们的月球任务"。

(六)非歧视地探索和利用的自由

为了促进第4条第1款,第11条第4款宣布:"各缔约方有权……探索和利用月球不得……受歧视"。第8条第1款宣称它们可以"在月球的表面或表面之下的任何地点……"这样做。尤其是,根据第8条第2款,它们可以:

(1)在月球上降落及从月球发射外空物体。

(2)将其人员、外空运载器、装备、设施、站所和装置放置在月球的表面或表面之下的任何地点。人员、外空运载器、装备、设施、站所和装置可在月球表面或表面之下自由移动或自由被移动①。

这些也可以被自由移动。同时,缔约方应谨慎避免妨碍其他缔约方在月球上的活动。发生此种妨碍时有关各缔约方应依照第

---

① 对此推测,无论在轨道上还是在大气层航行,应注意,协定适用于地球之外包括月球在内的太阳系内其他天体(第1(1)条)。

15条第2款和第8条第3款规定进行协商。

(七)建立配置人员及不配置人员的站所的自由

根据第9条的规定,在符合下列规定的情况下,可以建立配置人员及不配置人员的站所:

(1)仅可使用为站所需要的区域。

(2)立即将该站所的位置和目的通知联合国秘书长。

(3)每隔一年向联合国秘书长进行报告。

(4)不得妨碍其他缔约方自由进入月球所有地区。

(八)人员、运载器、装备、设施、站所和装置的法律地位

1. 对表面或表面下层无所有权

安置人员、外空运载器、站所等不产生对月球表面或表面下层或其任何领域的所有权①。

2. 管辖和所有权

这些人员和物项在其相应的缔约方管辖之下,至于运载器、装备、设施、站所和装置,它们的所有权不因其在月球上而受影响②。《月球条约》关于一个国家的人员的意思是不清楚的。这可以看作是指作为一个国家国民的宇航员。如果《月球条约》的第12条第1款与1967年《外空条约》第8条不一致,《外空条约》把管辖权授予人员所属运载器的登记国。如果《月球条约》所指也是运载器的登记国,它就不会明确一名不再构成航天器人员的宇航员的地位。他的管辖国是他的国籍国还是他所属站所的控制国?

3. 空间物体的返还

凡在预定位置以外的场地发现的运载器、装置及装备应依照

---

① 第11(3)条;详见以上第IV.D.2节。

② 第12(1)条;详见第3页注释①引文,IV.3 [Studies in International Space Law 第9章 V.C:登记国的管辖权]。

1968 年《宇宙航行员协定》第 5 条处理①。

4. 安全措施

各缔约方应采取一切实际可行的措施以保护在月球上人的生命和健康并且依照《宇宙航行员协定》对待他们②。

5. 危难

各缔约方应以其月球设施向在月球上遭难人员提供庇护③。

6. 紧急情况

各缔约方如遇足以威胁人命的紧急情况时可使用其他缔约方在月球上的设施。此种使用应迅速通知联合国秘书长或有关缔约方④。

7. 意外。第十三条规定：

一个缔约方获悉并非其本国所发射的外空物体或其组成部分⑤在月球上坠毁、强迫着陆或其他非出自本意的着陆时,应迅速通知发射该物体的缔约方和联合国秘书长。

该规定似乎可以被有力地扩展到月球上发生的所有已知的

---

① 第 12(2)条。详见 B. Cheng. 'The 1968 Astronauts Agreement', 23 YBWA (1969),第 185 页,第 201 页及其以下 [Studies in International Space Law 第 10 章, VI. B:关于空间物体]。

② 第 10(1)条。

③ 第 10(2)条。关于危难,见 Cheng, General Principles of Law,第 75～77 页。

④ 第 12(3)条。此处的"或"是针对已经利用另一方的设施但有关当事方没有外交关系的情况规定的,在设施权属明确的情况下,不直接通知其他当事方似乎有些吝啬,参见使用"和"的第 13 条。第 12(3)条无论如何仅仅是对一般国际法公认的必然行为(紧急避险)的宣示,它涉及获益或致害的偿付。详见 Cheng, General Principles of Law,第 69～77 页。

⑤ 译者注:此处的"或其组成部分"并未出现在《月球条约》的中文本中,但在英文本和法文本有相应的表达。

意外①。

(九)缔约方的各种义务

1. 任务通知

第5条第1款要求各缔约方应向联合国秘书长以及公众和国际科学界提供它们在月球上的活动情报。早期试图要求"发射前充分地"②提供这样的情报,遭到苏联的强烈抵制。现在的"尽快"③提供情报,似1967年《外空条约》④第11条规定的仅限"在最大可能和实际可行的范围内",给各缔约方留下了很多的自由。

2. 预先通知

第一个例外是:如一缔约方获知另一缔约方计划同时在月球的同一区域进行活动时,应立即将其自己进行活动的时间和计划通知该缔约方(第5条第2款)。第二个例外是:根据第7条第2款,各缔约方应尽一切可能预先将它们在月球上放置的一切放射

---

① 参见1968年《宇航员协定》第1条,该条似乎包括了此种情形,并且起草得更好。见以下第10章 VI.A.1:事故的通知。

② 参见美国工作文件,A/AC.105/C.2(XI)/WP.3(11.4.72),重印于A/AC.105/101,附录Ⅰ,第8页。

③ 译者注:贺其治先生的《外层空间法》所附《月球条约》中文本对应于英文本该条约第五条第一款中的"as soon as possible"的词语为"尽快"(贺其治:《外层空间法》,法律出版社1992年版,第339页),而联合国外层空间委员会秘书处网站上的中文本(http://www.oosa.unvienna.org/ Reports/ AC105_722C.pdf,2005-08-17; http://www.unoosa.org/pdf/reports/ac105/ AC105_722C.pdf,2008-08-21.)和联合国文献中心网站上的中文本(http://daccessdds.un.org/doc/RESOLUTION/GEN/NR0/374)对应于英文本该条约第五条第一款中的 as soon as possible 的词语为"立即"。考虑文章作者意图,将"as soon as possible"译为"尽快"。此全篇译文中,在引用《月球条约》条文时,除另有说明和尊重作者原意而稍有差异外,均采用上述外层空间委员会秘书处网站上的中文本)。

④ 参见15页注③Cheng 引文 V.4[Studies in international Space Law 第9章 VI.E:空间活动报告]。

性物质以及放置的目的通知联合国秘书长。

3. 危险现象或有机生命的报告

第 5 条第 3 款对 1967 年《外空条约》第 5 条第 3 款规定的义务略有扩充,要求各缔约方对其所发现的可能危及人类生命或健康的任何现象以及任何有机生命迹象进行报告。

4. 环境保护

根据第 7 条,各缔约方有义务在探索和利用月球时采取措施保护环境,并将它们所采取的措施通知联合国秘书长。如上所述,它们应尽一切可能预先将其在月球上放置的一切放射性物质以及放置的目的通知联合国秘书长。《月球条约》考虑了建立国际科学保护区的可能性。为此目的,各缔约方应就具有特殊科学重要性的地区向联合国秘书长和其他缔约方提出报告。在条约草案通过前,外层空间委员会在其 1979 年会议的讨论报告中说:

委员会同意第 7 条并非意在达到禁止开发地球以外天体上可能发现的自然资源,只不过是这种开发应以对现有的环境平衡产生任何最小限度的破坏或不利后果的方式进行[①]。

5. 发现自然资源的报告

为了便利建立月球自然资源开发的国际制度,各缔约方应在实际可行的范围内,尽量将它们在月球上发现的任何自然资源告知联合国秘书长、公众和国际科学界(第 11 条第 6 款)。

(十)本国行为的国家责任

在 1967 年《外空条约》第 6 条确立先例之后,《月球条约》的第 14 条第 1 款指出,各缔约方对于本国在月球上的各种活动应负直接责任。然而,像《外层空间条约》一样,它没有详细说明,这种责任是否仅扩展到国家领土管辖以及准领土管辖内的活动,或者它是否也适用于其国民在其领土外实施的未经其授权和甚至违反其法律的活动[②]。

---

① A/34/20,第 65 段。

② 参见第 3 页注释①Cheng 引文 IV. 6 [Studies in International Space Law 第 9 章 V. F:国际责任]。

(十一)相互监督

第 15 条承认"每一缔约方得查明其他缔约方的活动……确是符合本协定的规定",因而允许各缔约方之间相互参观它们在月球上的设施。参观国应于合理期间事先发出通知和采取最大限度的预防措施以保证安全和避免不合理的干扰。但是,与 1967 年《外空条约》第 12 条不同,不再受限于对等的条件[①]。

如果协商未果,第 15 条规定,应首先在有关缔约方之间磋商。如陷入僵局任何缔约方可无须征求任何其他有关缔约方的同意,单方面要求联合国秘书长协助解决争端。同样的程序适用于月球上活动的相互妨碍(第 8 条第 3 款)。

(十二)国际制度

全体人类的共同财产这一概念的难题可能在于在某些阶段一个规范的框架不再能满足需要,而需要一个制度性的结构。因此,当前的《月球条约》的规则在月球活动的探索阶段是可以满足需要的;缔约方认为一旦开发月球资源变为可行的时候,就需要更多的规则。因而,写入《月球条约》的全体人类共同财产这一概念的关键性因素是缔约方的承诺,第 11 条第 5 款规定:"一俟月球自然资源的开发即将可行时,建立指导此种开发的国际制度,其中包括适当程序在内"。

第 11 条第 7 款规定:

即将建立的国际制度的主要宗旨应为:

(1)有秩序地和安全地开发月球的自然资源。

(2)对这些资源作合理的管理。

(3)扩大使用这些资源的机会。

(4)所有缔约方应公平分享这些资源所带来的惠益,而且应当对发展中国家的利益和需要,以及各个直接或间接对探索月球做出贡献的国家所做的努力,给予特别的照顾。

根据第 18 条的规定,建立国际制度的问题应在为审查本协定召开的任何会议上予以考虑。召开此会议的问题应自动包括在本

---

① 详见第 3 页注释①V.4[Studies in International Space Law 第 9 章 VI. D:自由进入]。

协定生效后十年联合国大会的临时议程内。在本协定生效五年后的任何时候,经本协定三分之一的缔约方提出要求,并经多数缔约方同意,可召开此会议①。

(十三)导致损害的责任

如果在月球上发生损害,《月球条约》似乎依赖于 1967 年《外空条约》②以及 1972 年《责任公约》③中所建立的责任规则。但是,它承认在月球上更加广泛的活动使详细的安排可能变得必不可少。据第 14 条,它把该事项留给随后的审查会议去讨论④。

五、若干结论

从纯形式的观点看,《月球条约》可能是源于联合国外层空间委员会的五个条约中起草最糟的条约之一,胜于 1968 年的《宇航员协定》⑤。首先,条约对月球这一词语所做的特别扩展可能引起诸多的疑惑。其次,各个条款似乎是被无序地集合在一起。1974年,美国曾建议,为了产生更加"清晰和一致"⑥的效果,重新组织条约的条款。但是,该建议未被重视。

从实质的观点看,确实,条约已经宣布月球和太阳系内地球以外的其他天体为全体人类的共同财产。但是,它的重要性是什么?《月

---

① 见以上 III. C:时间范围。

② 参见第 3 页注释①Cheng 引文 IV. 6 [Studies in International Space Law 第 9 章 V. F:国际责任]。

③ 详参见第 7 页注释②引文,[Studies in International Space Law 第 11 章,尤其 V. B:宇宙的范围]。应当注意,在草拟 1972 年《责任公约》的讨论期间,因在月救或其他天体上由空间物体所导致的对宇航员的伤害和对设施与空间站的损害的问题被提出,但未做特别处理。见第 11 章注 189 相应正文。

④ 见以上 III. C:时间范围。

⑤ 见以上第 10 章。译者注:即 Studies in international Space Law 第 10 章。

⑥ A/AC. 105/C. 2/L. 91 和勘误表 1 (6.5.74),重印于 A/AC. 105/133,附录 I,第 2 页。

球条约》所界定的许多概念,看来好像已经被包括在 1967 年《外空条约》、1968 年的《宇航员协定》以及 1972 年《责任公约》的规则之中。

自然,关键的问题是资源。基于对宣布暂停海床和洋底资源开发活动的联合国大会决议①的考虑,联合国外层空间委员会已通过月球条约草案,关于是否在月球条约中强制实行类似的暂停,就在美国引发了一场大辩论。几乎紧随外层空间委员会的月球条约草案投票之后,美国的代表 Hosenball 先生(也是美国国家航空和航天局的总顾问)立即就说:

月球条约草案——作为国家航空和航天局(NASA)的一名成员,我为之特别高兴——作为许多代表做出妥协的部分,在建立一个国际机制的未决时期,没有暂停天体自然资源的开发。这就可以有秩序地尝试以确定这样的开发在事实上是可行的和实际的。这要通过可能的实验性的开始,然后,试点作业这样一个过程。如果它是实际的和可行的,我们相信,通过这样一个过程我们能学到对类似天体的矿物资源的开发②。

然而,这一观点却受到 Leigh S. Ratiner 先生的挑战。他是华盛顿的一名律师,担任第三次联合国海洋法会议美国代表团的成员并工作多年。他代表对空间潜能利用感兴趣的一个名字为 L-5 协会的组织,于 1979 年 9 月 6 日向美国众议院科学技术委员会的空间科学和应用小组委员会提交了事先准备的报告书。在该报告书中,Ratiner 先生说:

我坚定不移地认为,月球条约以其现在的形式对于与开发自然资源有关的私人企业的空间利用在事实上是强制实行暂停的③。

稍后,他继续陈述道:"也应当注意,它不仅是一个事实问题,

---

① 见第 13 页注释②相应正文。

② A/AC.105/PV.203(3.7.79),第 22 页;详见特别政治委员会美国代表 Petree 先生的发言,A/SPC/34/SR.19(1.11.79),第 25 段:"条约草案没有暂停国家及其国民对天体自然资源的开发。"

③ International Space Activities 1979. 美国第 96 届国会第一次会议众议院科学技术委员会空间科学和应用小组委员会听证会,1979 年 9 月 5~6 日[No.50],第 100 页,又见第 108 页。

而且是一个法律问题,月球条约可以被认为是一个暂停"[①]。Ratiner 先生援引 Hosenball 先生以上陈述的段落,进一步讲究修辞地说:

主席先生,通过其陈述,美国的代表已经明确条约本身不允许开发,有任何疑问吗?

正确的观点是什么呢? 首先,澄清"开发"[②]这一词语的意思是必要的。在条约所涉及的范围内,这一词语的意思尤其应源于第 11 条第 5 款。它规定,当"开发"即将可行时建立一个国际制度[③]。在这一背景中的开发,似乎超出了仅仅是"探索和利用"的范围,涉及为了商业或其他实际的目的,有计划有步骤地占有和利用月球的自然资源。无疑,Ratiner 先生在此意义上使用该术语。在上文引用的段落中,Hosenball 先生第二次使用这一词语时,即当他说"有秩序的尝试以使这样的开发在事实上的可行性和实际性被接受"时,也是在此意义上使用。然而,在同一段落,当他第一次提到"开发"时,即使他不在不同的意义上,也至少是在较为宽泛的意义上使用,它包括"实验性的开始"和"试点作业",与条约所称的"探索"更相符合。在较为宽泛的意义上使用该术语是可能的,例如,Petree 先生的使用。Petree 先生是美国在特别政治委员会的代表,他说:

月球条约没有暂停国家或其国民对天体自然资源的开发,但是,它的确规定,这种开发要按照第 11 条第 7 款和第 6 条第 2 款进

---

① 见第 24 页注释③。

② 见第 2 页注释③。在 Hosenball 先生用到过"开发(exploitation)"一词的两个场合,Ratiner 先生的援引使用了"探索(exploration)"这个词语。然而,这似乎不会以任何方式影响 Ratiner 先生的主张。详见,Ratiner 先生的口头证词中相同的段落被准确地援引,见第 25 页注释①。

③ 见以上四、(十二)。

行①。

包括在条约称为"探索和利用"的第6条第2款中的活动,在"开发"的意思范围内,他在说条约没有强制实行暂停开发,自然是正确的,因为这样的活动是条约明确授权的②。但是,仍然存在的问题是,对于第11条第5款意义上的"开发",条约是否强制实行暂停。

为了回答这一问题,任何人必须从头开始,这个开始就是规定在第11条第2款中的前提,它排除了私人对"其中的自然资源"的所有权③。就资源而言,条约在紧接着的第11条第8款中规定:

有关月球自然资源的一切活动均应适当进行,以便符合本条第7款所订各项宗旨以及本协定第6条第2款的规定。

处理月球的自然资源必须符合该条的规定以两种名义进行,即,或者是根据第6条第2款中规定的科学调查④;或者是符合根据第11条第7款中规定建立的国际机制的目的进行利用和占有⑤。如果这样的解释是正确的,作者亦如此认为,第11条第4款⑥中规定"探索和利用的权利"没有授予与自然资源有关的任何其他的权利,仅仅与探索和利用的形式有关,诸如降落、发射、放置人员和建立配置人员及不配置人员的站所等⑦。

就条约第6条第2款而言,如上文所提到的,暂停是不可能的。的确,Hosenball先生在其谈及以下内容时是正确的。

---

① A/SPC/34/SR.19(1.11.79),第25段以下内容:Hosenball先生在其对众议院科学技术委员会空间科学和应用小组委员会提出的第七个书面问题时似乎以同样的方式使用开发这个词语:见上第23页注释②,第99页。

② 见以上四、(五)。

③ 见以上四、(四)2。

④ 见以上四、(五)。

⑤ 见以上四、(九)。

⑥ 见以上四、(六)。

⑦ 见以上四、(六)和四、(七)。

第 11 条第 8 款通过援引第 6 条第 2 款,明确了:采集自然资源样本的权利并不侵害和没有限制各缔约方在进行科学调查时可使用适当数量的自然资源以支援它们的任务的权利①。

关于第 11 条第 7 款,看起来似乎是,尽管该段规定建立国际机制的主要目的,但它隐含着管辖三种不同的情况。

首先,假定自然资源的开发已经可行和国际制度已经按时建立,很明显,该国际制度将必须与第 11 条第 7 款规定的原则相一致。

其次,第 11 条第 8 款似乎明确了,第 11 条第 7 款同样适用于 Hosenball 先生谈及的开发前作业这一类型,关于此种类型的作业,看来好像条约没有暂停。存在制度没有包括进去的作业,此种类型的作业仍然要根据第 11 条第 7 款进行,是 Petree 先生明确设想的要点。他说:

第 11 条第 7 款,为此种类型的开发规定了框架,因为,预定制度范围以外的成员国(或地区)及其国民所进行的开发仍要符合该款的规定②。

它还可能导致第三种可能性,即对于第 11 条第 5 款意义上的开发已经可行的情况。但是,由于达成协议的不可能性,国际制度还没有建立。当然,国际制度的建立需要另一个条约。成员国(或地区)根据第 11 条第 5 款所承担的义务仅仅是缔约承诺,它意味着成员国(或地区)的义务仅仅是为达成这一制度而善意地谈判,没有义务不惜代价地达成协议③。鉴此,Hosenball 先生在被引用的演讲中说:

在需要为建立这一制度而谈判的情况下,我的政府,根据第 11

---

① 见第 7 页注释②引文,第 22 页。类似的,特别政治委员会美国代表,第 26 页注释①引文。

② 见第 26 页注释①引文,第 25 段;斜体字体为作者另加。

③ 见 Cheng, General Principles of Law, 第 111 页注 27,第 117 – 8。详见 Hosenball 先生对第 8 个书面问题的回答,见第 24 页注释③引文。

条和第 18 条,将竭尽全力务必成功地磋商这一制度①。

Petree 先生在特别政治委员会说得更明白。说他的政府,将"尽一切诚信的努力",以确保磋商"成功地完成"。他补充说:

关于这一制度的会议的每一参与者,应按照他们本国的利益评价会议所产生的条约,他的国家需要一个平衡和合理的,并且得到美国参议院批准的条约②。

因此,当时机成熟时,没有国际制度不是完全不可能的。

如果机会来了,但是仍然没有国际制度,还存在暂停开发吗?尽管倡议最大限度地分享开发利用的国家无疑会赞同一个肯定的回答,哎!客观地分析条约及其历史会倾向于一个相反的结论。首先,条约本身并没有指明有这样的暂停。第二,埃及、印度和尼日利亚在 1974 年提出了一项未被接受的共同建议,该建议所允许的仅仅是"为实验目的的探索"③。第三,考虑到联合国大会决议要求暂停海床和洋底的资源开发的相反性质④,在起草月球条约期间

---

① 见第 24 页注释②。
② 见第 26 页注释①;第 24 段。
③ A/AC. 105/C. 2/L. 97;重印于 A/AC. 105/133,附录 I,第 14 页。
④ 见第 13 页注释②相应正文。

两次重申美国代表主张的没有暂停开发——这一主张没有被驳斥①——肯定会被认为是起草者观点的明确表示。然而，即使处于这样的情势，第 11 条第 7 款的原则也是适用的，Petree 先生的陈述可以被解释为包含了这样的情势。

鉴此，Petree 先生就第 11 条第 7 款所继续讲的内容意义重大：

后者②提供了一种鼓励，因为它减少了国家和私人实体对从事高成本月球自然资源开发可取性的顾虑，以及承认、公平分享由此获得的惠益，需要对那些为开发月球做出直接贡献者、发展中国家和那些为开发月球做出间接贡献者，都予以特别考虑。在空间探索的其他领域，在现有的国际合作条件下，为开发空间应用而发展空间系统已耗费巨资的国家，已经在国际社会中公平地分享着惠益③。

任何人读了这段陈述就会感到空间强国已经在与国际社会其他国家（或地区）公平地分享着空间应用的惠益，以至于，当第 11 条第 7 款被适用的时候，或者甚至在国际制度本身之下，至少在惠益分享的范围内，没有巨大的变化可以期待。

---

① 见第 24 页注释②及相应正文。Hosenball 先生在其对 1979 年 9 月 6 日美国众议院科学技术委员会空间科学和应用小组委员会提交的预备陈述中指出，外空委员会 1979 年的会议之所以能就《月球条约》达成一致，原因之一是发展中国家达成协议不再坚持对自然资源开发施加暂停的条款而搁置建立管理此类开发的国际体制（24 页注释③引文，第 82 页，又见 84 页）。然而，基于上述理由（见第 7 页注释②及相应正文），并没有此协议的记录，如果任何这样的非正式谅解被作为条约预备工作资料对待就会被质疑。至于 Hosenball 先生在其陈述中援引的 1972 和 1973 年外层空间委员会法律小组委员会美国代表的陈述（见第 7 页注释③引文，见 85 页），可以指出（Ⅰ）它们必然会被认为以任何方式作为结论性的条约的适当解释在时间上距最终协议有些久远，以及（Ⅱ）它们在联合国发布的总结性记录中已经被较多地缩减[分别见 A/AC. 105/C. 2/SR. 188 (3. 5. 72)，第 31 页；同上/SR. 205 (19.4.73)，第 112 页]。

② 即，第 11 条第 7 款。

③ 见第 26 页注释①，第 25 段。

然而,这并不是说,国际制度不会建立起来,或者,它建成后,对月球及其以外的自然资源的开发,将不会产生重大的影响,或者对国际法在整体上不会产生重大的意义。但是,正如月球条约的缔结是一个政治勇气,它的实施也是如此。条约引入的全体人类的共同财产这一新概念是否会发展为绚烂的现实,或者退化为虚幻的神话,依赖于在未来的年岁里各缔约方是否能展示出必要的勇气,以不仅遵守条约的文字,而且发扬其精神。

如何探索、利用和开发月球自然资源,见表1。

表1 探索、利用和开发月球自然资源

1. 国家不得占有月球(第11条第2款)
2. 不得对其表面或表面下层或其中的自然资源享有所有权(第11条第3款)
3. 平等地探索和利用的权利(第11条第4款)
4. 有关月球自然资源的活动服从第11条第8款,它依次地提及与下列规定的相容性和一致性:

第6条第2款允许,在科学调查中,(a)采集和移动标本,以及(b)使用自然资源以支援任务。	第11条第7款明确规定建立的国际制度的主要宗旨,包括 (a)有秩序地和安全地开发 (b)合理的管理 (c)扩大使用这些资源的机会,和 (d)公平分享惠益		
	无开发可行性	有开发可行性	
		有国际制度(第11条第5款)	无有关国际制度的协议
没有施加暂停	对实验的和试点的方案没有暂停	制度授权的开发	看来好像:没有暂停符合第11条第7款的开发

联合国空间碎片减缓指南[①]

Stephan Hobe[②] 著   侯瑞雪 译   李滨 校[③]

一、引言

20世纪标志着空间时代的开始。早期只有非常有限的空间成员从事外空活动,并未对外空环境问题给予过多的关注。对于那个时代的两个超级大国而言,外空的资源在任何方面都是充裕的,技术挑战使各种手段合法化。外空中的活动最终被认为对人类自身的利益是有害的,比如说核爆炸可在一个相对小的团体[④]中通过

---

① 本文在提交给国际空间碎片跨学科大会(2009年5月7日—9日在蒙特利尔麦吉尔大学航空和空间法研究所召开)的两篇论文基础上进行了修改和更新。

② Stephan Hobe,德国科隆大学空间法研究所所长,德国科隆大学空间法研究所研究员。

③ 侯瑞雪,哈尔滨工业大学法学院副教授;哈尔滨工业大学空间法研究所副所长。感谢哈尔滨工业大学法学院赵海峰教授所提供的翻译资料和建议。李滨,北京师范大学法学院教授,哈尔滨工业大学空间法研究所副所长。

④ Subsequently Developed into the Multilateral Treaty Banning Nuclear Weapon Tests in the Atmosphere, in Outer Space and under Water, 5 August 1963, 480 U.N.T.S.43.

协商得到禁止。外空成员数量不断增长以及外空利用的多样化进一步增加了外空活动的复杂性和强度。因此,最终在20世纪70年代末产生了有关空间碎片的技术性问题论文。20世纪80年代末欧空局(1988)发布了几个权威性研究和报告,除此之外,美国国家安全理事会(1989,1995)、美国国会技术评估办公室(1990)、国际空间研究委员会(1988)、国际宇航科学院(1993,2001)确认了空间碎片所产生的风险[1]。在联合国和平利用外空委员会有关空间碎片的技术报告[2]中,这种发展至少初步达到了高潮。2007年联合国空间碎片减缓指南——这一报告的最初主题——归功于1999年该报告公布这一事实:"当前的空间碎片环境对地球轨道中航天器构成了风险,这已经成为一种共识。"[3]联合国空间碎片减缓指南进一步确认:"而且,如果碎片在重返地球大气层后继续存在,它对地面也有造成损害的风险。"[4]

然而,恰在21世纪开端之际,人类不得不见证了故意摧毁卫星的两个事例,一个是2007年1月由中国实施的,另一个是2008

---

[1] Perek, Luboś, "Ex Facto Sequitur Lex: Facts Which Merit Reflection in Space Law in Particular with Regard to Registration and Space Debris Mitigation", in: Benkö / Schrogl (eds.) Space Law: Current Problems and Perspectives for Future Regulation (2005) p. 29~46, 40.

[2] Technical Report on Space Debris, UN doc. A/AC.105/720, Report adopted by the STSC of the COPUOS (1999), online: UNOOSA < http://www.oosa.unvienna.org/pdf/reports/ac105/AC105_720E.pdf > accessed 19 March 2009.

[3] Space Debris Mitigation Guidelines of the Committee on the Peaceful Uses of Outer Space, as annexed to UN doc. A/62/20, Report of the COPUOS (2007), no. 1, para. 1.

[4] Ibid.; see also database on reported space objects discovered by Member States within their territories, online: UNOOSA < http://www.unoosa.org/oosa/en/natact/sdnps/unlfd.htmlof space debris impacts on Earth > accessed 6 April 2009.

年 2 月由美国实施的;再加上令人感到意外的 2009 年 2 月美国的一个正常运行的卫星和俄罗斯的失效卫星相撞,每个事件都相当明显地增加了空间碎片污染①。这些事件进一步表明空间碎片问题的助长者同时也是受害者这一二元论。即使假定人类在 21 世纪已经处理了地球轨道上的空间碎片,比光速还快的"曲速"被突然发现能够对空间构成带来巨大损害,而这正是虚拟的星河"舰队企业"的现代版演绎②。空间碎片和其他环境问题不会"消失",而是可预测到它们将成为与外空探测和利用及发展有不可分割联系的一些问题。它们需要由全人类来积极解决。

本文关注联合国空间碎片减缓指南本身在这方面做出的安排。本文首先简要思考有关空间碎片问题的空间法律的适用性;其次,概述指南的历史发展;第三,考察指南的内容;第四,分析指南的法律地位以及在有关空间活动的法律框架中的位置。

二、空间碎片和空间法

很显然,国际社会将空间碎片视为一个问题,因为它对地面和其他仍在履行使命并有功能的空间物体都具有造成损害的潜在可能性。特别重要的是宇航员的安全问题③。尽管联合国指南谈道:

---

① For coverage of these events see online: Center for Space Standards & Innovation < http://celestrak.com/ > accessed 6 April 2009.

② Scharf, Michael P. / Roberts, Lawrence D., "The Interstellar Relations of the Federation: International Law and 'Star Trek: The Next eneration'", 25 U. Tol. L. Rev. 577 (1994), p. 8, "... the Enterprise discovers that persistent warp (faster than light) travel in certain regions of space is causing damage to the very fabric of space, and consequently causing gravitational shifts that change the climates of nearby planets... Perhaps the closest analogy to the hazard described ... is the contemporary problem of orbiting space debris".

③ 见第 32 页注释③和④。

"为未来世代保护外层空间环境的谨慎和必要的一步"①。有争议的是:指南是否意在将外空作为一种没有人造空间碎片的原始状态加以保护,还是在仅仅为了未来世代能安全探测和利用这样一种状态下应该保护外空环境。指南表明,迄今为止的共识仅在于一个工具性的人类中心说视角,这种视角将空间碎片视为地球轨道上的航天器和地球上的地面所面对的一个问题②。在地球附近,空间碎片数量及其预计的增长已经警示国际社会,空间碎片问题是外空活动的一种潜在危险,也是造成地面损害的一种潜在原因③。

迄今为止规范空间活动的国际法律框架并未使用"空间碎片"这一术语——至少是在不考虑以联合国大会决议或其他国际文件和声明的形式体现出来的"软法"体系的时候④。然而,空间碎片和空间法之间的各种"紧密联系",存在于有关为应对空间碎片所导致的风险而采取预防措施的法律义务和权利中,也存在于当这种风险成为现实时所引起的法律后果中。前者处理由空间碎片引起的损害航天器以及地面损害的风险的预防和/或最小化,同时"它自身所要求的"对外空环境的保护。这方面涵盖非常广泛的法律问题,包括制造空间碎片的合法性问题、减缓和治理空间碎片环境的义务,到参与避免碰撞项目以及数据交换,再到积极清除和尽可能回收空间碎片以及资金负担的分摊和技术转让。后者主要提出

---

① UN Space Debris Mitigation Guidelines, supra note 4, no. 1, para. 1, sent. 5.

② See the reflections on the dominant anthropocentric approach in space activities, Viikari, Lotta, The Environmental Element in Space Law: Assessing the Present and Charting the Future (2008), pp. 12 et seq.

③ See the definition of space debris, infra part IV. no. 1.

④ Only the Treaty banning nuclear weapon tests in the atmosphere, in outer space and under water, 5 August 1963, speaks of "radioactive debris" under Article I. 1. (b).

对于空间碎片的责任和风险分担等问题。

下面我将评价联合国空间碎片减缓指南在法律框架中的潜在作用。

三、联合国空间碎片减缓指南的历史发展

关于外空保护和空间碎片减缓的观念多种多样。然而,导致联合国空间碎片减缓指南最终形成的基础是1993年机构间空间碎片协调委员会的成立,这一委员会目前包括10个重要的国家空间机构以及欧洲空间局①。1994年,和平利用外层空间委员会的科技小组委员会将空间碎片作为其议程的正式项目②。科技小组委员会③的1996—1998多年工作计划在1999年完成于有关空间碎片技术报告的公布④,这一报告最初基于空间碎片协调委员会的调查结果。尽管该报告首次从一个技术角度对空间碎片环境问题达成了一种共识,但它却未能以一种普遍接受的方式来界定空间碎片⑤。尽管存在法律小组委员会的强大支持(法律小组委员会在技术报告之后思考了"既存的外空条约对空间碎片的适用性"),然而仍不能达成一致意见,因为一些代表仍然认为这一步骤为时过早⑥。然而,欧洲空间法中心承担了一项有关空间碎片的法律研

---

① Online:IADC <http://www.iadc-online.org/> accessed 19 March 2009.

② UN GA doc. A/RES/48/39, para. 10; UN doc. A/AC. 105/571, Report of the STSC (1994), paras. 63 et seq.

③ UN doc. A/AC. 105/605, Report of the STSC (1995), para. 82.

④ Technical Report on Space Debris, supra note 3.

⑤ Technical Report on Space Debris, supra note 3, para. 6; see also supra note 15, para. 95.

⑥ UN doc. A/54/20, Report of the COPUOS (1999), para. 45.

究,这项研究的结果于 2002 年提交给法律小组委员会①。空间碎片协调委员会再次领先了一步,因为它已经开始考虑碎片减缓措施。科技小组委员会于 2002 年提交了议案②,该委员会于 2002—2005 年的多年工作计划确立了如下目标:"加快国际上对自愿减缓碎片措施的采纳",并预见在 2004 年"小组委员会可能希望对空间碎片协调委员会关于空间碎片减缓的建议的适用提供支持,以此作为指南通过国内机构在一种自愿基础上实施"③。

在 2004 年,科技小组委员会对空间碎片协调委员会的指南进行了评价,其观点可表达为"认可空间碎片协调委员会关于空间碎片减缓的建议为时过早,是因为以下事实:这些建议与一些成员国(或地区)的空间碎片减缓实践不相符,并需要根据成员国(或地区)的意见进行审核和更新"④。其中包含的观点是:"要开启制定一个新文件的工作,这一工作应该基于空间碎片协调委员会的指南,但要在小组委员会的框架下发展,并由和平利用外空委员会和大会批准⑤。"

甚至在 2004 年 10 月,通过空间碎片协调委员会与有利害关系的和平利用外层空间委员会成员国(或地区)之间在闭会期间的协商,科技小组委员会开始发展它们自己的一套减缓碎片指南,这一

---

① European Centre for Space Law, "Analysis of Legal Aspects of Space Debris", UN doc. A/AC. 105/C. 2/2002/CRP. 5(27 March 2002), in: Böckstiegel/Benkö/Hobe (eds.), Space Law: Basic Legal Documents (2008) Vol. 2 B. III. 14.; UN doc. A/56/20, Report of the COPUOS (2001), paras. 184 et seq.; UN doc. A/57/20, Report of the COPUOS (2002), paras. 176 et seq.

② Inter-Agency Space Debris Coordination Committee space debris mitigation guidelines, as annexed to UN doc. A/AC. 105/C. I./L. 260 (2002).

③ UN doc. A/AC. 105/761, Report of the STSC (2001), paras. 128 et seq.

④ UN doc. A/AC. 105/823, Report of the STSC (2004), para. 97.

⑤ Ibid, para. 98.

工作包含在其2005—2007年[①]的多年工作计划中,建立在以下几个因素之基础上:

(1)该指南将使用机构间空间碎片协调委员会空间碎片减缓指南(A/AC.105/C.1/L.260)的技术内容作为基础。

(2)该指南在技术上不会比机构间空间碎片协调委员会空间碎片减缓指南更为严格。

(3)该指南在国际法上不具有法律约束力。

(4)空间碎片减缓的实施保持自愿并应通过国内机构执行。

(5)该指南会确认例外可能被证明为合理。

(6)该指南是现行的文件,可以根据有关空间碎片减缓的国内和国际发展实践进行定期修正。

(7)该指南适用于任务规划、新设计的航天器和轨道级的运行,如有可能也适用于既存的航天器和轨道级(orbital stages)。

(8)该指南会考虑有关外空的联合国条约和原则。

(9)空间碎片减缓文件要成为一个包含高质量指南的简明文件,并参照机构间空间碎片协调委员会空间碎片减缓指南。该文件包括由工作组在其工作计划中所决定的几个附件[②]。

按照以上这些因素,科技小组委员会的指南在2007年[③]被通过,并在此后得到联合国和平利用外层空间委员会[④]和大会[⑤]的认可。最终,法律小组委员会对"与空间碎片减缓措施有关的国内机

---

① UN doc. A/AC.105/848, Report of the STSC (2005), para. 95 and annex II; UN doc. A/60/20, para. 126.

② UN doc. A/AC.105/848, Report of the STSC (2005), annex II para. 5.

③ UN doc. A/AC.105/890, Report of the STSC (2007), paras. 96 et seq. and annex IV.

④ UN doc. A/62/20, Report of the COPUOS (2007), paras. 117 et seq. and annex.

⑤ UN GA doc. A/RES/62/217, para. 26 "Endorses the Space Debris Mitigation Guidelines of the Committee on the Peaceful Uses of Outer Space".

构信息的一般交换"这一新议题达成一致。该议题将包括在其2009年的议程中①,但是仍未能讨论与空间碎片有关的法律问题。

四、联合国空间碎片减缓指南的内容

（一）空间碎片的定义

1999年关于空间碎片的技术报告所不能达到的目标,2007年联合国指南达到了。该指南提供了首个在国际上获得认可的空间碎片的定义,即"在地球轨道上或重新返回大气层的不具有功能性的所有人造物体,包括由此产生的碎片和成分"②。

尽管该定义仅限于空间碎片减缓文件的目的,但是,这一定义可引导对空间碎片的技术和法律含义的进一步探讨。由联合国指南所采纳的定义——来源于空间碎片协调委员会的指南③——排除自然的碎片,比如说流星（与美国所采纳的空间碎片定义相对比,美国空间碎片是指轨道碎片④)并且仅包括一个特定场所的物体,即地球轨道上的或那些重返大气层的碎片。然而,这一定义包括各种非功能性的物体。"功能性"到底是一个客观的标准,还是仅由登记国主观上决定,这个有争议的问题仍未解决。

（二）指南的适用

联合国指南仅适用于任务规划、新设计的航天器和轨道级(orbital stages)的运作,"如有可能"也适用于既存的那些航天器和轨

---

① UN doc. A/AC. 105/917, Report of the LSC (2008), para. 150; UN doc. A/63/20, Report of the COPUOS (2008), para. 117; UN GA doc. A/RES/63/90, para. 4.

② UN Space Debris Mitigation Guidelines, supra note 27, no. 1, para. 1.

③ IADC Space Debris Mitigation Guidelines, IADC – 02 – 01, Revision 1 (September 2007), online: IADC <http://www.iadc – online.org/>, no. 3.1.

④ ECSL, "Analysis of Legal Aspects of Space Debris", supra note 19, no. 1 lit. a.

道级①。通过采纳一种实践性的以未来为趋向的进路,这种进路很明显考虑了经济上的理由,适用的范围因此避免了一种"追溯效力"②。

（三）指南的范围

联合国指南并不关注宣布特定的空间活动不合法,甚至有关故意摧毁这种非常有争议的问题本身可能并不被禁止。它们关注的是:为了防止空间活动的有害影响、后果或副产品或至少使有害影响、后果或副产品等最小化,如何在原则上开展空间活动。

指南1在这方面是有代表性的,因为它规定"空间制度应当被设计为不在正常运转期间释放碎片",即在从事总体上完全合法的空间活动时,也应防止空间碎片的产生。指南2进一步规定"如果这不可行,任何碎片释放对外空环境的影响都应该被最小化",即如果不能在整体上防止空间碎片的释放,那么其影响要被最小化。其他指南也关注有关空间碎片产生的"可能性的减少"、可能性的"限制"和"潜在性的最小化"。

然而,联合国指南并未对空间碎片环境的补救(即对既存的空间碎片的积极清除以及对经济负担的分配)给出任何引导,这可能变成一个相关的问题,因为仅有减缓概念不能使空间碎片环境稳定化③。它对责任和义务、风险分配或有关保险事项等问题也未给出任何进一步的引导。指南并未提供任何关于如何平衡以下两方面需要的指导:一方面是适用对减缓空间碎片必要而严格的客观标准之需要;另一方面是使各国不论其经济和科学发展程度如何

---

① UN Space Debris Mitigation Guidelines, supra note 27, no. 3, para. 2, sent. 1,"These guidelines are applicable to mission planning and the operation of newly designed spacecraft and orbital stages and, if possible, to existing ones."

② See considerations on costs, e. g. in UN doc. A/AC.105/804, Report of the STSC (2003), para. 130.

③ Batista Virgili, B. / Krag, H., "Strategies for Active Removal in LEO", 5th European Conference on Space Debris, 1 April 2009.

都可以进入外空之需要。

尽管指南3致力于避免轨道上的偶然碰撞,并指出"可用的轨道数据",但对分享有关空间环境及物体的准确轨道方面的数据这种关键问题都未能提供指导。虽然大会"认为成员国(或地区)更加关注碰撞问题是必要的"[1],但是,监管引导的缺乏已经推动了一些空间操作者(这些操作者总共涵盖了对地静止轨道(GEO)中所有起作用的装备的三分之一)为了互相交换操作信息,来建立他们自己初期的数据中心[2]。正如空间监管数据的分享不仅有安全(safety,指自然属性的安全——译者注)的含义,还有安保(security,指社会属性的安全——译者注)的含义,前一个安全和后一个安全之间的相互关系在指南4中也是特别明显的。根据指南4,应该避免有意地摧毁和其他有害活动。指南并未涉及产生碎片的反卫星武器试验问题的核心。除此之外,能积极清除碎片的设备也增加了相当大的安保(指社会性安全——译者注)因素考量。

作为联合国指南的基本原理,它们指出一些空间碎片"损害航天器的潜在风险,在人造航天器的情况下导致任务失败或生命丧失。对于人造飞行器,空间碎片减缓措施与宇航员的安全非常相关。"[3]

聚焦于安全(safety)方面的问题,联合国指南并未设计成关于空间活动行为准则,因此不是解决与安全(safety)、安保(security)、环境、经济和公正等密切相关的空间碎片问题的一个对策。指南声明:"碎片减缓措施的立即执行被认为是为未来数代人而保护外空环境的谨慎且必要的一步[4]。"

---

[1] UN GA doc. A/RES/62/217, para. 28.

[2] SOCRATES – GEO powered by the Center for Space Standards and Innovation, online: CSSI < www.centerforspace.com > accessed 7 April 2009.

[3] UN Space Debris Mitigation Guidelines, see note [4] on page 37, no. 2, first paragraph.

[4] Ibid., no. 1, para. 1, sent. 5.

谨慎的第一步——不多不少。

五、联合国指南的法律地位

联合国指南的立场(这种立场与它们的法律地位相关)非常明确:"建议执行空间碎片减缓措施……""成员国(或地区)和国际组织应该自愿采取措施。"①指南明确声明:"它们不具有国际法上的约束力。"②

事实是,指南仅仅在科学技术小组委员会得到发展,并未与法律小组委员会合作,这一事实表明它们的技术性,而不必然具有法律含义。尽管本身缺乏技术说明,对空间碎片协调委员会指南的参照和对其技术内容的采纳,以及指南"根据新发现"和研究进行修正的条款进一步强调了联合国指南的"技术"性质③。

(一)外空法治及主权的概念

由于指南本身强调它们不具有法律约束力及其技术特征,这样就提出了如下问题:即指南是否表明了对外空法治的逐渐消失?

外空活动法律制定的第一个阶段从20世纪50年代持续到1979年,在此期间以五个国际条约的形式创造了硬法,尽管批准的数量在减少。从1980年到1995年的第二个阶段以几个联合国大会决议的通过为标志,这几个决议关注外空活动的具体领域以及以一种不太普遍的方式来阐述规则。尽管联合国大会决议可能有助于习惯国际法的产生,但是它们当然不具有与国际条约一样的

---

① Ibid., no. 2, para. 1, sent. 1; no. 3, para. 1, sent. 1.

② Ibid., no. 3, para. 2, sent. 2.

③ Ibid., no. 2, para. 2, "... The Working Group on Space Debris was therefore established (by the Scientific and Technical Subcommittee of the Committee) to develop a set of recommended guidelines based on the technical content and the basic definitions of the IADC space debris mitigation guidelines, and taking into consideration the United Nations treaties and principles on outer space"; no. 5 on updates, and no. 6 referencing the IADC guidelines.

法律约束力。在之后的第三阶段,为了解释或重新解释国际条约法,非约束性的联合国大会决议得到运用①。

当前的联合国指南未达到发展成为一个联合国大会决议的程度,而仅仅被联合国大会认可。在一种纯粹"技术标题"之下思考空间碎片问题,避免指南的法律约束力,甚至避免使法律小组委员会坚定地讨论空间碎片问题等,因而指南被认为严重偏离了外空活动的法治。当下这一更广泛的趋势进一步加深了上述印象:即通过召开有限成员参加的专门论坛,从一个"技术性"视角来思考空间活动问题,以便在和平利用外空委员会之外发现被视为"实用"的解决方法②。人们可能会质疑第四阶段是否会由那些取决于每个成员自身利益而被"大致"实施的非约束性和技术性的"共同理解"所构成?

诚然,空间碎片问题存在很强的科技成分,这一成分是通过和平利用外空委员会关于空间碎片的技术报告所提出的。正如科技小组委员会空间碎片工作组所要求的,科学研究和技术发展可能的确要求制定"能在一种常规基础上进行修正的动态文件,而非限于一套严格的规则"。然而,这种要求不可能阻止那些指南和技术标准与规范外空活动的国际法律框架更加密切相关。这一点通过如下实例可得到证明:通过将"标准和建议实践"附加到国际民用航空芝加哥公约来确保世界范围内的航空飞行安全和较小的环境影响③。

诚然,法律小组委员会最终已经正式思考空间碎片问题。然而,各种议程标题下的讨论限于"与空间碎片减缓措施相关的国内机构

---

① Hobe, Stephan, "The Importance of the Rule of Law for Space Activities", in: Proceedings of the 51st IISL Colloquium on the Law of Outer Space, Glasgow, 29. Sept. ~3 Oct. 2008, in print, quoted from manuscript.

② See Jakhu, Ram, "The Effect of Globalisation on Space Law", in: Hobe, Stephan (ed.) Globalisation: The State and International Law, Stuttgart 2009, p. 86, lit. H. who states that "the COPUOS is being abandoned".

③ See Art. 37, 38 of the Convention on International Civil Aviation, 1944.

之一般信息交换"①。争论并不直接关注以下问题:为既存的有约束力国际法律框架下的空间碎片减缓领域带来光明前景。有趣的是要注意国内机制给国际竞争环境(playing field)带来的结果。

当今时代已经超越了"荷花号案"中体现的,传统学说已经被超越,由曾经万能的主权国家构成的国际社会已经过渡到各个国家必须尊重共同体意义的国际社会,在这种情形下,阐明国际规则或共同体的规则就显得格外重要②。联合国指南究竟是向弱化外空活动法律规则迈进的又一步,还是对空间碎片减缓方面以规则为基础的体系这个问题的一种有益的努力,这依赖于指南在判定国际法律义务是否被违背方面的有用性。

(二)非约束性的联合国指南作为寻求利益平衡的"指导"?

关于各国探索和利用包括月球和其他天体的外层空间活动所应遵守原则的条约(外空条约)③在第1条的第1款中规定:"探索和利用外层空间,包括月球与其他天体在内,应本着为所有国家谋福利与利益的精神,不论其经济或科学发展的程度如何,这种探索和利用应是全人类的事情"。

第9条关于外空活动的行为进一步指出:成员国(或地区)要"适当考虑到其他所有成员国(或地区)的相应利益"。成员国(或地区)进一步有义务之避免对外空的"有害污染"。第9条也包含在有理由相信"有害干预"可能发生时进行磋商的程序权利和

---

① 见第38页注释①。

② For a description of this development towards a "sovereignty under law" and its impact on current space legislation see inter alia Hobe, Stephan, Art. I, in: Hobe, Stephan/Schmidt – Tedd, Bernhard/Schrogl, Kai – Uwe (eds.), Cologne Commentary on Space Law, vol. 1, Outer Space Treaty, forthcoming in fall 2009.

③ Treaty on Principles Governing the Activities of States in the Exploration and Use of Outer Space, including the Moon and Other Celestial Bodies, 27 January 1967, 610 U. N. T. S. 205.

义务。

　　作为绝对最低限度的要求，各国不得不采取适当的措施来使在它的管辖和控制范围外的国家和地区免受损害或至少使外空活动的风险最小化。这种义务几乎不能被视为一个限制甚或对每个国家探测和利用外空的自由之侵犯。这毋宁是与整个国际社会分享外空的结果。这是在由"地球"和外空构成的空间基础之上构建全球社会带来的启示。因此，这个最低限度的标准不仅适用于有关外空活动的特殊法律领域，同时也得到一般国际（环境）法的接受，其由国际法委员会于 2001 年通过的有关"防止危险活动的跨界损害"草案条款所编纂①。外空的法律环境并非在法律空白基础上从头开始，而是与国际法（根据外空条约第三条）紧密相关的②。

　　为了履行这项（行为的）义务，一个国家必须合理谨慎地行为③。而对于注意④与合理谨慎所要求的标准依赖于具体的情况，它通常

---

① International Law Commission, Draft articles on Prevention of Transboundary Harm from Hazardous Activities, with commentaries (2001) online: UN < http://untreaty.un.org/ilc/texts/instruments/english/commentaries/9_7_2001.pdf > accessed 7 April 2009; Art. 3 reads as follows: "The State of origin shall take all appropriate measures to prevent significant transboundary harm or at any event to minimize the risk thereof".

② For applicability and benefit of international environmental law in the space sector in general see Viikari, Lotta, supra note 10, pp. 119 et seq., on the principle of Sic Utere Tuo, Good Neighbourliness and Due Diligence in particular, pp. 150 et seq., 204.

③ ILC commentaries, supra note 49, Art. 3 para. 7; *Koivurova, Timo*, "Due Diligence" in: Max Planck Encyclopedia of Public International Law (2009), online: < www.mpepil.com >.

④ *Sands, Phillippe*, Principles of International Environmental Law (2003) p. 881, Sands distinguishes between "fault", i.e. intention or negligence, "strict", i.e. prima facie responsibility but qualifications and defences may be available, and "absolute" i.e. no mode of exculpation.

被认为应当是"合理的"或"良好"治理的行为,即一般而言对于风险程度而言是适当且相称的①。这些措施在不同国家可能不同,并随着时间而发生变化②。在外空境况下,各国有义务避免以有害污染的方式来探测和利用外空,合理关注其他各成员国(或地区)的利益,并由此能被认为是为了所有国家的福祉和利益而行为。

联合国指南考虑了与空间碎片对地球轨道上的航空器构成的风险有关的一种普遍理解,这种风险自从 1999 年和平利用外层空间委员会发布空间碎片技术报告时就存在。联合国指南进一步确认了对地面的损害风险。联合国大会认为"空间碎片是所有国家都关注的一个问题"并且"成员国(或地区)对空间碎片的这个问题给予更多关注是必要的"③。毫无疑问,空间碎片已经被国际社会确认为一种危害——这是各国必须减缓的一种危害,以使对超越其管辖权和控制的其他国家(或地区)或地区的损害风险最小化。作为对条约义务之功能的替代或补充,一些学者认为减缓空间碎片的义务已经成为习惯国际法的一部分④。

尽管各国受到国际义务的约束来防止损害或至少使风险最小化,因此必须减少其空间活动(包括空间碎片的产生)所出现的风险,但对于究竟需要什么样的措施具有相当大的不确定性。然而,不确定性在发展的前沿绝不是例外。国际法院为了跟上人类进步的步伐,从未拒绝求助于硬法和软法来规制国际环境法的快速发

---

① ILC commentaries, *supra* note 49, Art. 3 paras. 11, 17; Koivurova, Timo, *supra* note 51, paras. 16 *et seq*.

② Koivurova, Timo, see note ③ on page 44, paras. 19 and 20.

③ UN GA doc. A/RES/62/217, preamble, para. 28.

④ Mejía-Kaiser, Martha, "Informal Regulations and Practices in the Field of Space Debris Mitigation", 34 Air and Space Law 21~34, 26 (2009); Gable, Kelly A., "Rules Regarding Space Debris: Preventing a Tragedy of the Commons", in: Proceedings of the 50th IISL Colloquium on the Law of Outer Space, Hyderabad, 24~28 Sept. 2007, p. 257~265, 261.

展领域中的演变①。

根据联合国大会"反映许多国内和国际组织发展起来的既存的实践"②,联合国指南可能(尽管它们本身不具有法律约束力)在必须决定一个特定国家是否履行合理谨慎义务时充当一个参照点。指南不具有法律约束力的明确声明并不意味着不存在有关合理谨慎行为以及减缓空间碎片的国际法律义务。关于空间碎片减缓的技术发展的共识在决定一国遵守其国际义务方面是相当重要的一个因素,但并非唯一的因素。2001年国际法委员会关于防止有害活动的跨界损害的草案条款指出,为了通过谈判获得一种"利益的公正平衡"的目的,各国有协商的义务③。然而,国际法委员会草案条款的这一要素很大程度上被视为对一般国际法的一种相当

---

① Koivurova, Timo, see note ③ on page 44, para. 20 with references; Birnie, Patricia / Boyle, Alan, International Law & the Environment (2002), pp. 24 et seq., 108 et seq.; Viikari, Lotta, see note ② on page 34, pp. 242 et seq., 245, "In extreme cases, a breach of a non-binding instrument might even constitute evidence of a breach of due diligence and related obligations, and could thus have legal consequences".

② UN GA doc. A/RES/62/217, para. 27, "The General Assembly, ... agrees that the voluntary guidelines for the mitigation of space debris reflect the existing practices as developed by a number of national and international organizations, and invites Member states to implement those guidelines through relevant national mechanisms; see also UN guidelines" "A set of mitigation guidelines has been developed by the Inter-Agency Space Debris Coordination Committee (IADC), reflecting the fundamental mitigation elements of a series of existing practices, standards, codes and handbooks developed by a number of national and international organizations."

③ See Art. 9 on "Consultations on preventive measures" and 10 on "Factors involved in an equitable balance of interests" of the ILC draft articles on prevention, see note ① on page 44.

进步的编纂①,在空间法领域并无例外。不仅在空间从事航天活动的国家,而且所有国家,由此最终全人类的利益的公正平衡是各国在从事外空活动时需要努力达成的。联合国指南不会也从不意图成为一系列综合性的指南,以达到与整个空间碎片问题和有关的考虑相关的一种利益的公正平衡。指南本身谈到"例外",这通过诸如联合国条约的规定和外空原则来被证明具有合理性②。指南反映了技术水平最佳实践,已经将一定程度的经济因素包括进去,但是却未讨论"普遍但分化的责任",或者国家的不同经济和技术能力这个问题。

为了对联合国指南是向加强还是弱化外空活动的法治迈进了一步这个问题得出一个结论,人们必须承认指南已经为判断各国遵守国际法确定了某些参照点。然而,国际社会仍然没有一套综合且详细的规则,这些规则足够"清晰扼要",因此具有充分的操作性以判定一国的空间活动偏离国际法的要求。这样一种综合的框架会将预防效果最大化,确定责任,并为了全人类利益达致一种利益的公正平衡。最终,对于法治这个问题的答案依赖于我们欲将法治带向何方。非约束性的技术实践只会确保外空在未来使航天国家容易接近?或者这些实践会通过保护外空共同体利益的明确游戏规则得到补充?③

(三)通过国际条约及(或)国际习惯法的方式形成"明晰的"规则

在等待有关通过谈判建立一个基于体系的规则,从而以一种综合方式解决外空活动的环境问题和有害后果的国际共识和政治意愿形成的过程中,我们见证了国际习惯法的稳定出现。国际标准化组织试图将联合国和空间碎片协调委员会的指南转化为可衡

---

① Birnie, Patricia / Boyle, Alan, see note ① on page 46, p. 107.

② UN Space Debris Mitigation Guidelines, see note ④ on page 37, no. 3, para. 3.

③ See on the legal construction of the community interest in outer space Jakhu, Ram, "Legal issues relating to the Global Public Interest in Outer Space", 32 Journal of Space Law (2006), 31 et seq.

量及可验证的标准,其高水平的标准有待于 2009 年公布[①]。尽管这些还不具有约束力,但国内的执行和可能的相互承认可形成在法律认同基础上的统一国家实践,并由此形成国际习惯法规则[②]。由于联合国和空间碎片协调委员会的指南强调其非约束性并推荐"自愿"执行,各国在建立国内机制时,应该通过国际法明确表示它们要受约束的认识。由欧盟起草的外空活动行为准则包含这样一种信念:通过参与国来推进与外空活动相关的国际法,特别是通过参考联合国空间碎片减缓指南来实现。

"3.1. 签署国重申其承诺:……在接受和实施下列义务方面取得进展:

(b)声明和原则,特别包括:联合国大会 62/217 号决议所声明的联合国和平利用外空委员会的空间碎片减缓指南。

3.2. 为了促进对上述文件的普遍遵守,签署国也重申支持鼓励协调努力。"[③]

尽管与空间碎片相关的国际习惯法体系的扩展是一种受欢迎的发展,但仍旧存在这样的事实,即偏离习惯法规则比偏离明确的条约条款更难以证明。而且,空间碎片是一个复杂的问题,必须至少要从一种安全、安保(safety, security)及环境的视角去探讨。实质性规则和程序的发展要求一种为了具有充分的操作性而积极协商的框架。

六、结论

人类的活动经常产生意外的结果。在空间活动的初级阶段,

---

① Davey, J., "Status of the ISO Standards on Space Debris Mitigation", 5th European Conference on Space Debris, 2 April 2009.

② See note ④ on page 45.

③ Council of the European Union, draft Code of Conduct for outer space activities, approved 8~9 December 2008, online: EU < http://register.consilium.europa.eu/pdf/en/08/st17/st17175.en08.pdf > accessed 7 April 2009.

空间碎片已被确定为这样一种空间活动的意外且有害的副产品。在星际迷航的宇宙中,由于科学进步和新技术包括某种程度的风险和不确定性,意外的后果可能是"曲速运行"("warp travel")带来的有害后果。我们如何在这些风险发生之前面对它们,一旦有害的后果被确认后我们如何对待它们,以及我们是否将一种内在的价值归于空间环境,会反映出人类自身的许多问题。

  国际社会承认一般而言合法的活动必须以防止有害后果的风险或使之最小化这样一种方式来行为,以免这种风险扩展至一国领土之外或超越其管辖权或控制,这是一个伟大的成就。联合国指南被认为阐明了要采取的合适措施。然而,联合国指南的范围是受限的,并且指南并未对空间碎片的复杂问题给出一个综合性的解决方法。在一个关于偏离指南并有可能导致因违反国际法规则而引起法律后果的具体案件中,联合国指南不能被认为是"明晰的",即有法律约束力和明确的规则。

  作为弱化或强化法治的联合国指南的特点,取决于这些指南是否为一套可操作性的规则充当了一个踏脚石,或者满足于技术方式的普遍认同并依赖于行为主体对自我利益的考量。就模糊关于义务和责任的考量而言,后一种方式可能是有吸引力的。然而,只有法治才能使预防和压制效果得到最大化,并保护外空中的共同体利益。一套综合性的规则能处理这些复杂的问题,并处理诸如空间碎片减缓和空间碎片环境补救,以及故意毁坏、碰撞事故、数据分享、风险分配、赔偿基金和保险等问题。

  全球社会共同问题需要为了全球公共利益的全球性解决方法①。

---

  ① On the concept of global public interest see Jakhu, Ram, see note ③ on page 47, passim.

海洋发射:对于商业努力的一些思考

Armel Kerrst 著①　曹永根 译　张宇　李滨 校②

摘要:2009年6月,海洋发射公司寻求《破产法》第11章的保护,结束了其商业努力。然而,就空间法而言,海洋发射是非常有意思的情形。它是关于私人空间活动,尤其是发射活动法律问题的一个很好的案例。

在1998年,我们见证了空间物体发射领域的一个重要突破。这就是波音公司指导下的海洋发射。这项新技术动摇了既存的海洋法与空间法的界限,并促进了私人参与空间活动的趋势。这一发射计划是在国家管辖权之外的公海进行的,这促进了相关法律问题的发展。在此之前,发射空间物体一直是国家行为或国家控制的行为。总体而言,发射活动是国有的或接近国有的。

在海洋发射的情况下,两个主要问题就被凸显出来。第一个问题是关于"发射国"的定义和发射国对公海发射的潜在责任。第二个问题是关于由"适当国家"对由海洋发射空间物体的控制。

在海洋发射情形中,应适用的法律文件包括《美国商业空间发射法案》和《美国和乌克兰关于商业发射的协定》。这项活动的法律地位明显更加复杂,但仍可适用关于陆地发射的相关规则。从

---

① 法国西布列塔尼大学法律系,海洋经济和法律中心,国际法教授。
② 曹永根,哈尔滨工业大学法学院硕士毕业生。张宇,哈尔滨工业大学法学院教学秘书。李滨,北京师范大学法学院教授。

预测未来的角度上讲,如果一个发射基地位于公海上,那么关于空间活动的监管可能会被弱化。

在定义发射国时,《外空条约》和《责任公约》对其领土被用于发射空间物体的国家给予了非常特殊的地位。任何其他标准,诸如"实施发射的国家""促成发射的国家"以及有关设施的国籍国都很容易被一个私人公司选择。

潜在的威胁是类似于在海洋法前提下,私人财团希望规避有能力国家的控制,并通过规避行为获取利益。如此,既存的空间法的基本原理可能会受到影响,从而损害一个真正全面负责任的发射国的责任和登记国的控制。根据《登记公约》,登记国必须是发射国之一。

引言

技术革新会为重大的法律变革开辟道路,海洋发射似乎就是这样一个革新。它是一个私人商业计划,致力于将卫星由一个位于赤道上的半潜水的发射平台发射到轨道上。

其三级火箭是由知名的苏联(现归属于乌克兰)两级泽尼特火箭和俄罗斯博克 DM 上升第三级火箭组成的。这两者都是可靠的成功的科技产品。泽尼特火箭是最自动化的发射运载工具之一。它是重要的发射能力,因为它能够将与欧洲发射器阿丽亚娜 4 相同的荷载发射至轨道。一个自主动力的前北海钻井平台,在斯塔万格船厂经过改造后,充当了发射平台,它的空载排水量是 31 000 吨。一个集合指挥舰在苏格兰格拉斯哥的考克瓦纳·高湾船厂被建造出来,它的排水量达到了 30 000 吨,能为 250 名船员提供食宿。该船既将被用于将火箭和卫星从本港运送到发射点,又将被用作任务指挥和信息交流中心。实践中,在海上的船中将火箭组合起来并运到发射平台将是不可能的。

出发港位于加利福尼亚的长滩。在交互发射阶段,平台和集结指挥船停靠于此。出发港也为行政和商业服务提供场所。

发射行动的组织情况良好。发射平台位于夏威夷以南 1 000

英里的太平洋赤道上。火箭和运载工具在长滩被组装起来并被运到发射平台上。一台自动运送和提升设备被用于将发射器竖直安放于发射平台。火箭是自动加注燃料准备发射的。在发射阶段，每一步骤都是由数英里之外的集合指挥舰指挥的。发射过后，平台和指挥舰驶回出发港。我们不难发现，这些步骤是比当下常见的大型发射平台拥有更高的整合度，也更加经济。

这项工程致力于利用两大主要优势：通过移动平台由赤道发射和使用前苏联的空间产业（其火箭可靠而又廉价）。

海洋发射公司起初是一家有存续期间的公司，成立于英属殖民地鳄鱼岛。海洋发射公司的股东包括几家跨国公司。这中间就有波音商业空间公司（持股40%），它是位于西雅图的波音公司的一家子公司；还有挪威奥斯陆的克瓦纳公司，它是一家重要的造船公司，它提供了平台和集合指挥舰（持股20%），以及俄罗斯莫斯科的RSC能源公司（持股25%），它提供第三级火箭和第一二级火箭的部分零件并指挥这次发射，还有乌克兰尤佐耶的非营利性组织（持股15%），它提供被用作第一二级火箭的泽尼特火箭（该火箭有自主竖立的功能，这在本案中是十分有益的）。波音在团队中起的是领导作用，它提供了出发港、发射器的一些配件和载具上的食宿设备并将发射进行商业化。

这一新的项目提出了一些有意思的法律问题。

一、在国家主权之外发射的合法性

（一）自由原则

就空间法而言[①]，发射国的领土事实上是决定负责的发射国的

[①] 《关于探索和利用包括月球和其他天体在内的外空活动的基本原则的条约》，1967年1月27日开放签署，610 U.N.T.S. 205 18 UST 2410（1967）6ILM 386（简称《外空条约》）《空间物体所造成损害的国际责任公约》，1973年10月9日，961 U.N.T.S 2389（简称《责任公约》）。

标准之一。然而,即使发射的领土是被《责任公约》第5条第3款明确指出的重要一点,那么国家并不负有从其国土发射(空间物体)的义务。《外空条约》(1967)也未有相关限制,而是在第1条第2款规定了利用外层空间的自由。

有关公海自由的问题虽然并非显而易见,但仍具有相关性。《蒙特哥湾公约》规定:"公海自由包括:(1)航行自由。(2)飞越自由及其他。"其间既不包括发射空间物体的自由,不包括飞行器起降的自由。然而,文中有"其他"二字,对于自由的罗列就不是排他性的。发射空间物体并未被直接禁止,它是被《蒙特哥湾公约》允许的。

(二)使用公海从事发射活动

这方面的主要问题是由于安装(发射)平台的需要和设置以其他方法利用公海的限制引起的。

《蒙特哥湾公约》第87条包含了海洋的自由:"建设人工岛屿和其他国际法允许建设的设施的自由。"[①]纵然有该句最后部分的限制,关于安放平台的合法性问题似乎是清晰的。真正的问题在于是否可以建造被用于任何目的任何平台。在第三次联合国海洋法会议期间,在公海上安装平台的问题并未被明确,因为当时主要是在专属经济区的框架下讨论建设此类设施。

"根据国际法被允许的设施"这一表述应当作何理解?此种设施是被明确允许的,还是仅仅不被禁止?在公海上建筑巨大的平台难道不是具有法律意义的一种占有吗?此种设施又与国际海底有什么关系?(《蒙特哥湾公约》第6部分规定的区域)[②]这些规则

---

① 联合国海洋法公约,1982年12月10日于Montego Bay Jamaica开放签字(下文简称为蒙特哥湾公约)。

② 《蒙特哥湾公约》第137条(该区域的法律地位及其资源)第139条(确保遵守的义务和造成损害的责任)。

是否会通过第 147 条第 1、2、3 款而具有效力呢？①

在当时，人们是不可能预见以此种方式利用公海的。而且，在公海从事这些具有潜在危险的活动可能会产生一些困难。在这些计划中，一些非环境友好型的产业已经被投入使用，诸如冶炼厂或核电厂②。

然而，主要问题是对航行自由的限制。平台本身，以及更为重要的是，在发射期间在发射地点周围很大的空间内需要禁止航行，这对航行自由是很大的限制。被用于海洋发射的区域与主要的航海区域相隔甚远。然而，这一问题并未被《海洋法公约》严格规制。该公约只规定了公海上的矿产资源开发平台和科学研究平台。前者必须获得海底机构的授权，后者可以被建造但不得建立超过 500 米的安全区。我们似乎很难想象，一个私人的商业活动相对于经过许可且受人尊敬的科学研究，能够在更大的程度上限制航行自由。海洋发射活动并未澄清这一问题。

二、公海发射对空间法产生的影响

（一）发射国的定义

与海洋发射有关的主要难题之一就是"发射国"的概念。众所周知，发射国在确定发射活动的责任时具有重要意义。

就私人发射活动而言，根据《外空条约》第 6 条和第 7 条，由私人主体开展的外空活动被认为是由责任国实施的。该国不仅要负责监督、控制具有其国籍的非政府主体从事的空间活动，而且要对

---

① 参见 Armel Kerrest："Les aspects juridiques du projet Sea Launch de lancement de satellites depuis la haute mer" revue Droit et défense n°97/1 Paris. 及 A. Kerrest "The Launch of Spacecraft from the Sea" in："An Outlook on Outer Space Law in the Coming Thirty Years". Lafferranderie et Crowther edit. (Kluwer 1997).

② 虽然由于消耗大量能源，如此强劲的火箭的发射经常是危险的，但海洋发射似乎并不会对海洋环境造成特别大的损害。

这些活动承担与其自身从事的空间活动一样的责任。

私人公司能够成为发生主体的事实是一个新情况并应当被考虑。美国法律体系中《美国商业空间发射法案》的存在无疑是十分有益的。而其他国家(或地区)的相关国内法可能不存在相关规定或是过于概括。

如果私人团体从公海发射,这一情况就向发射国提出了问题。如果损害发生,那么责任结果就成为主要的利益所在和关注的焦点。如果我们使用《外空条约》和《责任公约》的标准,我们会得出第一条标准:"从事发射的国家"。此处,并非是国家而是私人公司从事发射活动。根据前面提及的规则,法人(本案中是海洋发射公司)的国籍使国籍国成为"发射国"。不是该公司的法律人格而是对给公司的有效控制问题在国际法上是不清晰的。

海洋发射公司起初是一家"有限定存续期间的公司",其注册于英属殖民地大鳄鱼岛,那么,英国就应当被认为是"发射国"①。之后,英国反对此种行为,公司转而注册于美国特拉华州,使美国成为发射国。

如果我们观察公司的真实管理情况,我们能够发现这项计划是由波音商业空间公司,即美国波音公司的一家子公司实施的。因此,美国也应被认为是发射国。

与其他各方的相关问题则尚不明确②。至于 RSC 能源公司,它在公司中起到了重要作用,提供了一些重要的部件,并为发射提供了技术指导。因此,俄罗斯也可以被认为是一个发射国。在本案中,俄罗斯和美国认为是"从事发射的国家"或"其设施被使用的国家"。

---

① 英国《外层空间法》在英属殖民地的适用情况尚不明晰。但一国的国内法问题并不能改变国际法上的情况(英国可能要承担责任)。

② 本文口头陈述之后的讨论表明,发射国的概念是不明确的,尤其是在考虑参与各方之后。一些律师认为该概念应包括任何参与方,其他律师认为参与方必须在空间活动中期待某种重要作用,才能符合"发射国"的条件。

乌克兰公司尤佐耶的非营利性组织提供了泽尼特火箭。那么，是否就可以据此认定乌克兰是发射国呢，这仍然有待讨论。因为这家公司仅占涉案公司15%的股份，这仍是不确定的。同样的情况也适用于挪威的克瓦纳公司，尤其是该公司提供了船只和平台，但并未悬挂挪威国旗。

第二条标准："促成发射的国家"不能在此处被考虑，因为其取决于航空器的负荷。考虑到此次海洋发射的商业目的，促成发射的实体可能是一个国家或一个将其国籍国作为发射国的私人公司。

定义发射国的最后两条标准是，其领土或设施被用于发射空间物体。公海等领土上不存在任何国家的领土主权①。因此，我们就不得不考虑"从其设施发射的国家"，此处事实上是指设施所属公司的国籍。这些设施首先必须包括平台和集合指挥舰，两者悬挂的都是方便旗——利比里亚国旗。在这个角度，利比里亚是发射国。

接下来，我们就必须讨论出发港的设施是否也是此种意义上的"设施"。将空间活动与一国领土连接起来无疑是一种可取的解决途径。然而，这真的是"从其上进行发射的设施"吗？支持对文本进行如此宽泛的解读是困难的，尤其是考虑到责任问题的结果。

（二）作为发射国之一的美国

1984年《美国商业空间发射法案》②的适用包括许多主体。各

---

① 船舶的准领土理论不再被国际法所认可。该设施的国籍不是被考量的唯一标准。

② 1984年《美国商业空间发射法案》，修改于与1988年，49 U. S. C. app. §§2601-2623（下文称之为 CSLAUSC §2303）(11)，"美国公民"是指(A)作为美国公民的任何个人(B)任何根据美国联邦法律或各州法律组织和存在的公司、合伙、合资联合或其他团体(C)任何根据外国法律组织和存在的公司、合伙、合资联合或其他团体，如果该组织的控制权（由国家即根据规则确定）是由上文第(A)、(B)条规定的个人或组织持有。

种国家空间法案的适用经常是非常宽泛的,而且在多数情况下是在疆界以外的。美国希望通过许可证程序避免对其不能控制的空间活动承担作为发射国的责任。这是空间法中客观责任规则的积极的副作用之一。《美国商业空间发射法案》,区别了由 USC 2603 第 11 条第(1)(2)两款定义的"具有美国国籍的自然人与法人"的"美国公民"实施的活动与第(3)款规定的由美国自然人和法人控制的外国法人的活动。

在海洋发射中,有一点必须被特别重视:这个项目使用了苏联的非常可靠和经济的技术。众所周知,由于担心滥用,美国与建立市场经济的各国就出售商业发射签署了一项协议。这些国家包括中国、俄罗斯和乌克兰①。

这些协议限制了这些国家的发射出售,然而,在美国公司和外国火箭制造商开展合作时适用特别的条款。在那种情况下,该企业必须由美国公司领导,并取得美国政府颁发的许可证,并根据 1984 年《美国商业空间发射法案》的框架成立。只有符合以上规定,美国才成为发射国。该发射机构没有必要在此方面规避适用美国法律。一起事故的潜在被害人会从这种有关美国责任的规定获得重大利益。

---

① 美国政府与乌克兰政府关于空间商业发射服务的国际贸易的协定,1995 年 10 月 15 日签署,1996 年 2 月 21 日生效,载于《空间法杂志》,24,1996 – 2(下文简称为《美乌协定》)。"完整的空间发射提供者"在第 2 条第 3 款被定义为:"包含美国公司和乌克兰公司的合资企业,通过完成火箭领域和空间技术领域的联合项目,提供商业发射服务或商业发射运载工具。其项目经费来源于投资、商业贷款和其他途径。在合资企业中,(1)企业获得了美国交通部颁发的商业发射许可证;(2)美方必须在合资企业中保持相当的利益与控制,并且合资企业发射活动所需商品与服务有很大一部分来源于美国;(3)合资企业发射活动所需商品与服务主要来源于市场经济国家。"

三、可能的趋势

似乎,发射活动的商业化,尤其是从国际平台进行的发射,可能会戏剧性地改变空间法的一些重要规则的适用。此时,发射国的领土成为这个体系中的"法锁"。鉴于航天器是在一个经济上技术上都很强大的国家[①]发射的,这些国家自然是有责任的发射国,而不论其本身是否愿意。潜在的被害人很有希望获得赔偿[②]。如果因为一个发射是从由国际领土上发射的,而将领土标准放置一边,这一"法锁"就将被抛弃,而唯一剩下的标准就是可由私人发射公司选择的国籍标准。当私人企业可以选择自己的国籍时,他们就可以选择发射国以及因此而产生的登记国[③]——因为登记国必须是发射国之一,以及对发射活动承担控制责任的"适当国家"[④]。这与公司可以在——事实上而非法律上——选择船只悬挂的国旗,以及因此需适用的国内法及国际法的做法非常相近。我们都明了这种"无政府状态"的危害:在这些国际领域上建立任何有效的规则都将是非常困难的。

更进一步讲,这种情况在空间中会比在公海上更加具有灾难性。一艘船舶被用于连接两块土地领土上的两个港口。如果国家想要,它们干涉任何一端。至于空间活动,从航天器被发射至其回归地球,它不与任何领土发生物理上的接触。它始终处于国际空间,并始终与一个或几个发射国保持着联系。

---

① 这种国家可能是"发达"国家,或是像印度、巴西、中国这样的"发展中"国家。

② 即使《责任公约》中的争端解决机制并不像在国际社会大体上那样充分。

③ 外空物体《登记公约》,第1条:"登记国一词是指一个依据第2条进行空间物体登记的发射国"。

④ 根据1967年《外空条约》第6条。

一些学者建议修改现行的发射国责任体系[①],免除发射国的负担。这似乎并不适宜。当然,我们必须考虑空间活动的商业化现象,确定从事空间活动的私人公司的责任,并保持一个或几个发射国承担绝对责任的安全网。这种保护必须被建立起来,以区别本质是高危险的空间活动与并未直接参与空间活动被公约规定的绝对责任加以保护的潜在被害人。这一规则具有两大优势:其一是对被害人提供保障;其二是在很大程度上确保一国控制该活动整体。《外空条约》第6条已经规定了控制义务,然而此项义务的遵守并不是像绝对责任那样清晰的一项国际责任。因为会招致责任,一国必定会小心从事这项活动。被害人可以起诉真正的空间活动实施者,然而,正如我们知道的那样,获得证明过错存在的判决或从公司获得一项合理的赔偿将会是非常困难的。除去那些可能性之外,维持发射国责任的安全网将会是有益的。如果它能像保险系统那样运作,那就更好了;即便它不能,被害人仍可或是在国内法院或是根据《责任公约》通过被害人的国籍国起诉发射国。

四、结论

海洋发射(公司)在公海进行发射。为了遵守《美乌协定》,公司必须遵守美国法并取得美国政府颁发的许可证,这使得美国成为应当承担责任的发射国。如果这一特殊情况不存在,另一家受商业竞争影响更严重的公司,可能会通过悬挂方便旗取得公司方

---

① See Henri A. Wassenbergh: A launch and a transportation law separate from outer space law. It is time to legally unburden the "launching state." Air and space law 21 1996 1 p. 28~32. Frans von der Dunk: Commercial space activities: an Inventory of Liability, an inventory of Problems, Proceedings of the thirty-seventh Colloquium in the law of Outer Space (1992) 161-71. and Loopholes in Liability? Aspects of Liability for Damages Sustained in the Course of Satellite Telecommunications Activities. 2 Telecommunications & Space Journal (1995) 153-74.

便国籍等方法选择逃避真实的控制。

正如在海上已经发生过的那些情形一样,如果在空间发射领域或其他空间活动领域的竞争是激烈的,那么选择逃避强力监管将会是有所助益的。从国际领土发射,将会使选择"发射国""适当国家"和"登记国"变得更加容易。我们必须注意到,选择国家意味着选择包括国际法和国内法在内的可适用于该活动的法律,也意味着选择负责控制的政府。出于这一原因而选择毫无空间能力的政府作为唯一的发射国将会引起困难。如果我们希望维持安全的高水平和对空间活动的控制,我们就应避免这样的困境。因为空间活动的主要使用者是强大的"发达"国家和强大的"发展中"国家。即使我们应该在空间活动领域,尊重最大限度的自由并鼓励私人企业,但是从长远角度来看,我们打开迅速发展的空间活动及相关领域中的无规则状态这个潘多拉盒子将是没有益处的。所幸的是,海洋发射并未打破既有的控制体系和责任体系,这表明这些体系可能继续维持下去。

Responsibility and Liability of GNSS Provider States in Air Navigation under International Air and Space Law[①]

Nie Jingjing[②]

Abstract: The Global Navigation Satellite System (GNSS) is one of the most critical technologies in the twenty-first century. Originally as military system, it now applies directly and indirectly to various sectors for civil use, one of the most important of which is air navigation. However, the system is not one hundred percent safe. Incidents in recent years indicate the risk of the GNSS signals malfunction, leading to damage.

The purpose of this paper is to examine the international responsibility and liability of GNSS primary signal provider states in air navigation under the current legal regime. It is therefore divided into the following five chapters. The first chapter is a brief introduction to GNSS, including its definition, working principles and application, especially its application in air navigation. The second chapter discusses the respon-

---

① This article is a part of the author's LLM thesis in partial fulfillment of the requirement of LL. M. (Adv.) Degree awarded by International Institute of Air & and Space Law, Leiden University, the Netherlands.

② Nie Jingjing, Lecturer of Civil Aviation University of China.

sibility and liability of GNSS primary signal provider states under international law, inter alia international air and space law. Chapter Three turns to recent trends towards a uniform set of GNSS rules, referring to the Eleventh ICAO Air Navigation Conference and studies carried out by UNIDROIT. Chapter Four discusses some substantive liability issues that the future uniform GNSS rules would need to cover. I would like to come to a conclusion in the last chapter.

中文标题:国际航空法与空间法中全球卫星导航系统信号提供国在飞行导航中的责任

中文摘要:全球导航卫星系统(GNSS)是21世纪最重要的技术之一。它原本是军用系统,如今也广泛应用于民用方面,其中最重要的应用之一就是飞行导航。然而,GNSS系统并非绝对安全,近年来发生的事件表明存在GNSS信号失灵的风险,导致损害发生。

本文旨在探讨现有国际航空法与空间法框架下GNSS信号提供国在空中航行活动中的责任。全文分为五部分。第一部分简要介绍了GNSS的定义、工作原理和应用,尤其是飞行导航中的应用。第二部分分析了国际空间法和航空法中GNSS信号提供国是否应当承担责任以及承担何种责任。第三部分通过介绍国际民航组织第十一次航行会议以及国际统一私法协会的研究,讨论建立统一规则的趋势。第四部分讨论将来统一规则中必须涉及的一些实质问题。结论部分认为,在国际法没有明确规定的情况下,GNSS信号提供国的责任问题有待于国家实践去解决。

关键字:GNSS;飞行导航;国际空间法;国际航空法;国家责任

1. Introduction

GNSS stands for Global Navigation Satellite System, which is considered as one of the most critical technologies in the twenty-first century. Like most other space technologies, GNSS was first developed for military application, and now its civilian applications have brought rapid development and huge benefits to the world. Interest in GNSS has increased in recent years, with UNISPACE III 1999 providing an impetus on the international stage[1]. The application of such systems was listed as one of the key actions of "using space applications for human security, development and welfare", mentioned in the resolution adopted by UNISPACE III[2].

1.1 What is GNSS?

Global Navigation Satellite Systems are space-based positioning and navigation systems designed to provide worldwide, all weather, passive, three-dimensional position, velocity and timing data[3].

According to the ICAO definition, GNSS is a worldwide position and time determination system that includes one or more satellite constellations, aircraft receivers and system integrity monitoring, augmented as necessary to support the required navigation performance for the intended operation[4]. It comprises two types of elements: core satellite constellations and augmentation systems (aircraft-based, ground-based and satellite-based) needed to achieve the level of performance suitable for

---

[1] Francis. Lyall and Paul. B. Larsen, Space Law: A Treatise (2009), at 389.

[2] Report of the Third United Nations Conference on the Exploration and Peaceful Uses of Outer Space, Vienna, 19~30 July 1999, Chapter I Resolution 1: The Space Millennium: Vienna Declaration on Space and Human Development, A/CONF.184/6, at 7.

[3] E. D. Kaplan and C. Hegarty, Understanding GPS: Principles and Applications, (2nd ed., 2005), cited in Lyall and Larsen, supra note 1, at 391.

[4] ICAO Annex 10, Volume I, cited in Jim Nagle, ICAO policy on GNSS, GNSS SARPs and global GNSS developments, presentation on the second ICG meeting 2007: http://www.oosa.unvienna.org/pdf/icg/2007/icg2/presentations/38.pdf (last visited 30 July 2009).

civil aviation applications①.

1.2 How does a Satellite-based Navigation System Work?

The basic principle of the navigation satellite system is satellite ranging distance measuring and in order to do this it is necessary to have accurate timing in the system②. A navigation satellite system consists of three components: the control segment, the space segment, and the user segment③. The control segment consists of a system of tracking stations located around the world④. The space segment consists of GNSS satellites. To provide global navigation service, the space segment consists of a constellation of at least 24 satellites to ensure that signals from at least four satellites are available at any location⑤. User segment consists of the GNSS receivers and the user community. The receiver converts space vehicle signals into position, velocity and time

---

① See Action Team on GNSS UNISPACE III Recommendation No. 10, Fifth Meeting, 15 November 2002, Vienna Austria: http://www. itu. int/jive/servlet/JiveServlet/download/453 - 1249 - 287286 - 763/5th _ AT10 _ draft _ minutes. pdf (last visited 30 July 2009). See also Javier Benedicto, Philippe Michel and Javier Ventura-Traveset, 'EGNOS: Project Status Overview', (1999) Vol. 1 No. 1 Air and Space Europe 58, at 58.

② Reinhard Schnabel, 'Satellite-based Navigation Systems', (1999) Vol. 1 No. 1 Air and Space Europe 65, at 65.

③ Bradford W. Parkinson and James J. Spilker Jr. (eds.) Global Positioning System: Theory and Applications, Volume I (1996), at 36 ~ 48. Brady M. Orschel, 'Assessing a GPS-Based Global Navigation Satellite System within the Context of the 2004 U. S. Space-based Positioning, Navigation and Timing Policy', (2005) Vol. 70 Journal of Air Law and Commerce 609, at 609.

④ See note③, pp. 63, at 8.

⑤ Paul D. Groves, Principles of GNSS, Inertial, and Multisensor Integrated Navigation Systems (2008), at 10 ~ 11.

estimates[①] (See Chart 1).

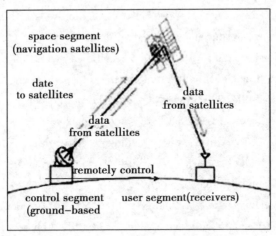

Chart 1　Three components of GNSS

Satellite-based navigation service requires a network of earth-orbiting satellites that transmit data to users' receivers[②]. Using radio waves, these navigation satellites communicate with each other and with ground stations in order to generate position information[③]. The satellites then transmit this position information to receivers located, for example, on a ship, a car or a plane. The receivers can use such data to provide users with their locations[④].

1.3 Applications of GNSS

Satellite navigation technology was originally developed by the United States and the former Soviet Union for military purposes.[⑤] There are

---

① See note ③, pp. 63.

② B. D. K. Henaku, The Law on Global Air Navigation by Satellite (1998) at 171.

③ Ibid.

④ Orschel, see note ③, pp. 64.

⑤ EUROSPACE, 'European Strategic Dependence as Related to Space Technology: Navigation', (1999) Vol. 1 No. 2 Air and Space Europe 45, at 45.

now two broad types of users: the military users, who use it for navigation, and the civilian users, who use it for hundreds of high-precision scientific, engineering and commercial applications[1].

In the military domain, a satellite navigation system offers the advantage of high precision both for positioning and navigation, thus enhancing the capability or weapon system[2]. The public became aware of its power during the Gulf War, where satellite navigation was shown to be an extremely important means of achieving superiority in the use and precision of weapons, in the flexibility of manoeuvring and in the efficiency and reliability of operations[3].

GNSS has changed from a limited military navigation tool to a highly flexible measurement system capable of literally hundreds of applications[4]. It applies directly and indirectly to various sectors including transport, communication, land surveying, agriculture, fisheries, environmental protection, scientific research, tourism, and other activities[5].

---

[1] Vidal Ashkenazi, 'The Challenges Facing Galileo', (2000) Vol. 16 Space Policy 185, at 186.

[2] Ibid, at 46.

[3] P. Hartl and M. Wlaka, 'The European Contribution to a Global Civil Navigation Satellite System', (1996) Vol. 12 Space Policy 167, at 167.

[4] Hervé Berthelo and Vidal Ashkenazi, 'GPS to Galileo: A European Path', (1999) Vol. 1 No. 3 Air and Space Europe 66, at 68~69.

[5] See e. g., Communication from the Commission to the European Parliament and the Council-Galileo at a Cross – Road: The Implementation of the European GNSS Programmes, COM (2007) 261 Final, para. 2; Stephanie Andries, 'The European Initiative Galileo', (2000) vol. 25 Annals of Air and Space Law 43, at 51~52; D. Brocklebank et al, 'Institutional Aspects of a Global Navigation Satellite System', (1999) Vol. 53 Journal of Navigation 261, at 261; Berthelo and Ashkenazi, supra note 19, at 69; Lyall and Larsen, see note [1], pp. 63, at 389~390. P. Hartl and M. Wlaka, 'The European Contribution to a Global Civil Navigation Satellite System', (1996) Vol. 12 Space Policy 167, at 167.

Specifically, GNSS contributes significantly to sustainable mobility of transport applications[①].

1.4 GNSS and Air Navigation

The first economic sector to acknowledge the potential benefits of GNSS was aviation[②]. The two essential functions of the satellite-based navigation system are to increase safety, which is of paramount importance in aviation[③], and to increase efficiency.

Safety is a fundamental condition for civil aviation. The advent of GNSS could very meaningfully enhance the safety of air navigation[④]. GNSS for air traffic management, which provides the air traffic controller accurate, precise and real time information (air-to-ground and vice versa), makes international civil aviation safer in all phases of flight[⑤], from initial climb out, through the en-route phases into the terminal area and down to the precision approach decision height[⑥]. Some of the most serious aeronautical disasters of the past decades could have been avoided if more precise and reliable means supporting air navigation

---

① Berthelo and Ashkenazi, see note ④, pp. 66, at 68.

② Frans G. von der Dunk, 'Liability for Global Navigation Satellite Service (GNSS): A Comparative Analysis of GPS and Galileo', (2004) Vol. 30 No. 1 Journal of Space Law 129, at 129 ~ 130.

③ Andries, see note ⑤, pp. 66, at 52.

④ Michael Milde, 'Institutional and Legal Problems of the Global Navigation Satellite System (GNSS): Solutions in Search of a Problem?', in Chia-Jui Cheng and Doo Hwan Kim (eds.), The Utilization of World's Air Space and Free Outer Space in the 21st Century (2000) 337, at 337.

⑤ Ibid.

⑥ S. J. Leighton et al, 'GNSS Guidance for All Phases of Flight: Practical Results', paper presented at The Third Europe Symposium on Global Navigation Satellite System, Edinburgh, Scotland, 1 ~ 4 May 2000.

had been available at the time and place of the accident①.

At the same time, GNSS will improve the efficiency of air transport. The high accuracy of satellite navigation will lead to a more efficient use of airspace and an increased air traffic capacity which will constitute one answer to the ever-growing air traffic demand problem②. Moreover, the exclusive utilisation of satellite-based guidance systems would reduce costs considerably③, because the optimisation of flight profiles will save fuel for operators, reduce flight times and reduce noise impact for cities④.

Ultimately aiming at one seamless, global and comprehensive system for the provision of positioning, navigation and air traffic management services to civil aviation fundamentally based on a satellite system and the signals it generates, ICAO quickly realised the potential of satellites for this purpose, and established the first Committee on Future Air Navigation Satellites (FANS) as early as 1983⑤, which is now known as the ICAO Communications Navigation Surveillance/Air Traffic Management System (ICAO CNS/ATM), to design a new air navigation infrastructure capable of meeting the anticipated challenges. GNSS, the

---

① Milde, see note ④, pp. 67, at 337. The list of such disasters include the collision of the Saudi B-747 with the Kazakh IL-76 close to New Delhi in 1996, the fatal crash of AA B-757 near Cali, Colombia in 1995, the fatal crash of Thai and Pakistani Airbuses in Nepal in 1992, and the collision of KLM and PANAM B-747s in 1977, all of which were attributable to the lack of knowledge of the precise position of the aircraft in real time.

② Andries, see note ⑤, pp. 66, at 52.

③ See note ⑤, pp. 65, at 46.

④ See Andries, see note ⑤, pp. 66, at 52.

⑤ Frans G. von der Dunk, The European Equation: GNSS = Multimodality + Liability, in Marietta Benk (ed.), Luft-und Weltraumrecht im 21. Jahrhundert (2001) 231, at 231.

backbone of ICAO's CNS/ATM, is able to provide the infrastructure needed to support future air navigation and will replace the current existing ground-based air navigation aids[①].

2. Responsibility and Liability of GNSS Primary Signal Providers in Air Navigation under International Law

While GNSS brings great convenience and benefit to the whole world, it may also cause significant damage due to signal malfunction. The purpose of this chapter is to examine the responsibility and liability of GNSS primary signal providers under current international law, especially international air and space law, in the case of accidents caused by GNSS signal malfunction.

2.1 Potential Risk of GNSS Signal Malfunction

No system is perfect. Neither is the GNSS. A signal malfunction, such as an absence of signal or an error or degradation in the signal could lead to a plane crash or shipping accident causing substantial loss of life and damage to property and the environment.

A report from the US Government Accountability Office predicts that if the Air Force does not meet its schedule goals for development of GPS IIIA satellites, there will be an increased likelihood that in 2010, as a number of older satellites begin to fail, the overall GPS constellation will fall below the number of satellites required to provide the level of GPS service that the U. S. government commits to[②] and warns that we

---

① Andries, see note ⑤, pp. 66, at 45.

② United States Government Accountability Office, 'Global Positioning System: Significant Challenges in Sustaining and Upgrading Widely Used Capabilities', report to the Subcommittee on National Security and Foreign Affairs, Committee on Oversight and Government Reform, House of Representatives, April 2009: http://www.gao.gov/new.items/d09325.pdf (last visited 3 July 2009).

could face "wide-ranging impacts on all GPS users"①.

This is not merely a warning; the problem did occur. There was one un-reported incident occurring in January 1998, when a number of flight crews complained about loss of GPS signals in the vicinity of Albany, New York. Some FMS (Flight Management System)/GPS receiver integrity monitoring systems were not notifying the crews of the problem resulting in aircraft heading changes of up to ninety degrees. Interestingly, some FMS systems reinitialized after reacquiring the satellite signals, sending the aircraft direct to Silicon Valley, California, the manufacture's location. It is clear that this anomaly could have significantly affected safe air traffic separation②.

Unfortunately, this was not the only incident. In mid June this year, a large group of car GPS users in China complained about the positioning failure. Regions suffering from the GPS failure include Chongqing (southwestern China), Liaoning (northeastern China), Hebei, Shanxi, Shandong (north China), and Taiwan (southeastern China). All of the big GPS receiver manufacturers received such complaints from their customers and they believed that the problem was caused by computation error of the positioning chips or other receiving components in the GPS receiver, which was a direct result of the change of satellite data and orbit, ageing satellite components and other problems in the GPS updating process. Although GPS receiver manufacturers eventually solved the problem by updating the software and the package, quite a

---

① See note ②, pp. 69.

② FAA Incident Summary, New England Region, January 30, 1998, cited in Gregory E. Michael, Legal 'Issues Including Liability Associated with the Acquisition, Use and Failure of GPS/GNSS', (1999) Vol. 52 Journal of Navigation 246, at 249.

few customers expressed the view that they had lost confidence in GPS①.

It was stated in 2003 that approximately 3000 aircraft have been equipped with satellite communication systems② and now there are many more. So there is an evident risk that the satellite navigation system fails thereby leading to a plane crash causing damage to its passengers③.

2.2 Potential Liable Parties, Potential Victims and Possible Damage

Liability in such a complex system as satellite-based air navigation involves many different players and many different sets of legal rules④.

A study carried out by European Commission on the legal implications of operating a global service, considered liability in terms of the supply chain beginning with those who provide the basic GNSS signals⑤. Following this supply chain, the potential liable parties could be the primary signal provider (space segment provider), secondary signal provider (navigation service provider), air traffic control agencies, airlines, as well as equipment designers and manufacturers, and other related organizations. Potential victims can be categorized as: primary (e.g., aircraft operators), secondary (e.g., passengers) and tertiary

---

① See Cong Hui, 'GPS Failure due to the Ageing Satellites: Who Will Lead the Navigation Industry?', Phoenix News Online, 22 June 2009: http://auto.ifeng.com/usecar/carsupplies/20090622/53676.shtml (last visited 3 July 2009, original in Chinese).

② Tare C. Brisibe, 'Legal and Regulatory Development in Aeronautical Communication and Navigation', presented in United Nations / Nigeria Workshop on Space Law "Meeting International Responsibilities and Addressing Domestic Needs", Abuja, 21st to 24th November 2005.

③ See ibid.

④ von der Dunk, see note ⑤, pp. 68, at 232.

⑤ Brocklebank et al, see note ⑤, pp. 66, at 269.

(third parties) ①. Moreover, loss of or damage to properties on board the airplane and on the surface of the earth, as well as the aircraft itself, are possible damages from the perspective of the 1972 Liability Convention.

The following chart is to demonstrate the relationship among different players in GNSS activities in air navigation (See Chart 2).

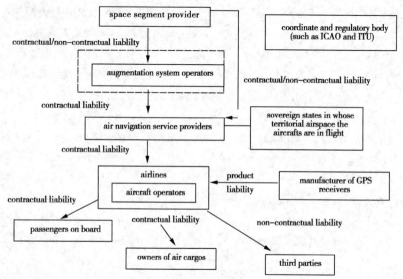

Chart 2   Relationship among participants of the satellite-based navigation activity and types of liability

2.3 International Responsibility of GNSS Signal Provider States

One of the main legal issues of GNSS is responsibility. In this section I will try to examine the international responsibility of the GNSS signal provider states under, inter alia, international air law and space law.

---

① Brocklebank, et al, see note ⑤, pp. 66, at 269.

2.3.1 The Notion of State Responsibility

State responsibility is regarded as "a general principle of international law, a concomitant of substantive rules and of the supposition that acts and omissions may be categorized as illegal by reference to the rules establishing rights and duties"①. When we speak of responsibility, "we are dealing primarily with obligations imposed on people and institutions who are supposed to carry out certain activities or are accountable in given situations, though not necessarily in the form of compensation for damages"②.

Under the ILC Draft Articles on Responsibility of States for Internationally Wrongful Acts, "every internationally wrongful act of the state entails the international responsibility of that state"③, and such an internationally wrongful act exists "when conduct consisting of an action or omission is attributable to the State under international law, and constitutes a breach of an international obligation of that State".④ This principle has been recognised by international tribunals in cases such as Spanish Zone of Morocco Claims, Chorzow Factory Case, and Corfu Channel Case⑤.

Navigation has traditionally been the responsibility of sovereign states,

---

① Ian Brownlie, Principles of Public International Law (6th edition, 2003), at 420.

② Stephen Gorove, Developments in Space Law: Issues and Policies (1991), at 224~225.

③ Draft Articles on Responsibility of States for Internationally Wrongful Acts, with Commentaries, 2001 Yearbook of the International Law Commission, Vol. II 31, at 32, Article 1 [hereinafter ILC Draft Articles on State Responsibility].

④ ILC Draft Articles on State Responsibility Article 2.

⑤ See Brownlie, see note ① above, at 421.

and satellite navigation will be no exception.① The following functions are relevant to responsibility: provision of primary signals; provision of space segment capability for secondary signalling; provision of secondary signals, State ATS authority to regulate for safety of air navigation, usage of GNSS services by the ATS and by aircraft operators, international regulation of satellite navigation services②.

International responsibility relates both to breaches of treaty and to other breaches of a legal duty.③ The basis of international responsibility of the primary signal providers lies in both the realms of international air law and space law.④ Such responsibility also generates from non-treaty obligations.

2.3.2 International Responsibility under Space Law

There is no doubt that satellite-based navigation is space activity and is therefore regulated by international space law. Although no specific provision in the space treaties deals with the international responsibility of GNSS signal provider states, the following articles in the 1967 Outer Space Treaty⑤ still imply such responsibilities.

Under Article III of the 1967 Outer Space Treaty, states shall carry on space activities in accordance with international law. The term "inter-

---

① Brocklebank, et al, see note ⑤, pp. 66, at 263.
② Henaku, see note ②, pp. 65, at 178.
③ Brownlie, see note ①, pp. 73, at 421.
④ See Henaku see note ②, pp. 65, at 187. See also Kim Murray, 'The Law Relating to Satellite Navigation and Air Traffic Management Systems-A View from the South Pacific', (1998) Vol. 53 Journal of Navigation 329, at 330; Michael, see note ②, pp. 70, at 247.
⑤ Treaty on Principles Governing the Activities of States in the Exploration and Use of Outer Space, including the Moon and Other Celestial Bodies, 610 UNTS 205 (1967) [hereinafter Outer Space Treaty].

national law" should be understood here in a broader sense, not limited to international conventions. The operation of the primary signal provision system shall not only be consistent with the Outer Space Treaty, but also other UN space treaties, other international treaties such as air law treaties, general principles of international law, customary international law and judicial decisions.

Article VI provides for international responsibility of States for their national activities in outer space, whether they are carried on by governmental agencies or non-governmental entities. It further provides that States are responsible for "assuring that national activities are carried out in conformity with the provisions set forth in the present Treaty" and the activities of non-governmental entities in outer space "shall require authorization and continuing supervision by the appropriate State Party to the Treaty". Moreover, when activities are carried on in outer space by an international organization, such responsibility "shall be borne by the international organization and by the State Parties to the Treaty participating in such organization".

Two concepts need to be clarified here. The first one is "national activities". In general international law, states are only responsible for their own activities; in case of private activities, a state is only responsible for its failure to control such activities[①]. Under this article, on the other hand, states are internationally responsible not only for their own activities, but also for activities carried on by private entities. That is to

---

[①] Armel Kerrest, 'Remarks on the Responsibility and Liability for Damages Caused by Private Activity in Outer Space', (1997) Proceedings of the Fortieth Colloquium on the Law of Outer Space 134, at 138. He further provides an example that in the well-known US-Canada Trail Smelter Case, the Arbitral Tribunal decided that Canada was responsible for a lack of efficient control of the smelter's activity, but Canada was not held responsible for the pollution as such.

say, the states are responsible not only for lack of "authorization and continuing supervision", but also for the consequence of the activities. Current and planned Global Navigation Satellite Systems are all owned and operated by States or international organisations. However, if in the future such a system is owned and operated by private entities, their national states shall still bear international responsibility under Article VI of the Outer Space Treaty.

The second concept is "space activities". Such activity in relation to contracting States' responsibility "is not necessarily restricted geographically, or cosmographically to only what occurs in outer space"[①]. That is to say, the international responsibility of States under Article VI would include "all the concomitant activities associated with what actually occurs in outer space, both before and after"[②]. Therefore, although not every step of the satellite navigation activities occurs in outer space, space segment operator states are still responsible for the entire process of navigation.

Moreover, Article IX of the Outer Space Treaty provides that state parties shall conduct their activities in outer space "with due regard to the corresponding interests of all other States Parties to the Treaty" and the obligation to "undertake appropriate international consultations", if it "has reason to believe" that space activities "would cause potentially harmful interference with activities of other States".

Based on the above articles in the Outer Space Treaty, it can be concluded that a GNSS signal provider state is internationally responsible for the navigation activities and for assuring such activities are carried

---

[①] See Bin Cheng, 'Article VI of the 1967 Space Treaty Revisited: "International Responsibility", "National Activities", and "The Appropriate State"', (1998) Journal of Space Law 7, at 27.

[②] Ibid.

on in conformity with the existing international norms. Even if the provider is a private company, its national state shall still bear such responsibility.

2.3.3 International Responsibility under Air Law

International air law also has a set of rules for GNSS in air navigation. The international responsibility of GNSS signal provider states are generated from Article 28 of the Chicago Convention[①] and relevant standards and recommended practices. Article 28 of the Chicago Convention requires States to provide air navigation facilities and services to facilitate international air navigation, in accordance with the standards and recommended practices, pursuant to the Convention. Another relevant article here is Article 37, which gives binding force to the ICAO standards in the Annexes.

This forms the basis of responsibility of GNSS primary signal providers. Although Article 28 requires States to provide air navigation facilities and services "in its territory", the practice of States and international agencies has led to the consensus that "Article 28 of the Chicago Convention does not prevent a contracting State from delegating its functions thereunder to a non-governmental entity, another State or an international agency"[②]. Despite that Article 28 "places primary responsibility on the States in whose territories the services are provided"[③],

---

　　① International Convention on Civil Aviation, Chicago, 15 UNTS 296 (1944) [hereinafter Chicago Convention].

　　② Jiefang Huang, Aviation Safety and ICAO (2009), at 36. He further points out that one example is Annex 11 to the Chicago Convention, which provides that "a State may delegate to another State the responsibility for establishing and providing air traffic services in flight information regions, control areas of control zones extending over the territories of the former".

　　③ Huang, ibid, at 37.

the GNSS primary signal provider states bear a "factual responsibility"[①] to provide GNSS signals to users in accordance with ICAO standards, due to the fact that the only primary GNSS signal providers are the United States and the Russian Federation, and therefore most States will have to rely on primary signals provided by others if the ICAO CNS/ATM systems are implemented.

The primary signal provider states bear an obligation to provide an acceptable level of service to users, in accordance with ICAO standards. The requirements of civil aviation include continuity, availability, integrity, accuracy and reliability[②]. The content of the responsibilities is irrelevant with whether the system is state owned or private. Nor does it make a difference whether the GNSS signals are used free of charges[③]. Therefore, GNSS primary signal provider states bear international responsibility for provision of GNSS signals for air navigation service in accordance with ICAO standards, under international air law.

2.3.4 International Responsibility Resulting from Service "Offers"

Both GPS and GLONASS were offered to the international civil aviation community to be used freely for a determined period. The offers, in the form of exchange of letters, have been accepted by the ICAO for and on behalf of its member states. These exchanges of letters provided contracting States of ICAO with assurance of universal accessibility to GPS

---

① See note ③, pp. 77.

② Charter on the Rights and Obligations of States Relating to GNSS Services, ICAO Assembly Resolution A32-19.

③ See Henaku, see note ②, pp. 65, at 188. See also Brocklebank, et al, see note ⑤, pp. 66 at 269.

and GLONASS①. This subsection will look into the question whether these offers generate international responsibility of primary signal provider states.

2.3.4.1 The Legal Effect of the Offers

In order to answer the above question, it is necessary to examine the legal effect of the offers: Do they provide legal obligations, or are they merely moral and political commitments?

Obviously, the offers are not "treaties" defined in the 1969 Vienna Convention of the Law of Treaties②, since ICAO is not a "state". However, as the Vienna Convention is a codification of international custom③, its provisions are generally accepted and binding.

There are no substantive requirements of form and thus, "an agreement may be recorded in an exchange of letters"④. The real issue is the substance of the agreement and whether language has been employed that clearly reveals the intention of the parties⑤.

The United States delegation stressed that the United States was not willing to sign a binding agreement on the GPS with the ICAO, which

---

① Jiefang Huang, 'Development of the Long-term Legal Framework for the Global Navigation Satellite System', (1997) Vol. XXII Annals of Air and Space Law 585, at 586.

② Vienna Convention on the Law of Treaties, 1155 UNTS 331 (1969) [hereinafter Vienna Convention]. Article 2 (a) "'Treaty' means an international agreement concluded between States in written form and governed by international law, whether embodied in a single instrument or in two or more related instruments and whatever its particular designation".

③ Brownlie, see note ①, pp. 73, at 63.

④ See ibid, at 581.

⑤ Henaku, see note ②, pp. 66, at 183.

clearly showed that the exchange was "in lieu of agreement" [1]. Thus the offer per se "is not meant to be a treaty"[2], "making the legal efficacy of this situation not reassuring"[3]. However, it is not to suggest that no obligation arises therefrom or from any of the numerous promises. Indeed the relation has been described as "a non-binding international agreement" in US law[4], but "a strong commitment if not an enforceable international agreement"[5] and "a mere intention to make GPS-SPS available"[6].

The exchange of letters between ICAO and Russian Federation, on the other hand, may be considered as a binding agreement, because it is a clear expression of an intention to be bound by the terms of the agreement[7].

2.3.4.2 International Responsibility for the Offers on the Basis of a Unilateral Act

Acts and conduct of governments may not be directed towards the formation of agreements and yet are capable of creating legal effects[8]. Promises and other unilateral acts do not necessarily constitute binding

---

[1] See note [5], pp. 79.

[2] Ibid.

[3] Murray, see note [4], pp. 74, at 332.

[4] Jonathan M. Epstein, 'Global Positioning System: Defining the Legal Issues of Its Expanding Civil Use', (1995) Vol. 61 Journal of Air Law and Commerce 243, at 276.

[5] Ibid, at 277.

[6] Scott Pace et al, The Global Positioning System: Assessing National Policies (1995): http://www.rand.org/pubs/monograph_reports/2007/MR614.pdf (last visited 29 June 2009).

[7] See Henaku, see note [2], pp. 66, at 107.

[8] Brownlie, see note [1], pp. 73, at 612.

legal obligations, but the content of the unilateral acts and the circumstances surrounding them will by and large determine whether and to what extent they are binding on the declarant state①. In the context of GNSS signal provision, even if the United States and Russian Federation "based their offer to the international community on a unilateral statement"②, promises made by such unilateral acts concerning legal or factual situations may have the effect of creating legal obligations. ③

The ILC Draft Articles of State Responsibility states that there is a breach of an international obligation when the act in question is not in conformity with what is required by that obligation "regardless of its origin"④. As this phrase indicates, the articles are of general application⑤. Thus States "may assume international obligations by a unilateral act"⑥. This principle was recognized by ICJ in, for instance, the Nuclear Tests Case⑦.

The ILC's Guiding Principles applicable to unilateral declarations of States capable of creating legal obligations⑧ also recognise that unilater-

---

① Robert Jennings and Arthur Watts (eds.) Oppenheim's International Law (9th ed 1992), at 1028.
② Milde, see note ④, pp. 67, at 352.
③ K. Skubiszewski, 'Unilateral Acts of States', in M. Bedjaoui (ed.) International Law: Achievements and Prospects (1991) 221, at 229; I. Detter, The International Legal Order, at 192. cited in Henaku, supra note 12, at 184.
④ ILC Draft Articles on State Responsibility Article 12.
⑤ See note ③, pp. 73, at 55.
⑥ Ibid.
⑦ Nuclear Tests (Australia v. France), ICJ Reports 1974; Nuclear Tests (New Zealand v. France), ICJ Reports 1974.
⑧ Guiding Principles Applicable to Unilateral Declarations of States Capable of Creating Legal Obligations, with Commentaries Thereto, 2006 Yearbook of the International Law Commission, Vol. II, at 369~381.

al declarations may create international legal obligations[①]. Elements to determine the legal effects of such declarations include the content, circumstances, and reactions[②], and only certain persons are competent to make such declarations[③]. After examining the elements consisting of a unilateral declaration that would arise to international obligation, it is safe to conclude that the unilateral acts by the United States, in the form of exchange of letters, give rise to its international responsibility.

2.3.4.3 International Responsibility Resulting from Agreements

Different from GPS, the GLONASS service offer is regarded as a binding agreement. The future Galileo will provide signals in air navigation based on contracts as well. That is to say, there is a contractual relationship, i.e. an agreement, between users and providers. If the users are states or other subjects of international law, treaties will be concluded. Pacta sunt servanda is a general principle of international law and is codified in Vienna Convention, which states that "every treaty in force is binding upon the parties to it and must be performed by them in good faith"[④]. In this case, their responsibilities will be provided in respective contracts.

2.3.5 Concluding Remarks on International State Responsibility

This section deals with the responsibility issues. Based on the above analysis, it is safe to conclude that GNSS primary signal provider states are internationally responsible under both lex specialis and lex generalis. In addition, international responsibility also derives from their non-treaty obligation if the service provision is unilateral, and treaty obliga-

---

① See note ⑧, pp. 81, Principle 1.
② Ibid, Principle 3.
③ Ibid, Principle 4.
④ Vienna Convention Article 26.

tion, if the service is based on agreement.

2.4 International Liability of GNSS Signal Provider States

Another important issue is liability. In this section, I will examine the liability of GNSS primary signal provider states for damage caused by signal malfunction. As there are no explicit provisions for liability of navigation service providers in international air law conventions, I would like to focus my discussion mainly on the space treaties, especially the Liability Convention.

2.4.1 The Notion of Liability

In connection with liability, we are dealing with legal consequences (mostly in terms of damages) arising from a particular behaviour[①]. Liability is generally defined as a "condition of being responsible for a possible or actual loss, penalty, evil, expense or burden" and as "the state of being bound or obliged in law of justice to do, pay, or make good something"[②] and "the accountability of a person or entity for damage caused to another person or entity as defined and regulated by a particular set of rules of principle"[③] It depends upon a specific legal regime, which itself determines the boundaries of the particular liability regime at issue regarding where it applies, which persons or legal entities are involved, what type of liability is provided for, and how compensation is being dealt with[④].

---

① Gorove, see note ②, pp. 73, at 224~225.

② Black's Law Dictionary (5th edition 1979), at 823.

③ Working Group Paper 3 Definition of the Requirements for a Liability System for GNSS -2, 28 June 1999 European Commission at 1.2 at 63, cited in Andries, see note ⑤, pp. 66, at 63.

④ von der Dunk, see note ②, pp. 67, at 133.

2.4.2 International Liability under Space Law

The issues we are concerned are that: Should the primary GNSS signal provider bear any liability to compensate the damage to the victims (e. g. in a plane crash due to the malfunction of a GNSS satellite)? If so, what is the legal basis? If not, is there any legal basis for other liable parties, such as the airline, to seek indemnification from the GNSS signal provider state?

The liability of a launching state for damage is generally provided in Article VII of the Outer Space Treaty. This is further specified in the 1972 Liability Convention①. The only possible applicable provision is Article II of the Liability Convention, which imposes absolute liability on the launching State "for damage caused by its space object on the surface of the Earth or to aircraft in flight". There are four elements in this article: (1) The liable party is a "launching State" in Article I; (2) the "damage" falls within the scope of "damage" in Article I; (3) the damage is "caused by" a "space object"; (4) the damage occurred on the surface of the Earth of aircraft in flight.

Let us suppose that elements 1 and 4 are satisfied. Then, in order to apply this article, it is necessary to examine the two questions respectively in the following two sub-subsections: (1) Can damage caused by GNSS signal malfunction be considered as damage "caused by a space object" under the Liability Convention? (2) Is there any causal link between damage and GNSS signal malfunction?

2.4.2.1 The Scope of Damage "Caused by a Space Object"

Pursuant to the Liability Convention, the term "damage" is defined as "loss of life, personal injury or other impairment of health; or loss of or

---

① Convention on International Liability for Damage Caused by Space Objects, 961 UNTS 187 (1972) [hereinafter Liability Convention].

damage to property of States or of persons, natural or juridical, or property of international intergovernmental organizations"①. To determine applicability of Article II of the Liability Convention, it is necessary to identify whether these damages are "caused by a space object". The Liability Convention defines space object as "include component parts of a space object as well as its launch vehicle and parts thereof"②. It is difficult to identify whether the GNSS signal is a "space object"; it is even difficult to identify whether it is an "object" because the signals are intangible, but objects are most often tangible. In short, it is not very realistic to consider the GNSS signal "a space object". However, since the signals can be traced to the navigation satellites, the damage could still be considered to be "caused by a space object".

2.4.2.2 The Causal Link between Damage and GNSS Satellites

Then the question is raised whether "caused by" means that "direct contact" must be made or whether it is enough that the damage was a consequence of a space object③. In other words, will the Liability Convention cover proof of causation only in case where the said damage is suffered on "direct impact or hit"④? Will indirect, consequential damage fall within its scope?

Most of the discussions on the Liability Convention have tended to settle on the issue of direct and indirect damage. No agreement was reached at the sixth session of UNCOPUOS as for whether or not to include in

---

① Liability Convention Article I (a).

② Liability Convention Article I (c).

③ See e.g., Bruce A. Hurwitz, Space Liability for Outer Space Activities in Accordance with the 1972 Convention on International Liability for Damages Caused by Space Objects (1992), at 17.

④ See e.g., Gorove, see note ②, pp. 73, at 149; Carl Q. Christol, Space Law: Past, Present and Future (1991), at 223.

the definition a reference to indirect damage and delayed damage①. At its seventh session in 1967, the majority of delegates regarded the matter as one of adequate causality which need not be expressed in the convention②.

The language of directness concentrates on physical contact③. Article II might "at first sight appear to apply to damage caused by reliance on faulty GNSS"④. However, the Liability Convention has been interpreted by some "to apply only to direct damage attributable to a crashing space object or a collision between space objects in outer space"⑤. They believe that only those types of damages, which can be substantiated as having occurred on "physical impact with the space object or parts of the space object", can be covered under this article⑥. According to this view the Liability Convention would not apply to damage caused indirectly through an orbiting GNSS space object transmitting faulty navigation and positioning information⑦.

On the other hand, some are of the view that the Liability Convention applies to both direct and indirect damage caused by space objects⑧. They identify the GNSS satellite as an "indirect" cause of the damage,

---

① Nandasiri Jasentuliyana and Roy S. K. Lee, Manual on Space Law, vol. 1 (1979), at 115.
② Ibid.
③ See Henaku, see note ②, pp. 66, at 230.
④ Lyall and Larsen, see note ①, pp. 63, at 405.
⑤ Ibid.
⑥ See e. g. , Frans G. von der Dunk, Private Enterprise and Public Interest in the European "Spacescape"-Towards Harmonized National Space Legislation for Private Space Activities in Europe (1998). See also, Gorove, see note ②, pp. 73, at 149.
⑦ Lyall and Larsen, see note ①, pp. 63, at 405.
⑧ Bin Cheng, Studies in International Space Law (1997) at 506.

based on the fact that "the signals can be traced to a particular satellite and the satellite can be identified"① and believe that "governments would be liable for their navigation satellites under the Outer Space Treaty, Art VII, and under the Liability Convention"②.

In relation to the US GPS, the view was expressed that:

"…the U. S. would probably refuse to recognize the validity of a claim filed against it for damages arising indirectly from incorrect GPS data. …While the U. S. might be willing to consider claims for indirect damages, it is under no obligation to settle them by virtue of any provision in the Convention."③

Here I would like to share Henaku's interpretation of the above statement④:

– that damage can be (proximately) caused by a GNSS satellite;

– and that direct or immediate damage would be easily accepted;

– but that the indirect damage (i. e., damage remotely removed from the act or a loss which cannot be attributed to the act) was not covered by the Liability Convention;

– therefore the indirect damage will not be accepted by the US.

Therefore, to a certain extent, the conclusion that direct damages will be allowed clearly assumes that GNSS signals can cause damage⑤. That

---

① Henaku, see note ②, pp. 66, at 225.

② Paul B. Larsen, 'Legal Liability for Global Navigation Satellite Systems', (1993) Proceedings of the Thirty-Sixth Colloquium on the Law of Outer Space at 89.

③ K. K. Spradling, 'The International Liability Ramifications of the US NAVSTAR Global Positioning System', (1990) Proceedings of the Thirty-third Colloquium on the Law of Outer Space 93, at 98.

④ See Henaku, see note ②, pp. 66, at 227.

⑤ Ibid.

is to say, although the issue whether "indirect damage" also falls within the scope of "damage" under the Liability Convention is not yet determined, the causation link between damage and a GNSS satellite could be expected.

Based on the above analysis, as long as there is sufficient evidence in the facts to prove the causal link, State A is liable for Damage 1 ~ 5 in the table under the Liability Convention, and therefore it is obliged to compensate the victims "with international law and the principles of justice and equity, in order to provide such reparation in respect of the damage as will restore the person, natural juridical, State or international organization on whose behalf the claim is presented to the condition which would have existed if the damage had not occurred"[1].

2.4.3 International Liability under Air Law

International air law deals with both third-party liability and inter-party liability[2]. The 1952 Rome Convention[3] deals with liability to third parties, focusing on the "operator of the aircraft"[4]. One article in this Convention provides for the right of recourse of the liable party against other persons[5]. If the state in whose territory the accident occurred is a contracting State to the Rome Convention, the operator of the flight in question has the right of recourse against the GNSS signal provider (the real liable party as well) under this provision in terms of damage occurring on the surface.

---

① Liability Convention Article XII.
② von der Dunk, see note ⑤, pp. 68, at 236~237.
③ Rome Convention on Damage Caused by Foreign Aircraft to Third Parties on the Surface, 478 UNTS 371 (1952) [hereinafter Rome Convention].
④ Rome Convention Article 1.
⑤ Rome Convention Article 10.

As for inter-party liability, we have to refer to the Warsaw System[①] and Montreal Convention[②]. There is no provision in any of these conventions for the liability of the air navigation service provider in case of an accident or delay. Neither do they provide for rights of air carriers to claim indemnification against the party at fault.

When it comes to state practice, court decisions resulting in successful claims are rare, while a handful of cases exist where air navigation service providers have voluntarily agreed to compensation gestures in the name of customer services.[③] Currently the only primary signal provider which is capable to provide global air navigation service is the United States, but there have been no reported cases holding the US Government responsible for failure of aviation navigational aids[④]. But there are examples under domestic case law to impose liability on air navigation service providers. One example is Ingham v. Eastern Airlines in the United States, in which the Court held that the failure of an air traffic controller to provide accurate weather forecasts was the proximate cause of the crash. It further stated that while establishment of an air traffic system was discretionary, once established, employees are required to act in a reasonable manner, and the Government was liable

---

① Convention for the Unification of Certain Rules Relating to International Carriage by Air, Signed at Warsaw on 12 October 1929 [hereinafter Warsaw Convention]. It was amended by the Hague Protocol, Guatemala City Protocol and Montreal Additional Protocol.

② Convention for the Unification of Certain Rules Relating to International Carriage by Air, Signed at Montreal on 28 May 1999 [hereinafter Montreal Convention].

③ Francis P. Schubert, 'An International Convention on GNSS Liability: When Does Desirable Become Necessary?', (1999) Vol. XXIV Annals of Air and Space Law 245 at 246.

④ Michael, see note ②, pp. 70, at 247.

for failure to do so. Similarly, it is reasonable to conclude that the Government would be liable if the failure of the signal was the proximate cause of a crash①.

Another example is EC Regulation 261/2004②. This regulation is not targeted directly at the activities of air navigation services providers and its scope is explicitly limited to the liability of air carriers. It is legitimate that airlines should either be exempted from paying compensation for damages attributable to third parties or able to recover these amounts from the parties responsible for the loss③. Therefore EC Regulation 261/2004 creates potential liability exclusively for air carriers while reserving their rights of recourse④. Air carrier's right of redress from the party at fault is provided in Article 13⑤.

2.4.4. International Liability on the basis of the Good Samaritan Principle

The principle of good faith is also recognised in domestic law. In the

---

① See note ④, pp. 89.

② REGULATION (EC) No. 261/2004 OF THE EUROPEAN PARLIAMENT AND OF THE COUNCIL of 11 February 2004 establishing common rules on compensation and assistance to passengers in the event of denied boarding and of cancellation or long delay of flights, and repealing Regulation (EEC) No 295/91 [hereinafter EC Regulation 261/2004].

③ Francis P. Schubert, 'The Liability of Air Navigation Services for Air Traffic Delays and Flight Cancellations: the Impact of EC Regulation 261/04', (2007) Vol. XXXII Annals of Air and Space Law 65, at 74.

④ Ibid.

⑤ EC Regulation 261/2004 Article 13: "In cases where an operating air carrier pays compensation or meets the other obligations incumbent on it under this Regulation, no provision of this Regulation may be interpreted as restricting its right to seek compensation from any person, including the third parties, in accordance with the law applicable."

United States, there is a principle called "good Samaritan doctrine", which holds that one who undertakes, gratuitously, or for consideration, to render services to another which he should recognize as necessary for the protection of the other's person or things, is subject to liability to the other for physical harm resulting from his failure to exercise reasonable care to perform his undertaking if: a) this failure to exercise such care increases the risk of such harm or: b) the harms is suffered because of the other's reliance upon the undertaking[①].

This principle has been applied in many US cases, among which some involving air traffic control[②]. The Good Samaritan doctrine can be applied by analogy to the promise to provide GNSS signals to the civil aviation community[③]. By undertaking to offer the signals to the international civil aviation community, the signal provider states have placed themselves in the position of the parabolic good Samaritan and have consequently assumed a duty of care involving taking all necessary measures not to cause injury to any state or any user for that matter. As has been intimated here above, any unannounced interference by signal providers which resulting damage to any state or citizen of any state will

---

① Section 323 Restatement of the Law (second) Torts, vol. 2 American Law Institute Publishers, 1965.

② Henaku, see note ②, pp. 66, at 197. For example, in Ingham v Eastern Airlines Inc. the US Court of Appeal held that "when the government undertakes no perform services, which in the absence of specific legislation would not be required, it will nevertheless be held liable if these activities are performed negligently. … In light of this reliance, it is essential that the government properly perform those services it has undertaken to provide albeit voluntarily and gratuitously …" In another case, the court construed similar constraints: "… once the government takes an action, such as marking a reef or placing a navigation aid, it must act reasonably with respect to those who are likely to rely upon it."

③ Henaku, see note ②, pp. 66, at 198.

result in liability claims being brought against the provider states. Thus the provider is required to act as any private person, or private company will act when involved as promisor and provider of satellite navigation service[①].

2.4.5 Contractual Liability

If the provider state has concluded a bilateral agreement on air navigation services with the augmentation service provider state or the air traffic control agency, the liability will be attributed on the basis of the liability clause in the agreement, as long as the liability clause is compatible with the provisions in international law.

2.4.6 Concluding Remarks on International State Liability

This section examined liability issues. There is no specific provision in either international space law or international air law. The only way to establish GNSS signal providers' liability under international space law is to prove the causal link between the signal malfunction and the accident, regardless of the existence of the physical impact. In the realm of air law, although there is no provision in relevant international conventions, the liability issue of signal provider is left to state practice. In addition, if the GNSS signal providers have concluded agreements with users, their liability will be determined by the agreements.

2.5 Concluding Remarks

No system is a hundred percent safe and GNSS is not an exception. Current incidents caused by GPS signal malfunction indicate the potential risk of signal malfunction in air navigation.

GNSS primary signal providers are the starting of the service supply chain and GNSS activities are regulated by both international air law and space law, but there is no specific provision on their international

---

① See note ③, pp. 91.

responsibility and liability. In terms of responsibility, signal provider states are obliged to bear State responsibility under both lex specialis and lex generalis. It is also possible to establish their liability, under the current legal regime. Moreover, their responsibility and liability are provided in bilateral or multilateral agreements with users, if any. However, the current regulatory regime for GNSS primary signal providers is insufficient.

3. Uniform International Rules on GNSS Liability?

Since neither in international law nor domestic law can we find rules specifically dealing with the liability of GNSS signal providers, the issue of uniform rules on GNSS liability has been raised from time to time. Whether or not we need an international convention specific to GNSS issues, especially liability issues, has been discussed in the international society over years. International organisations, such as ICAO and UNIDROIT, put this issue on their agendas. States expressed different views during the discussions and no consensus was reached. This chapter will summarize the discussions in ICAO and UNIDROIT.

3.1 ICAO

The Eleventh ICAO Air Navigation Conference was held in 2003 in Montreal, Canada. The need for an international GNSS liability regime was one of the vital subjects addressed in this Conference. Even though there is no consensus on the form of any new instrument, there has been much discussion on what features it might contain[①].

---

① LEGAL ASPECTS OF GNSS presented by African States in the Eleventh Air Navigation Conference, Montreal, 22 September to 3 October 2003, AN-Conf/11-WP/143, para. 1.3.

3.1.1 Views of Member Sates

Member states expressed different views on the future international legal framework on GNSS service. User states such as African states make a strong case for an international convention which should be binding and enforceable and clearly spell out the rights and responsibilities of all parties involved in the GNSS, CNS/ATM service. They proposed that in the statement, they share the view that certain principles may be considered in establishing the Convention relating to GNSS service[①]: The consideration of the legal framework resulted in the consensus on the text of a draft Charter on the Rights and Obligations of States Relating to GNSS Services, which was adopted by the 32nd Session of the Assembly in the form of Resolution A32-49, was proposed by African states.

The "Contractual Framework" is an interim framework proposed by European states, referred to as "a middle ground" and "a realistic stepping stone" towards an international convention[②]. It is based on a two-tier approach. On one level, it offers a regulatory agreement dealing with public law matters including certification, liability and jurisdictional maters. Another level consists of private contractual agreements between the various stakeholders in which they would have a very large degree of autonomy subject to certain mandatory elements determined

---

① See note ①, pp. 93, para. 2.5.

② GNSS LEGAL FRAMEWORK: CONTRACTUAL FRAMEWORK FOR THE IMPLEMENTATION, PROVISION, OPERATION AND USE OF THE GLOBAL NAVIGATION SATELLITE SYSTEM FOR AIR NAVIGATION PURPOSES, presented by the European Organisation for the Safety of Air Navigation-EUROCONTROL, on behalf of its Member States and those of ECAC, in the Eleventh Air Navigation Conference, Montreal, 22 September to 3 October 2003, AN-Conf/11 – WP/153 para. 1.2.

by the regulatory agreement①. European states made this proposal taking into account their specific regional requirements, namely the future provision of EGNOS and Galileo②.

As for the contractual framework, it is proposed that the framework agreement would establish the state responsibility for GNSS implementation pursuant to Article 28 of the Chicago Convention, and that they have to verify that GNSS service providers and operators comply with the requirements set out in private law contracts when performing activities over their territory③. The framework agreement aims at the introduction of mandatory common elements which will need to include in contracts involving system operators or service providers④.

The view was expressed by the US delegation that "the United States believes that this conference should do no such thing, for both procedural and substantive reason"⑤ and that "the conference is invited to agree ⋯ that ICAO's long-term legal framework-the Chicago Convention, its Annexes, and ICAO guidance materials-offers continued serviceability and no deficiencies have been found to impede technical implementation of CNS/ATM"⑥.

3.1.2 Discussion after the Eleventh Air Navigation Conference

The ICAO Study Group on Legal Aspects of CNS/ATM Systems submitted its final report in 2004, which contained the issue of liability. This

---

① ICAO Doc A36-WP/140.
② See note ②, pp. 94, para. 1.4.
③ Ibid, para. 2.2.
④ Ibid, para 3.2 and 3.3.
⑤ LEGAL AND INSTITUTIONAL ISSUES AND THE STATUS OF CNS/ATM, presented by the United States in the Eleventh Air Navigation Conference, Montreal, 22 September to 3 October 2003, AN-Conf/11-WP/160, para. 1.
⑥ Ibid para 6.1 (c).

report was presented to the 35th ICAO General Assembly in 2004 for the adoption of a resolution[①]. In Subsection 3.3.3 of the report, the Group identified three possible approaches to the problem of liability relating to GNSS, including: (1) to ensure that the doctrine of sovereign immunity and related principles will not be an obstacle to bringing all potential defendants; (2) to establish an adequate recourse action mechanism for the state having jurisdiction and the aircraft operator to take recourse against other party at fault; (3) to ensure adequate compensation coverage[②].

The European Civil Aviation Conference (ECAC) acting on behalf of its 41 members also submitted a working paper to the 35th ICAO General Assembly with the draft on a "contractual framework" as Appendix B and a draft convention as Appendix C to the working paper[③]. The 35th ICAO General Assembly in 2004 resolved to finalise a contractual framework in line with the ECAC proposal[④]. However, the 36th ICAO General Assembly in 2007 no longer regarded the finalisation of the contractual framework as a task for the ICAO. Finally the 36th ICAO General Assembly in 2007 downgraded the priority of this project[⑤]. Till

---

① Hans-Goerg Bollweg, Initial Considerations regarding the Feasibility of an International UNIDOIT Instrument to Cover Liability for Damage Caused by Malfunctions in Global (Navigation) Satellite System, (2008) Vol. XIII Uniform Law Review 917, at 926~927.

② REPORT ON THE ESTABLISHMENT OF A LEGAL FRAMEWORK WITH REGARD TO CNS/ATM SYSTEMS INCLUDING GNSS, ICAO Doc A35 - WP/75, Appendix para. 3.3.3.

③ DEVELOPMENT OF A CONTRACTUAL FRAMEWORK LEADING TOWARDS A LONG-TERM LEGAL FRAMEWORK TO GOVERN THE IMPLIMENTATION OF GNSS, ICAO Doc A35 - WP/125.

④ Bollweg, see note ① above.

⑤ Ibid.

today there is no consensus as to whether an international legal regime on GNSS service is in need.

3.2 UNIDROIT (International Institute for the Unification of Private Law)

At the suggestion of the Italian Government, the UNIDROIT Governing Council held initial consultations at its 85th session in 2006 on the inclusion of a new project in the UNIDROIT Work Programme: the elaboration of an international instrument to cover liability for damage caused by malfunctions in global (navigation) satellite service. At its 86th session in 2007, the UNIDROIT Council received a feasibility study entitled "The civil liability and compensation for damage resulting from the performing of European GNSS Services", which came to a positive assessment. In the following year, it took up this issue at its 87th session, under the proposal that the Triennial Work Programme 2009-2011 might include "work on liability for malfunctions of navigation systems and other satellite-based services". Another study paper was compiled under the request by the 86th UNIDROIT Governing Council in 2007. [1]

With reference to studies prepared by ICAO, ECAC and preliminary work on a European Community Regulation, the author of this study paper came to the conclusion that it is not a good time for such a UNIDROIT GNSS liability convention, based on three reasons. Firstly, among current and planned GNSS systems, Galileo is the only commercial one. It is too unusual to have an international convention on just one single subject of liability. Secondly, if the regulation under European Community law is formed, it would have the disadvantage of applying only to areas covered by the law-making competence of the Com-

---

[1]　See note [4], pp. 96.

munity and would not cover cases of damage occurring outside the Community. Finally, a UNIDROIT convention would come too late for Galileo supposing the system comes into operation in 2013 as planned①.

3.3 Concluding Remarks

This chapter dealt with issues concerning the future GNSS liability regime. Different States, representing different interest groups, take different positions. The discussion in international organisations such as ICAO and UNIDROIT indicate that it is not easy to reach consensus in the near future as to whether an international GNSS convention is in need and whether it is feasible.

4. Topics that a GNSS Liability Convention Would Need to Cover

A number of legal issues, both substantive and procedural, were addressed in the discussion above, such as the form of the legal instrument to be adopted, the basis of liability, the question of state immunity, jurisdiction, the scope of damage, or the channeling of liability②. As a liability regime is always victim-oriented, such a legal regime should ensure the prompt payment of a full and equitable measure of compensation to victims③ and provide recourse to remedy to the greatest extent possible. In this section, I would like to discuss issues concerning basis of liability, joint and several liability, and state immunity.

4.1 Absolute Liability or Fault Liability

If we want to establish fault liability to a party, fault or negligence of

---

① See note ④, pp. 96.
② See Milde, see note ④, pp. 67, at 354; Henaku, see note ②, pp. 66, Chapter 8.
③ Liability Convention Preamble.

that party must be proven. On the other hand, if the liability is absolute (or strict), there is no need to proof fault or negligence. The victims only need to demonstrate the loss, the wrongful act, and the causal link between them.

Under normal circumstances, international law does not impose liability on States for lawful activities[①]. Space activities are an exception to this principle, as States may be held liable even if their activities are not prohibited under international law. In this case, liability was usually based on fault, that is to say, liability is attached to the person causing harm intentionally or negligently[②]. However, when the nature of the activity is "ultra-hazardous", the liability shall be absolute, and the liability therefore is incurred irrespective of the perpetrator's compliance with the required standards of care[③].

There already existed a generally accepted rule that "ultra-hazardous activity in an act of conduct necessarily involves a risk of serious harm to a person, land or chattels of others which cannot be eliminated by the utmost care and which is not a matter of common usage"[④]. Although space activities have rapidly developed in the past decades, it is still regarded "ultra-hazardous". In the case of air navigation, if the accident occurred due to the GNSS signal malfunction, the lives of hundreds of people on board the plane are threatened and there is little possibility for them to survive. That is why States pay much more attention to safety regulation of air navigation as compared to, for example, personal vehicle positioning. In addition, it is unreasonable to impose

---

① Manfred Lachs, The International Law of Outer Space (1964), at 78.
② Hurwitz, see note ③, pp. 85, at 27.
③ See ibid.
④ I. H. Ph. Diederiks-Verschoor, An Introduction to Space Law (3rd edition 2008), at 31.

the burden of proof of fault/negligence on victims, because the proof is almost impossible for ordinary people and they can never foresee such danger.

Moreover, the absolute liability regime is supported by international conventions dealing with "ultra-hazardous" activities or catastrophes. An example is the Nuclear Damage Convention[①], which imposes strict liability on nuclear installation operators. Support for an absolute liability may also be found in international judicial decisions.[②] The most famous case is the Trail Smelter Case in which the arbitral tribunal held Canada liable to pay damages despite the fact that there was no negligence in the pollution of the US territory[③].

In fact Article II of the Liability Convention is an even better example. From the analysis in Subsection 2.4.1, this article is applicable to accidents caused by GNSS signal malfunction. Based on these reasons, therefore, it is reasonable to establish absolute liability in a GNSS convention.

4.2 Joint and Several Liabilities

There is a need to establish joint and several liability in a GNSS convention. Joint and Several Liability means that victims can claim compensation for damages from any potential liable party, and that party is obliged to compensate; after that, it can claim indemnification from the real liable party.

The rationale behind this is yet again that such a liability convention is victim-oriented. More importantly, due to the complicated navigation technology, it is not that easy to prove which party/parties is/are lia-

---

① Vienna Convention on Civil Liability for Nuclear Damage (1963) [hereinafter Nuclear Damage Convention].
② Hurwitz, see note ③, pp. 85, at 29.
③ Kerrest, see note ①, pp. 75.

ble. It is possible that the accident is solely caused by the malfunction of signal from GNSS satellite. It is also possible that there is nothing wrong with the primary signal system, but the secondary signal system, namely augmentation system, fails. It is also possible that the problem does not lie in the signals, but the receivers on board the plane. It is also possible that the pilot of the aircraft does not follow the safety regulations or there is design deficiency of the plane. It is even possible that two or more causes jointly led to the accident. In such case, where there is no joint and several liabilities, victims have to wait long until the result of the investigation comes out before they can bring a lawsuit, and sometimes the result will never come out. That would be unfair to the victims.

Another situation also supports the need for a joint and several liability regime. Currently, many parties are researching the interoperability and compatibility among different global navigation satellite systems. International bodies such as UNOOSA are also making such efforts. Now we already have receivers that can receive signals from both GPS and Compass, or both GPS and GLONASS. The future Galileo system is designed to be interoperable with GPS. The advantage of an interoperable and compatible system is that the superposition of signals will make it more accurate. However, the other side of the technology is that it is impossible to identify the source of the absent or error signals. In such case, the best solution, for the sake of victims, is that all the signal providers are jointly liable, while they are entitled to claim indemnification to other signal providers after the investigation, if there is any result.

Due to the possible scenarios described above, I believe that a joint and several liability regime is necessary.

4.3 Immunity

As current and planned GNSS primary signal providers are States and international organisations, it would be necessary to examine the issue of immunity. States and international organisations enjoy immunity from the jurisdiction of local courts and the local agencies of law enforcement①. The state immunity rules were codified by the ILC②. Under this convention, which tends to reflect communis opinio of different countries, only actions that can be defined as commercial transactions may be excluded from judicial immunity③. This rule also applies to international organsations. Therefore, it implies that damage deriving from commercial services may be subject to claims for compensation whereas damage caused by sovereign acts would benefit from procedural immunity④.

If the provision of signals is based on contract, like the case of Galileo, the service falls within the scope of "commercial transactions", and the provider states (or international organisations) are therefore not subject to immunity. If it is a non-contractual service, like the case of GPS, it is possible to be considered as sovereign acts and benefit from procedural immunity. However, whether or not the provider states enjoy state immunity depends on the domestic legislation of policy of that state. For instance, under the Federal Torts Claims Act of the United States, the government has waived immunity for claims caused by its wrongful acts.

---

① Brownlie, see note ①, pp. 73, at 319.

② United Nations Convention on Jurisdiction Immunities of States ad Their Property (2004).

③ United Nations Convention on Jurisdiction Immunities of States ad Their Property Article 10.

④ Pietro Manzini and Anna Masutti, 'An International Civil Liability Regime for Galileo Service: A Proposal', (2008) Vol. XXXII Issue 2 Air and Space Law 114, at 117~118.

4.4 Concluding Remarks

There are a number of issues that future GNSS liability rules need to cover, either an international convention or domestic legislation. Since the purpose of the liability rules is to provide full and equitable measure of compensation to victims, the basis of liability should be absolute liability and the joint and several liability rule should also be adopted. As for the issue of state immunity, in the case of service based on contract, the provider states are not subject to immunity; in the case of service without a contract, the issue depends on the domestic rules.

5. Conclusion

This paper examined the international responsibility and liability of GNSS signal provider states, which is placed on the starting point of the relationship chain, in air navigation under the current legal regime. First of all, in Chapter Two, I searched for legal basis under international law for such State responsibility and liability. After examining, inter alia, international air and space law, I conclude that although state responsibility and liability can be established under current international air and space law regime, as well as general international law, the international regulatory regime is insufficient to regulate GNSS activities.

Obviously the current legal regime, whether international or domestic, is insufficient to regulate GNSS activities. Therefore in Chapter Three, I looked into the proposed new GNSS liability convention. However, the study by ICAO and UNIDROIT indicates that there is no consensus as to whether such an international convention is necessary and feasible. The conclusion of the studies by UNIDROIT is not so positive, either. Finally in Chapter Four, I addressed some substantive liability issues mostly related to GNSS signal providers among the liability issues that could be included in such a new convention.

I would like to conclude that with the rapid development of GNSS technology and wide applications, especially in air navigation, a set of uniform international rules should be established. Considering the fact that it is not just a matter of law, but also a matter of politics and policy, it is reasonable to put the idea of a GNSS convention aside at the moment. Instead, states can gradually adopt rules regulating GNSS activities in their domestic legal regime. It is possible that new international custom will derive from the state practice.

世界各主要空间法中心硕士点课程体系和考核情况分析[①]

李杜[②]　赵海峰[③]

自1957年10月14日世界上第一颗人造卫星在苏联Sputnik 1（斯普特尼克1号）发射以来，越来越多的国家开始不同程度地开展外层空间活动，外层空间法也开始逐渐形成[④]。《关于各国探索和利用包括月球和其他天体在内外层空间活动的原则条约》于1963年通过之后，空间法开始慢慢出现在大学的教学提纲中，有的学校将空间法作为国际公法的一部分，有的学校则将其纳入航空法的教学范畴之中，也有一部分大学的研究中心将其本来的航空法研究中心拓展成为航空法与空间法研究中心，如加拿大麦吉尔大学的航空法和空间法中心等。至今，越来越多的空间法研究中心在全球范围内形成，其在空间法研究和教育上发挥越来越大的

[①] 本文为黑龙江教育科学规划课题"国际化法学人才培养研究"以及哈工大法学院首届教师创新基金项目世界各主要空间法中心教学体系及对我国的启示的部分成果。

[②] 李杜，巴黎第十一大学法学博士，现任华中科技大学法学院讲师。

[③] 赵海峰，国家法官学院教授。

[④] 外层空间法最开始是因为政治原因而在联合国的框架下形成的。参见 Kerrest（A.），L'Espace extra-atmosphérique-le cadre juridique de droit public，Editions du Juris-Classeur，2000，Fasc. 141-10.

作用。本文将对世界上现存的主要空间法中心的硕士教育进行研究,分析其课程体系及考核制度等,以求对中国的大学和空间法研究所开展空间法硕士教育提供借鉴。

一、北美空间法的硕士教育

北美地区是空间法研究的一个重要地区,因为美国和加拿大目前在外层空间活动领域都占有十分重要的地位。而北美也是空间法教育开展最早的地区之一。

(一)加拿大麦吉尔大学航空法和外层空间法研究所

加拿大麦吉尔大学于1951年成立航空法研究所(McGill Institute of Air Law)。该研究所在1957年扩展了研究教学领域并更名为航空法和外层空间法研究所(Institute of Air and Space Law)。至今,共有900多名学生从该研究所毕业,这些学生在全球120多个国家的律师事务所、公司、政府和跨政府机构中任职,不少担任要职。该研究所负责空间法的主任是Ram Jakhu副教授。

航空法和外层空间法研究所提供两种不同的硕士教育,论文硕士(Master of Laws with Thesis)教育和非论文硕士(Master of Laws Non-Thesis)教育。论文硕士教育更加注重研究,学生只针对其选择的法学领域进行深入调查,因此需要选择的课程也相对较少。而非论文硕士教育综合性强,学生可以选择更多的课程,广泛学习各种法律学科的知识。该研究所的硕士教育主要由三个部分组成:必修课、理论研究和选修课。其中必修课主要有三门,国际航空公法、国际航空私法以及空间法(一般原则)。可供选择的选修课程包括比较航空法、法学的理论研究方法、航空运输的政府调控、空间应用法、空间活动的政府调控、航空业和法律等。学生可根据自己感兴趣的方面来选择选修课来对该法学领域进行更加深入的了解和研究。航空法和空间法研究所十分注重培养学生的研究能力,理论研究在整个课程体系中占了相当重要的位置。攻读论文硕士的学生必须完成约30 000字的论文。在论文的完成过程中,学生还必须完成论文选题准备、文献评论准备、论文研究报告、论文的完成和最后的论文研究报告等阶段性成果。攻读非论文硕士的学生必须完成 15 000 字左右的与时事相关的研究报告。

该硕士项目的考核形式以笔头考试为主。必修课中的国际航空公法和国际航空私法均采取 24 小时内完成家庭作业形式,而空间法则采取 3 小时开卷考试形式。在选修课中,大部分课程均以期末开卷考试作为考核方式,但是也有少数课程以口头方式进行考核,如航空业和法律等。另外,论文或者研究报告的完成情况也构成取得学位与否的关键因素。

通过对麦吉尔大学航空法和外层空间法研究所的课程体系和考核方式进行研究我们可以发现,该硕士点的教育侧重点在于理论研究,并且学生在课程选择和研究领域的选择上有很大的自由。但是这种教育体系在对学生的实践素质的培养上稍显欠缺。

(二)美国提供空间法课程的研究中心

美国是一个超级空间大国。美国大学中有不少学校提供空间法教育,如密西西比大学,乔治·华盛顿大学[1],内布拉斯加大学等[2]。还有一些军事院校也提供空间法课程[3]。提供硕士研究课程的主要是新近的内布拉斯加大学法学院。

密西西比大学也是较早开展空间法研究的大学之一。自 20 世纪 60 年代起,密西西比大学法学院的一些教授像 Stephan Gorove 等就开始了空间法的研究,并且组织了一些空间法方面的学术会议。1999 年,密西西比大学法学院创立了国家遥感、航空和外空法研究中心(The National Center for Remote Sensing, Air, and Space Law at the University of Mississippi),成为全美国唯一提供航空法和

---

[1] 乔治·华盛顿大学的伊里亚德国际事务学院下设空间政策研究所,主要提供美国外层空间政策方面的研究生课程。

[2] 如乔治·顿大学法律中心,南加利福尼亚大学和麻省理工学院。

[3] 赵海峰,"国外国际空间法的教学与研究",《中国航天》,2006 年第 7 期,第 15 页。

空间法教育的教学机构。中心的前主任为 Joanne Irene Gabrynow-icz 教授。

该中心提供的空间法课程主要是由法学院的空间法的法律博士(Juris Doctor)①项目提出的;此外,该中心举办了国家遥感、航空和空间法中心证书项目(Certificate Programs),该证书项目课程由核心课程和选修课程组成。核心课程包括国际空间法、美国国内空间法和遥感法等。该证书提供的选修课科目十分丰富,以保证学生对美国法律制度和国际法的全面了解。课程包括行政法、通讯法、环境法、欧盟法、国际贸易仲裁、国际环境法、知识产权、国际法、国际安全法和政策、国际贸易、武装冲突法、遥感法等。该项目的学生还必须完成一篇与航空航天法有关的研究报告或者进行一个为期3个学分的实习。②

密西西比大学最新的进展是,它也在2014年兴办了航空和空间法硕士项目。密西西比大学法学院积极推进与中国的关系,从2010年起,与哈尔滨工业大学、北京理工大学的学生举办了学生空间法论坛,由各校每年派三个学生,就有关空间法的论题进行研究,共同开会,由学生发言、老师评论。2010、2012年在密西西比大学,2011年在北京理工大学举办了三届论坛。

---

① 美国大学的法学院学位一般分为三种,法学硕士(Master of Laws),法律博士和法学博士(Doctor of Juridical Science)。美国教育体系中没有法律本科学位,只有获得了其他专业本科学位的学生才能申请法律博士学位。申请该学位的学生需要提供语言考试成绩和 LSAT (Law School Admission Test) 法学院入学考试成绩。该学位学制一般为三年,其课程侧重于训练学生的法律实务技能。该学位的获得者可以参加美国任何一个州的律师资格考试而成为该州的执业律师。

② CERTIFICATE IN REMOTE SENSING, AIR, AND SPACE LAW NATIONAL CENTER FOR REMOTE SENSING, AIR AND SPACE LAW UNIVERSITY OF MISSISSIPPI SCHOOL OF LAW available at http://law.olemiss.edu/img/pdfs/Space% 20Law% 20Certificate% 20Web% 20description% 202009.pdf, last visited Aug. 28, 2011.

内布拉斯加大学（University of Nebraska-Lincoln）法学院于2006年春开始筹划设立一个空间法和电信法的硕士点。硕士点的设立于2007年被法学院及大学其他相关机构正式批准，并且自同年12月开始接受入学申请。著名的空间法学家 Frans von der Dunk 在这里任教。第一批空间法与电信法的学生于2008年秋正式入学。该学院提供三种学位，空间法和电信法法学硕士、专业方向为空间法和电信法的法律博士以及专业方向为空间法和电信法的法律硕士。学院开设了很多与空间法、电信法相关的科目，包括空间法、国家空间安全法、国家空间立法、欧洲空间法和电信法规定、电信法、国际电信法、空间法研究、网络法和国际法等。其中，法学硕士的学生必须修满国际法、空间法这两门基本课程、以及国家空间安全法、电信法、国际电信法/电信法 II、空间法研究等专业课，并且完成达到发表标准的论文。

在美国大学中，考核评定大致由两个方面组成：平时表现和期末考试。平时的表现体现在课程参与以及作业的完成程度上。学生的出勤率低和作业完成情况不佳将直接影响学生该门课程的最终成绩。期末考试和中国大学的考试类似，一般均安排在学期末的一段特定的时间内进行。除了完成课程之外，论文的完成也占有相当比重的学分。

二、欧洲的空间法硕士教育

在欧洲开设硕士点的大学主要有两个，荷兰莱顿大学和法国巴黎第十一大学。不少其他的教育机构也开设与空间法相关的课程。

（一）荷兰莱顿大学国际航空法与空间法研究所（International Institute of Air & Space Law at the University of Leiden）。

荷兰莱顿大学也是较早开展空间法教学的教学机构之一。该校所属的国际航空法与空间法研究所自1938年起开始教授航空法课程,自 1986 年起,开始同时研究航空法与空间法。2000 年 9 月,该所正式开展航空法和空间法硕士项目。这个硕士项目的学习方式主要有两种,全职在校学习以及远程与在校相结合的学习方式①。这两种学习方式的学生成绩合格都能获得学位。中心现在的副主任是由 T. L. Masson-Zwaan 教授担任,她也同时担任国际空间法学会的会长。

莱顿大学国际航空法和空间法研究所的航空法和空间法硕士项目是站在世界性角度和欧洲角度对航空公法、航空私法和空间法进行的整体教育。与其他研究所的课程相比,该硕士项目的课程有一个很大的特点,就是课程中包括了模拟法庭竞赛,且这门课程在两个学期都有占到相应的学分。每个学生都必须参加模拟法庭竞赛以达到法律实践的效果,使学生能够活学活用,并且锻炼了学生的法律实务能力。除了模拟法庭之外,航空私法、航空公法、航空运输竞争法和政策、欧洲航空航天法、空间法和政策、案例分析、空间法和政策等也是硕士项目的主要课程。最后,学生还必须完成论文和参加实习以得到这两项所对应的学分。其教学方法相教于北美的一些空间法研究所比较多样,不仅包括了传统的授课法,还有来自实践部门人员的讲座、研讨会、模拟法庭、报告等方式。

航空法和空间法的硕士项目的考核方式十分多样,除了传统的笔试之外,还有做报告形式和课堂讨论形式。如空间法和政策、欧洲航空航天法这两门课程,即是采用的做报告形式和笔试相结合的考试形式。而空间法和政策——案例分析,则是按照学生在课堂的参与讨论程度来直接决定某学生通过该门课程进而拿到学分与否。

莱顿大学国际航空法和空间法中心也接收博士生,由中心的教授指导。

从莱顿大学航空法和空间法硕士项目的课程设置和考核方式可以看出,虽然该硕士点与空间法相关的课程比较基础性,但是实用

---

① 该学习方式自 2005 年 9 月开始施行。

性很强,通过整个课程和考核的安排,使学生对航空法和空间法的应用能力得到加强。但是在研究能力的培养上,似乎还有所欠缺。

(二)法国巴黎第十一大学空间法和电信法研究所

巴黎第十一大学的空间法和电信法研究所(Institut du droit de l'espace et des télécommunications)是法国最重要的空间法的硕士教育机构。该所隶属于法学院的国际研究院,自2002年起创办了空间法和电信法的硕士点,并且在不断的自我完善中。所长为Philippe Achilléas副教授。每年,该硕士点都会与不同的政府机构或者公司合作,如欧洲空间局、法国电信等,来保障学生能与空间法和电信法相关行业的专业人士得到一定的接触,并通过这种方式对该行业的实际情况得到相应的了解。

该硕士点提供两种不同的硕士教育,研究型硕士和实践型硕士[①]。他们的课程几乎相同,只是研究型硕士的课程比实践型硕士的课程数量稍少。但是实践型硕士最终需要完成为期3到6个月的实习并且提交实习报告,而研究型硕士最终则需要完成80页左右的论文并且参加答辩。空间法和电信法研究所开设的硕士课程十分全面,几乎涵盖了这两门法律的所有基本面。硕士课程分为两个方向,空间法方向和电信法方向。这两个方向的硕士的基础课程都相同,涵盖了空间法和电信法的主要内容,包括欧洲竞争法/国际和欧洲知识产权法(两门课程选择一门)、知识产权原则、国际空间公法、空间法和空间应用法、电信法和信息法等。其他一些基础课程都是以专题讲座的形式进行的,主题包括科学技术,法律和机构、合同、市场、管理、政策等。每个主题都有相关的两到三个专题讲座。这些讲座的实用性非常强,其中不少都是由在相关行业工作的专业人士来进行的,有的甚至是在专业机构或者公司

---

① 在法国的硕士教育中一般都有包含这两个方向。其中,实践型硕士的教育比较侧重实践技能,具有实用性,为学生毕业后进入工作岗位打下基础,而研究型硕士主要是一些理论的深入教育,为这些学生之后进行博士研究做准备。

进行的。学生通过这些讲座,不仅了解了相关的知识,还得到了和专业人士面对面沟通的机会。除了这些基础课程之外,研究所还提供一些专门讲座。依照学生的选择方向不同,空间法方向的专业讲座主题为空间应用,包括新空间项目的相关法律和政策、卫星传播和卫星网络的管理、卫星定位法律和政策、外层空间和国防、航空法等;电信法方向的专业讲座主题为信息社会,讲座内容有视听传播法、电子通讯和地方机构①(collectivités territoriales)、电子商务法、信息社会经济学、竞争和电子通讯等。

空间法和电信法硕士的考核方式非常多样,有开卷笔试形式、闭卷笔试形式、作独立报告形式、小组课题报告形式、独立书面作业形式、小组书面作业形式等。其中理论性较强的课程,比如国际空间公法、欧洲竞争法、空间法和空间应用法、知识产权原则等都采取闭卷笔试形式,以要求学生达到一定的理论水平。也有一些课程采取的是 séminaire(席明纳)的形式。比如对于实践性较强的科目,一般采取的是各种形式的口头测试,既有独立完成的,也有集体完成的,充分锻炼了学生在未来工作中作口头报告的能力和团体协作能力。除此之外,在法律和机构这一主题下有一项课程是会议和研讨会,要求学生在硕士学习过程中,参加一些相关方面的会议等来了解这个方面的动态并和一些专业人士进行交流。这门课程则是通过参与程度来评分的。

中心也接收博士生,由中心的负责老师等指导。

总的来说,空间法和电信法研究所的硕士点教育非常详尽和全面,同时考虑到了实用性和研究性两个方面。但也是由于课程安排太多,一定程度上限制了学生研究的自由性。另外一点就是,该项目大部分课程是法语授课,外国学生要进行学习,必须先达到

---

① Collectivités territoriales 是法国特有的行政现象,在法国宪法第 34 条和第 7 部分有相关规定。地方机构是独立于国家机关行政机构,它对所管辖的地区人民的整体利益负责。其特点是它是法人,有相应的能力,且有决策能力。

一定的法语水平。这一点也为很多其他国家(或地区)的学生进行学习造成了较大的难度。

(三)欧洲其他空间法研究中心

作为一个整体来讲,欧洲在外层空间的研究和实践方面十分活跃,因此,欧洲也有不少的空间法研究中心,其中包括最早进行空间法研究的大学,如德国科隆大学等。同时,也有越来越多的研究教育机构开始对空间法感兴趣,进而设立了空间法研究中心,并开始提供相关的课程,如国际空间大学,法国的西布列塔尼大学等。还有其他的一些大学或者教育机构,虽然并未开设专门的空间法专业,但是也将空间法纳入了法学学位的课程当中,如法国的西布列塔尼大学,意大利的帕多瓦大学(Universitá degli Studi di Padova)、罗马大学(Universitá degli studi di Roma, "La Sapienza")、芬兰的拉普兰德大学(University of Lapland)、英国伦敦大学贸易法学习中心等。

德国科隆大学(University of Cologne)法学院于1925年设立航空法研究所。该研究所于1959年扩展了研究领域并于同年12月1日正式更名为航空法和空间法问题研究所。在1975年,科隆大学校方正式接受空间法和航空法是两个不同的法律分支,航空法和空间法问题研究所再次更名为航空法和空间法研究所。研究所所长为Stephan Hobe教授。今天,该研究所并不提供空间法的相关学士学位或硕士学位,只接受该方向的博士研究生。但是,该所向法学院的学生提供一些空间法的基础课程,主要有三门,航空法和空间法基础课程,航空法和空间法讲座以及航空法和空间法学术讨论会。这些课程都是普及型的,旨在对学生灌输最基本的空间法的理论。科隆大学法学院虽然在空间法的教学方面不十分突出,但其所引导的相关研究还是值得赞赏的。

国际空间大学(International Space University)位于法国的斯特拉斯堡。它虽然是一所私立的大学,但是它在空间法教育方面享有很高的声誉。自1987年创立以来,已经培养了来自100多个国家的2 900多个学生。该学校设有两个硕士项目,空间学习硕士和空间管理硕士。这两个硕士项目的学生会有相同的基础课程,以对外层空间这一个部门有初步了解。但是在深入学习中,空间学习硕士的课程更加侧重于空间科学技术,而空间管理硕士的课程更多的则是与空间政策、管理等方面相关。硕士课程主要分为五个部分。第一个部分是基础课程,使学生对外层空间部门有一个大概的了解。第二个部分的课程重点在于是学生较深入的了解一个空间项目的展开和执行,以及与之相关的政策,法律,贸易和技术等各方面的内容。课程有国家空间政策、空间技术的军民两用,空间站和空间旅游介绍、知识产权法、全球卫星电子通信、地球观测和卫星定位的法律相关方面、财经分析和资金流动、空间贸易的法律相关方面、发射卫星服务市场等。课程的第三部分是对第二部分课程的深入,包括知识管理、创新和技术转让、网络和信息法、证券债券市场、空间应用的法律相关方面、战略联盟、空间站的商业化和空间旅游的市场策划等。学习的第四部分是小组作业,学生根据选择的课题组成小组,互相协作来共同完成一项任务。最后,学校还要求学生进行独立作业,即进行实习,来完成学习的最后一个部分。该硕士点的课程十分全面,不仅仅包括了空间法的内容,还包括了一些基础的空间技术,与空间活动相关的经济贸易方面的课程,十分符合该硕士项目的创办宗旨,即培养未来的空间活动部门的领导者。该项目的缺点是费用非常昂贵,但是大部分的学生都能够申请到一部分的奖学金。

三、世界其他地区的空间法教育

现在,处于战略考虑以及看到空间活动对人民生活品质带来的大幅度提升,越来越多的国家开始积极开展空间活动。很多国家也随之开始了空间法的研究和教育。

在亚洲,不少国家都是空间活动的活跃分子。如曾与美国在空间领域激烈竞争的俄罗斯,已是空间大国正在向空间强国迈进的中国,空间活动快速发展的日本和印度,以及在空间活动中具有雄心壮志的韩国等。但总的来说,在亚洲,空间法的研究和教育较为落后,大部分的教育机构,如俄罗斯的莫斯科国家国际关系研究所和人民友谊大学,我国的中国政法大学、哈尔滨工业大学、北京航空航天大学、北京理工大学、深圳大学等,日本的庆应义塾大学、印度的尼赫鲁大学等,都只是在一般的法律教育中,特别开设空间法及其相关的课程,仅有韩国的韩国航空航天大学(Korea Aerospace University)和最近日本的庆应义塾大学设有专门的空间法硕士点。我国北京理工大学开设了空间法博士点教育。

韩国航空航天大学的空间法的教授中有麦吉尔大学航空航天中心很久以前的毕业生。该硕士点主要课程有国际航空公法、国际航空私法、空间法、卫星通信和法律、航空航天工业、国际航空航天组织、国内航空法、航空和空间政策、航空私法、航空公法、航空事故调查和法律、产品责任、外国航空法、航空刑法等。从以上课程可以看出,韩国航空航天大学的空间法硕士点侧重点还是在航空法及其相关的方面,对空间法的教学还稍嫌笼统。

世界的其他部分,南美洲、大洋洲、非洲等空间活动较为不发达,因此空间法的研究和教育业相对落后。但是一些国家,如巴西、智利、南非等,也开始慢慢活跃在空间活动部门,空间法的研究和教育也正在起步,如非洲的南非共和国、南美洲的阿根廷和大洋洲的澳大利亚。在非洲,南非的金山大学教授空间和卫星法课程给通信法专业硕士的学生。阿根廷的布宜诺斯艾利斯大学,每年3月—11月期间都有面向博士生和青年教师教授的空间法课程,而阿根廷国家航空和空间法研究所则设立了航空法和空间法的硕士点。大洋洲的澳大利亚国立大学和西悉尼大学也开始在传统的法律课程当中加入了空间法相关的科目,如西悉尼大学教授的空间法的经济相关方面等。

值得注意的是,各空间法中心各自的历史存在有很大的不同,培养的学生的数量也是很不相同的。

总结

通过了解世界上各个空间法硕士点等的课程设置情况和考核

体系,我们可以了解到,空间法的研究和教育还是在欧美等国家和地区较为发达,整体的教育体制设置比较合理,有很多在我国未来设置空间法教学点时值得借鉴的地方。

中国是一个航天大国,航天活动比较活跃。经过数十年的发展,中国航天事业取得了以载人航天、月球探测等为标志的辉煌成就,为经济建设、社会发展、国家安全和科技进步做出了重要贡献。这都对空间法提出了更高的要求,时代要求我们在空间法方面有更大的进步。

首先,应该在法学本科的课程中开设一门国际空间法的课程,使学生对空间法的基本原则有所了解。这一点在我国的一些学校中已经做到。中国需要做的大概就是在空间法的专业硕士学位上取得突破。在硕士课程的设置上,可以单设空间法专业,也可以与航空法一起共设航空法和空间法专业,或者空间法与其他的专业。建议借鉴欧洲一些空间法硕士点的较为完整课程体系,不仅开设空间法课程,也开设与空间活动相关的其他法律课程,如空间应用法、进出口管理、知识产权法、发射服务市场、空间机构等。这样能使学生更加全面的了解整个外空活动部门,从而使学生毕业之后能够更加容易地融入相关的职业。在教学的过程中,最好能开办如模拟法庭类似的活动,使学生能够实践所学的知识,考核制度也应该尽可能不单单采取笔试这样的传统方式。对于一些理论性较强的学科,如国际空间法、知识产权法等,可采取笔试,对于实践性较强的科目,如进出口管理等,可采取席明纳小组(小组课题)的方式,以锻炼学生的小组工作能力。而对于一些与经济、市场相关的科目,可采取席明纳独立(独立做报告)等形式,开发学生的独立思考和演讲能力,使其日后能尽快适应工作岗位。

学术信息

国际法与外层空间的和平利用研讨会在哈尔滨召开

2010年7月10—11日,由中国空间法学会、哈尔滨工业大学法学院主办的"国际法与外层空间的和平利用"研讨会暨中欧社会论坛空间法小组会议在哈尔滨市凯莱花园酒店隆重召开。来自哈尔滨工业大学、中国政法大学、北京理工大学、武汉大学、深圳大学、中国民航大学等20余所高校和研究机构的专家、学者,以及来自法国西布列塔尼大学、意大利罗马大学等欧洲国家知名高校的4位欧洲学者、来自香港大学的学者和来自亚太空间合作组织的官员等代表参加了会议。会议期间,与会代表就"外层空间和平利用的国际法问题""空间立法及法律规制的研究""探月与载人航天等空间活动的法律问题研究""空间碎片及其他空间法问题研究"等议题进行了深入的交流和探讨。

开幕式于7月10日上午举行。哈尔滨工业大学法学院院长、空间法研究所所长、中欧论坛空间法小组组长赵海峰教授主持了开幕式。哈尔滨工业大学副校长张洪涛,哈尔滨市法学会会长陆文君,欧洲空间法中心副主席、法国西布列塔尼大学法律系教授阿迈尔·克里斯蒂(Armel Kerrest)分别致开幕词。致辞嘉宾充分肯定了召开本次会议的重要意义,希望通过本次研讨会中欧专家、学者能够为促进外层空间的最优利用和法制建设的进一步完善提供宝贵的意见。

大会主题报告由哈尔滨工业大学法学院国际法教研部主任葛勇平教授主持。首先，中国外交部条法司处长徐宇做了题为"国际空间法的最近动向"的报告。徐处长对2010年召开的外空委小组会议和外空委大会做了介绍，并对会议体现的外空法的新动向进行了归纳总结。同时，他还就如何使外空委更加有效工作及外空委未来发展方向两个问题同与会代表进行了交流。接着，亚太空间合作组织（APSCO，以下简称亚空组织）对外联络与法律事务部部长艾哈迈德·泰勒巴扎蒂（Ahmad Talebzadeh）博士针对"亚空组织的法律框架及其最新发展"进行了大会发言。发言中，泰勒巴扎蒂部长介绍并分析了亚空组织的发展历程、现状、组织结构、国际地位及主要活动与对外合作情况，展望了亚空组织的扩展情况与未来空间法活动的发展趋势。同时，他还通报了在亚空组织的框架下建立亚洲空间法中心的可能性，并希望哈尔滨工业大学法学院能在该机构中发挥重要作用。与会代表对两位发言人的报告内容表现出极大的兴趣并纷纷踊跃提问，就空间活动和法律建设的前沿问题进行了热烈的交流和互动。

7月10日下午，与会代表分两个小组分别进行了两场小组发言和讨论。第一小组主要由中欧社会论坛中方和欧方空间法小组成员组成。法国西布列塔尼大学法律系阿迈尔·克里斯蒂教授和中国政法大学国际法学院凌岩教授分别主持了第一小组两个单元的会议。意大利罗马第一大学法学院赛尔究·马可修（Sergio Marchisio）教授、哈尔滨工业大学法学院赵海峰教授、法比欧·特隆凯蒂（Fabio Tronchetti）副教授、法国西布列塔尼大学克里斯蒂教授、北京理工大学法学院李寿平教授、中国政法大学国际法学院李居迁副教授、凌岩教授等多名专家学者针对"国际法与和平利用外层空间"这一议题进行了发言，与会代表之间并进行了深入而细致的探讨。与此同时，第二小组与会代表就"外层空间和平利用的国际法研究"和"探月与载人航天的法律问题"两个议题也分别进行了两个单元的发言和讨论。讨论是由上海航天技术研究院研究员李琰处长和武汉大学法学院冯洁菡副教授主持的。深圳大学法学院尹玉海教授、北京理工大学空间法研究所王国语副所长、西安交通大学法学院苏金远博士、哈尔滨工业大学空间法研究所侯瑞雪副所长、研究生聂明岩同学、中国民航大学法学院王立志老师、聂晶晶老师等进行了精彩的发言,第二小组成员也就两个议题积极发表了自己的想法和意见。

7月11日上午,会议进行大会发言和闭幕式。大会发言由北京理工大学法学院副院长李寿平教授主持。香港大学法学院赵云副教授、哈尔滨工业大学法学院葛勇平教授、李晶珠老师分别做了大会发言,会议还宣读了法国第戎大学法学院院长劳伦斯·海威云教授提交的论文。大会发言结束后,多名专家、学者针对发言内容提出了自己的观点和建议,现场气氛活跃。

闭幕式由哈尔滨工业大学法学院赵海峰院长主持。首先,两个小组的报告员:哈尔滨工业大学空间法研究所副所长法比欧·特隆凯蒂副教授和北京理工大学空间法研究所王国语副所长分别就各自小组讨论情况和学术成果向大会做了总结报告。随后,徐宇处长致闭幕词,他在充分肯定本次会议重要性的同时,对空间法的研究意义及其在国际法和国内法层面上的新发展做了总结,并希望与会代表今后继续关注空间活动的发展,从而推动空间法研究的与时俱进。接着,艾哈迈德·泰勒巴扎蒂部长和阿迈尔·克里斯蒂教授也向大会致闭幕词并做总结性发言。各位发言人对哈尔滨工业大学学院对会议的精心组织和妥善安排都表示了衷心的谢意。最后,赵海峰院长对本次研讨会做了全面总结。在对所有与会嘉宾、代表、会务人员致以真诚的感谢后,赵院长全面回顾和评析了本次会议的讨论内容和在学术上所获得的突出成就。他认为,高水平的参会者和高质量的论文,是本次会议的突出特点和成功的根本保障。他期待类似的讨论会在将来得以继续进行。

研讨会在与会者们热烈的掌声中落下了帷幕。

国际空间站政策与法律问题研讨会在北京召开

2010年6月25日,由北京航空航天大学法学院主办、外层空间法研究所承办的"国际空间站政策与法律问题研讨会"在北京航空航天大学举行,来自北京航空航天大学和美国密西西比大学、香港大学、中国政法大学、北京理工大学、中国空间法学会、《中国航天报》等单位的共20余位代表与会。研讨会开幕式由法学院副院长孙新强教授主持。北京航空航天大学法学院外层空间法研究所所长高全喜教授和中国空间法学会秘书长戚永亮研究员分别致辞。

研讨会分为两个单元。第一单元由孙新强教授主持,美国密西西比大学国家遥感、航空与空间法研究中心主任约娜·加布里诺维奇(Joanne Irene Gabrynowicz)教授做了题为"国际空间站政府间协议"的报告。她从历史发展的角度,梳理了《国际空间站政府间协议》的发展历程,深入分析了该协议的关键性条款。中国政法大学国际法学院李居迁副教授对加布里诺维奇教授的报告进行了点评。第二单元由高全喜教授主持,香港大学法律学院赵云副教授、北京航空航天大学法学院外层空间法研究所副所长高国柱副教授与北京理工大学空间法研究所王国语博士分别进行了主题发言。赵云副教授分析了中国加入《国际空间站政府间协议》的可能性,并以俄罗斯加入该协议时面临的法律问题为例,对中国可能面临的法律困难进行了分析,并针对这些困难提出了若干解决方案。高国柱副教授从对《国际空间站政府间协议》第6条和第7条的分析入手,认为该协议有关空间站组件所有权的规定可能超越了1967年《外空条约》的规定。如果将这种关于所有权的规定扩大适用于人类可能在月球和其他天体上建造的各种设施,必然使某些国家事实上占有了月球或其他天体的一部分,从而构成了《外空条约》中"不得据为己有原则"的违反。王国语博士从国际私法的角度出发,分析了围绕空间站产生的法律问题的管辖权和解决方式,并指出在确定国家管辖权时,"国籍联系原则"起着关键性作用。中国政法大学国际法学院梁淑英教授分别对上述发言进行了精彩点评。

研讨会闭幕阶段,北京航空航天大学法学院院长助理、外层空间法研究所副所长李斌博士进行了总结发言,指出本次研讨会时间安排紧凑,讨论的议题范围很广,就空间站管辖权、所有权、争端解决方式等方方面面的问题进行了卓有成效的研讨,取得了一定成果。

研讨会在热烈掌声中圆满结束。

亚太空间合作组织国际研讨会在泰国举行

2009年7月21日,"亚太空间合作组织促进亚太地区空间合作国(或地区)际研讨会"(以下简称"研讨会")在泰国开幕。研讨会由亚太空间合作组织和泰国信息与通信技术部主办,中国工业和信息化部、联合国外空司、联合国亚太经社会是研讨会的支持单位。泰国信息与通信技术部副部长尼密特、亚太空间合作组织秘书长张伟、工业和信息化部军民结合推进司副司长林森、联合国外空司遥感项目负责人尼古拉斯·海德曼、联合国亚太经社会代表李开金等先后在开幕式上致辞。

本次研讨会是亚太空间合作组织成立后举办的首次重大专题会议,受到与会各方面的高度重视。亚太空间合作组织9个公约签署国以及日本、马来西亚等国派团与会。我国从事空间技术和应用的相关单位将在研讨会上就遥感和通信卫星技术、遥感卫星数据应用、卫星地面接收站建设等进行详细介绍和推介,为今后开展实质性合作奠定了良好基础。

研讨会第一天的主题为"空间活动,现状及未来发展",亚太空间合作组织、联合国外空司、泰国、孟加拉国、伊朗、巴基斯坦、秘鲁、印尼、土耳其和我国的代表相继做专题报告,介绍各自空间活动的概况及最新进展等。

此次研讨会将进一步促进亚太国家在空间技术、卫星应用等领域的合作,为各国分享应用经验,提高应用水平,增强各成员国(或地区)应对自然灾害、气候变化、环境保护等方面的能力,促进区域经济社会的发展,将做出积极贡献。

第 51 届国际空间法年会在英国格拉斯哥召开

2008 年 9 月 29 日，第 59 届国际宇航联大会暨第 51 届国际空间法年会在英国格拉斯哥召开。本届国际宇航联大会的主题是"从想象到现实"。与该次宇航联大会同时举办的是由国际空间法学会主办的第 51 届国际空间法年会。本次年会分 6 个主题，分别是外空活动中的国际私法问题、外空武器化与外空条约第 4 条、营救协定的 40 周年及其前瞻、近地自然物体的法律方面、技术与法律、其他空间法律问题等。会议持续到 10 月 3 日。来自世界各地的空间法研究人员参加会议。

在穿插充满苏格兰文化与艺术特色和诗情画意表演的国际宇航联大会开幕式中，英国首相布朗通过电视屏幕预祝大会取得成功。在国际宇航联主席的开幕发言中，作为空间活动的最新发展，他明确提到了中国神七宇宙飞船航天员成功的太空行走。这是第四次在英国举办国际宇航联大会。

第 53 届国际空间法年会在捷克布拉格召开

2010 年 9 月 27 日至 10 月 1 日,第 61 届国际宇航联合会(IAF)大会在捷克布拉格举行,来自世界各国航天界的近 3 000 名代表将在 5 天的时间内,围绕航天工业、科学和教育等方面的最新动态展开交流和对话。本届国际宇航联大会的主题是"造福人类及探索未来的航天"。包括"政府航天政策对工业界的影响"、推进全球探索战略发展下一代航天系统运行构想、国际空间站上科学实验研究等议题。除了继续关注民用空间技术,同时也将目光投向了未来空间科学探索。大会不仅包括涉及空间科学、空间技术、空间应用、空间人文等方面的技术分组和互动分组讨论会,还包括航天展览,各国航天局官员、专家学者参与的高端讲坛、青年学者计划、学生会议以及丰富多彩的民族文化活动等。会议还宣布,第 64 届国际宇航联大会(第 54 届国际空间法年会也将在此期间召开)将于 2013 年在中国举办。

大会期间,国际空间法学会也组织召开了第 53 届国际空间法年会,主题为"合作型人类空间项目的法律问题",这也是由国际宇航联合会与国际空间法学会共同举办的跨学科研讨会。此外,第 19 届 Manfred Lachs 空间法模拟法庭世界总决赛也同时举行。

法律文件

加拿大政府、欧洲航天局成员方政府、日本政府、俄罗斯政府和美国政府签署的关于民用国际空间站合作的政府间协定（中、英文）

王晶[①]译

加拿大政府（以下简称"加拿大"）。

比利时、丹麦、法国、德国、意大利、荷兰、挪威、西班牙、瑞典、瑞士、英国和北爱尔兰等国家的政府，也是欧洲航天局成员的政府（以下共同称为"欧洲的政府"或者"欧洲的合作国"）。

日本政府（以下简称"日本"）。

俄罗斯联邦政府（以下简称"俄罗斯"），及

美利坚合众国政府（以下简称"美国政府"或者"美国"）。

回顾在1984年，美国总统下令美国航空航天局（NASA）开发永久性载人空间站并将其放置于轨道，而且邀请美国的友国和联盟国参与它的开发和使用，并分享所获利益。

[①] 王晶，哈尔滨工业大学人文与社会科学学院社会学专业（法学方向）2008届硕士毕业生。

回顾在 1985 年 3 月,加拿大总理与美国总统聚首于魁北克,并在会议上接受了上述邀请,而后于 1986 年 3 月华盛顿召开的首脑会议上相互确认了合作的意向。

回顾欧洲航天局(ESA)理事会于 1985 年 1 月 3 日和 1995 年 10 月 20 日召开了部长级的会议,在欧洲航天局的机构内部通过了相关决议的条款,并与其公约第 2 条中规定的宗旨相一致,哥伦布项目和欧洲参与的国际空间站的开发项目都已经开始实施,并将会开发民用国际空间站的组成部分。

回顾日本对于空间站项目的兴趣开始于 1984 年和 1985 年美国航天局局长在日本的访问,而且,日本通过首次材料加工实验开始参与美国的空间项目。

回顾欧洲航天局和加拿大对于美国航天运输系统的参与,欧洲通过开发第一个载人宇宙空间实验室——太空实验室,而加拿大通过开发遥控操作器系统。

回顾于 1988 年 9 月 29 日在华盛顿签订的《美国政府、欧洲航天局成员国(或地区)政府、日本政府、加拿大政府关于永久性载人民用空间站的详图设计、开发、操作和利用的合作协议》(以下简称"1988 年协议"),以及美国航天局和加拿大国家科技部门(MOSST),美国航天局和欧洲航天局,美国航天局和日本政府之间签订的相关谅解备忘录,这些建立了各个政府之间的合作关系。同时,认识到 1988 年协议于 1992 年 1 月 30 日在美国和日本之间生效。

回顾美国航天局、欧洲航天局、日本政府和加拿大国家科技部门是依据 1988 年协议和相关的谅解备忘录开始实施合作活动以实现在空间站项目的合作关系,并且认识到加拿大航天局(CSA)在 1989 年 3 月 1 日成立之时,它就承担了实施国家科技部门转移过来的加拿大空间站项目的责任。

鉴于俄罗斯在人类太空飞行和太空长期任务领域中的独特经验和造诣,包括俄罗斯和平号空间站的长期成功运作,俄罗斯在空间站的参与将会极大地加强空间站造福所有合作者的能力。

回顾1993年12月6日,加拿大政府、欧洲政府、日本政府和美国政府向俄罗斯政府发出邀请,邀请其参与空间站协议规定的框架内的空间站详图设计、开发、实施和使用,俄罗斯政府在1993年12月17日对于此邀请做出了肯定的答复。

回顾俄罗斯联邦政府总理和美国副总统做出了一系列安排以促进在重要的人类太空飞行活动中的合作,包括俄罗斯－美国的和平号空间站－航天飞机项目上的合作,以便于为国际空间站的建设做准备。

回顾《关于各国探索和利用外层空间包括月球与其他天体活动所应遵守原则的条约》(以下简称为《外空条约》),生效于1967年10月10日。

回顾《营救宇宙航行员、送回宇宙航行员和归还发射到外层空间的物体的协定》(以下简称为《营救协定》),生效于1968年12月3日。

回顾《空间物体所造成损害的国际责任公约》(以下简称为《责任公约》),生效于1972年9月1日。

回顾《关于登记射入外层空间物体的公约》(以下简称为《登记公约》),生效于1976年9月15日。

坚信民用国际空间站的合作,将会通过建立一种长期和互惠的关系来进一步加强合作,并且将会进一步促进在外层空间的探索和和平利用方面的合作。

认识到美国航天局和加拿大航天局、美国航天局和欧洲航天局、美国航天局和日本政府,以及美国航天局和俄罗斯航天局(RSA)之间已经签署了谅解备忘录(以下称为"谅解备忘录"),以协助他们的政府在本协定中的谈判,而且,谅解备忘录对于本协定的执行做出了详细的规定。

认识到,综上所述,在加拿大政府、欧洲政府、日本政府、俄罗斯政府和美国政府之间建立一个关于空间站设计、开发、实施和使用的框架是合乎情理的。

协议如下:

第1条 目标和范围

1. 本协定的目标是在真正的伙伴关系基础上建立一个长期的国际合作框架,以规定一个用于和平目的,符合国际法的永久性载人民用国际空间站的详图设计、开发、实施和使用。此民用国际空间站将加强对于外层空间的科学、技术和商业的应用。本协定明确界定了民用国际空间站的项目及这种合作关系的本质,包括合作当事方在这次合作中各自的权利和义务。为了确保目标得以实现,本协定还规定了一些机制和安排。

2. 各合作国(或地区)将会在美国领导的整体管理和协调之下共同努力,以建立一个联合的国际空间站。美国和俄罗斯在人类太空飞行方面的丰富经验将会成为国际空间站的基石的重要部分。欧洲的合作国(或地区)和日本将会制造能够大大提高空间站性能的组成部分。加拿大对于空间站的贡献也将是不可或缺。本协定在附件中列出了各合作国(或地区)提供的构成国际空间站的组成部分。

3. 永久性载人民用国际空间站(以下简称"空间站")将会是一个在低地球轨道上的多功能设备,它是由所有的合作国(或地区)提供的飞行要素和空间站专用的地面组成部分构成。由于提供飞行要素,依据本协定,谅解备忘录和实施安排,每一个合作国(或地区)可以要求具有一定的使用空间站和参与其管理的权利。

4. 空间站被构思为具有循序渐进的特性。对于这种演变,合作国(或地区)的权利和义务应当依据第14条的具体规定。

第2条 国际权利和义务

1. 空间站的开发、实施和使用应当依据国际法,包括《外空条约》《营救协定》《责任公约》和《登记公约》。

2. 本协定的任何规定不得作如下解释:

(1) 更改条约的上述第1条中规定的合作国(或地区)的权利和义务,无论是相互之间还是与其他国家(或地区)之间,除了第16条中的例外规定。

(2)影响进行探索或利用外层空间活动的合作国(或地区)的权利和义务,无论是单独的或与其他国家(或地区)合作的与空间站无关的活动。

(3)为国家发表对外层空间或外层空间任何据为己有的宣言提供法律依据。

第3条 定义

基于本协定的目的,应当适用下列定义:

(1)"本协定":

当前这个协议,包括附件。

(2)"合作国(或地区)"(或者,在适当情况下称为"各合作国(或地区)"):

加拿大政府、在本协定的序言中列出的成为本协定当事方的欧洲政府,以及根据协议第25条第(3)款可能加入本协定的任何其他欧洲政府,可以作为一个合作国(或地区)共同活动;日本政府,俄罗斯联邦政府及美国政府;

(3)"合作国(或地区)":

根据本协定第25条,本协定对其已经生效的各缔约方。

第4条 合作机构

1. 各合作国(或地区)同意加拿大政府的加拿大航天局(以下简称"CSA")、欧洲有关国家政府的欧洲航天局(以下简称"ESA")、俄罗斯政府的俄罗斯航天局(以下简称"RSA"),美国政府的美国国家航空和航天局(以下简称"NASA",美国航天局),这些机构成为负责实施空间站合作的合作机构。日本政府为了实施空间站合作设置的合作机构规定在下面第2款提及的《NASA与日本政府之间的谅解备忘录》中。

2. 合作机构实施空间站合作,应当按照本协定的相关条款,按照美国航天局和加拿大航天局,美国航天局和欧洲航天局,美国航天局和日本政府,美国航天局和俄罗斯航天局之间关于民用国际空间站的各个谅解备忘录的规定,以及按照美国航天局和其他合作机构之间实施谅解备忘录的多边或双边安排(实施安排)进行。谅解备忘录应当遵守本协定,而实施安排应当符合和遵循谅解备忘录。

3. 如果谅解备忘录中的某一项条款提出的权利和义务被一个合作机构(或者,在日本的情况是日本政府)所接受,这个机构却并不是该谅解备忘录的当事方,则此条款没有该合作机构(或者,在日本的情况是日本政府)的书面许可,不可被修改。

第 5 条 登记、管辖和支配

1. 根据《登记公约》第 2 条,各合作国(或地区)应当对其提供的、并列于附件中的飞行要素作为空间物体进行登记,欧洲各合作国(或地区)委派欧洲航天局以它的名义代表其履行这一职责。

2. 根据《外空条约》第 8 条和《登记公约》第 2 条,各合作国(或地区)对于依照以上第 1 款进行登记的设备和空间站上的本国人员应当保留管辖权和支配权。这种管辖权和支配权的行使应当遵守本协定、谅解备忘录和实施安排的相关规定,包括其中设立的相关程序机制。

第 6 条 组成部分和设备的所有权

1. 加拿大、欧洲的合作国(或地区)、俄罗斯和美国通过他们各自的合作机构,日本委派的实体按照第 25 条第 2 款规定交存它的器械时,也拥有在附件中列出的他们各自提供的组成部分,除非本协定另有规定。各合作国(或地区)应当通过其合作机构相互通知关于空间站的设备的所有权。

2. 欧洲合作国(或地区)应当委托欧洲航天局以它的名义代表其拥有它所提供的组成部分的所有权,以及为了空间站,为了它的实施或使用而进行的欧洲航天局项目的开发和资助的设备所有权。

3. 附件中列出的组成部分或者空间站设备的所有权的转移,不应当影响本协定、谅解备忘录或实施安排中规定的合作国(或地区)的权利和义务。

4. 参与或置于空间站的设备所有人及附件中列出的组成部分所有权的受让人,未经其他各合作国(或地区)事先一致同意,不得是非合作国(或地区)或者非合作国(或地区)管辖内的私人实体。附件中列出的任何组成部分的所有权转移都应当事先通知其他各合作国(或地区)。

5. 用户提供的设备或物资的所有权不应仅仅因为这种设备或物质放置于空间站而受到影响。

6. 组成部分的所有权或登记,或者设备的所有权,绝不应当被视为包含因为空间站的实施活动而产生的材料或数据的所有权。

7. 组成部分和设备的所有权的行使应当遵守本协定、谅解备忘录和实施安排的相关规定,包括其中设立的相关的程序机制。

第7条 管理

1. 空间站的管理将建立在一种多边的基础上,各合作者通过其合作机构,在依照谅解备忘录和实施安排的如下规定而设置的管理部门中分担和履行责任。依照本协定和谅解备忘录,这些管理部门应当计划和配合影响空间站设计和开发的活动,以及安全、高效和有效的实施和使用的活动。在这些管理部门,应当把一致同意做出的决策作为目标。若各合作机构很难达到一致同意,则使用在谅解备忘录中有详细说明的、设置于这些管理部门内部的决策机制。各合作者和其合作机构对于其提供的组成部分有决策的职责,这在本协定和谅解备忘录中有详细说明。

2. 美国通过美国航天局并依照谅解备忘录和实施安排,应当负责自己项目的管理,包括它的使用活动。美国通过美国航天局并依照谅解备忘录和实施安排,还应当负责:空间站总体项目的管理和协调,除了在本协定和谅解备忘录中另有规定;整体的系统工程和整合;制定整体安全的要求和部署;空间站的全面综合操作的执行的总体策划和协调。

3. 加拿大、欧洲的合作者、日本和俄罗斯通过其合作机构,并按照谅解备忘录和实施安排,应当负责:其自己项目的管理,包括其应用活动;其提供的组成部分的系统工程和整合;为其提供的组成部分制定和执行详细的安全要求和部署;而且,根据上述第2款的规定,支持美国履行其整体职责,包括参与空间站综合运作的实施方面的策划和协调。

4. 就设计和开发事项来说,如果只涉及加拿大、欧洲合作国(或地区)、日本或俄罗斯提供的空间站组成部分,而没有包含在谅解备忘录的商定的项目文件里,合作国(或地区)可以通过它的合作机构做出与该组成部分相关的决定。

第8条 详图设计和开发

依据第7条和本协定的其他相关条款,以及依据谅解备忘录和实施安排,各合作国(或地区)通过其合作机构,应当设计和开发它所提供的设备,包括空间站独特的地面组成部分能够足以支撑持续的运作,以及飞行要素的全面的国际性的利用,而且应当与其他合作者相互配合,通过其合作机构,以达成关于其各自组成部分的设计和开发的解决方案。

第9条 使用

1. 使用的权利源自合作国(或地区)对用户组成部分或者基础设备组成部分的提供,或者两者兼有。任何提供空间站用户组成部分的合作国(或地区)可以保留那些组成部分的使用权,除非此条款另有规定。各合作国(或地区)为空间站的运作和使用提供了资源,并成为空间站基础设备组成部分,应当换取对于某些用户组成部分的固定份额的使用权。各合作国(或地区)对于空间站的用户组成部分和空间站基础设备组成部分的资源的具体分配,在谅解备忘录和实施安排中应有具体说明。

2. 各合作国(或地区)有权交换或出售其各自配额内的任何部分。任何交换或出售的条件和要求应当由交易方自己逐个决定。

3. 基于符合本协定的目标及谅解备忘录和实施安排的条款的规定,各合作国(或地区)可以在配额内使用和选择用户,除了下列情形:

(1) 由一个非合作国(或地区)或非合作国(或地区)管辖下的

私人实体提出的任何使用用户组成部分的提议,应当事先通知所有的合作国(或地区),并通过其合作机构及时达成共识;并且

(2)提供组成部分的合作国(或地区)应当确定该组成部分的预期使用是否是为了和平目的,除了为防止任何合作国(或地区)使用源于空间站基础设施的资源,本项不得援引。

4. 在使用空间站的时候,各合作国(或地区)应当通过其合作机构遵循谅解备忘录中设置的机制,以避免对其他合作国(或地区)的空间站的使用造成严重的不利影响。

5. 各合作国(或地区)应当保证其他合作国(或地区)根据其各自的分配,能够进入和使用属于它的空间站的组成部分。

6. 就本条来说,欧洲航天局的成员国(或地区)不应当被视为一个"非合作国(或地区)"。

第 10 条 操作

依照本协定第 7 条和其他相关条款,以及依照谅解备忘录和实施安排,各合作国(或地区)对于其各自提供的组成部分的操作应当负有责任。依据谅解备忘录和实施安排,各合作国(或地区)应当通过其合作机构,以对空间站的使用者和操作者来讲安全、高效率和有效的方式制定和实施空间站的操作程序。此外,各合作国(或地区)应当通过其合作机构,负责维持其所提供的组成部分的功能发挥。

第 11 条 工作人员

1. 各合作国(或地区)在公平的基础上均有权提供合格的人员在空间站工作。关于合作国(或地区)的工作人员的飞行任务的选择和决定应当按照谅解备忘录和实施安排的程序规定进行。

2. 《空间站工作人员行为规范》应当依照谅解备忘录的规定,根据各合作国(或地区)的内部程序,由所有合作国(或地区)共同制定和批准。各合作国(或地区)在提供空间站工作人员之前必须批准《行为规范》。各合作国(或地区)在行使其提供工作人员的权利时,应当保证其工作人员遵守行为规范。

第12条 运输

1. 各合作国(或地区)均有权利用其各自政府和私营部门的空间运输系统进入空间站,前提是它们能与空间站相互协调。美国、俄罗斯、欧洲的合作国(或地区)和日本通过其各自的合作机构,应当为空间站提供发射和回收的运输服务(这种空间运输系统如美国的航天飞机、俄罗斯的质子号和联盟号飞船、欧洲的阿丽亚娜5号火箭、日本的H-II号火箭)。最初,美国和俄罗斯的空间运输系统将被用来为空间站提供发射和回收的运输服务,此外,当其他的空间运输系统可供利用时也将被使用。进入和发射与回收的运输服务应当按照相关的谅解备忘录和实施安排的规定进行。

2. 那些在有偿或其他的基础上,向其他合作国(或地区)和其各自的用户提供发射和回收运输服务的合作国(或地区),提供的服务应当符合相关的谅解备忘录和实施安排规定的条件。在可比较的的条件下,那些在有偿基础上向另一个合作国(或地区)或其用户提供发射和回收运输服务的合作国(或地区),应当在同样的基础上向任何其他合作国(或地区)或其用户提供此种服务。各合作国(或地区)应尽最大努力协调其他合作国(或地区)提出的要求和飞行时间表。

3. 美国通过其航天局,与管理部门中其他合作国(或地区)的合作机构合作,按照谅解备忘录和实施安排规定的综合运输计划程序,策划和协调空间站的发射和回收运输服务。

4. 各合作国(或地区)对于其空间运输系统进行运输的标有适当标记的数据和货物,应当尊重其所有权和保密性。

第13条 通讯

1. 为了指挥、控制和操作空间站的组成部分和有效载荷,以及其他空间站通讯的目的,美国和俄罗斯应当通过其合作机构提供两大主要的数据中继卫星系统的空间和地面通信网络。如果符合空间站的要求,并且与前两个主要网络的使用相协调,其他合作国(或地区)也可以提供数据中继卫星系统的空间和地面通信网络。

有关空间站通讯的提供应当依照相关的谅解备忘录和实施安排的规定进行。

2. 在有偿的基础上,按照相关的谅解备忘录和实施安排规定的条件,合作机构应当通过其通信系统,尽力满足相互之间关于空间站的具体要求。

3. 美国通过它的航天局,与管理部门中其他合作国(或地区)的合作机构合作,应当按照谅解备忘录和实施安排规定的有关程序文件,策划和协调空间站的空间和地面通讯服务。

4. 根据谅解备忘录的规定,对于经过空间站信息系统和其他与空间站相关的通讯系统的数据,可以采取一些措施以确保数据利用的机密性。当向另一个合作国(或地区)提供通讯服务时,每个合作国(或地区)对于通过它的通信系统,包括它的地面网络和它的承包商的通讯系统的使用数据,应当尊重这些使用数据的所有权和保密性。

第 14 条 改进

1. 各合作国(或地区)要通过增加空间站性能而使其得到改进,并且力求通过所有合作国(或地区)的努力最大限度地实现这种改进。在适当的情况下,一个合作国(或地区)在它的提议下向其他合作国(或地区)提供合作机会以便于增加改进性能,到最后,这应当是每个合作国(或地区)的目标。带有增加的改进性能的空间站应当仍然是一个民用空间站,它的实施和使用应当基于和平目的并符合国际法。

2. 除了本条款和第 16 条应当适用于任何改进性能增加的情况以外,本协定规定的权利和义务只是涉及附件列出的组成部分。本协定未委托任何合作国(或地区)参与,或者以其他方式授权任何合作国(或地区)参与改进性能的增加。

3. 关于各合作国(或地区)各自的改进研究的协调程序,以及改进性能增加的具体建议的审查程序,都规定在谅解备忘录中。

4. 在上述第 3 款规定的协调和复查以后,在双方或多方合作者之间关于分配改进性能增加的合作,还应当要求修正本协定或者与美国另行达成协议,以确保任何增加都与总体规划相一致。

此外,提供空间站组成部分或空间运输系统而又受运作上或技术上影响的任何其他合作国(或地区)都应当成为当事方。

5. 在上述第 3 款规定的协调和复查之后,一个合作国(或地区)的改进性能的增加应当要求提前通知其他合作国(或地区),并要求和美国达成协议,以确保任何增加都符合总体规划,而且还要求与提供空间站组成部分或空间运输系统而又受运作上或技术上影响的任何其他合作国(或地区)达成协议。

6. 对于上述第 4 款或第 5 款规定的可能会受到改进性能增加影响的合作国(或地区),可以依据第 23 条的规定,要求与其他合作国(或地区)进行协商。

7. 对于根据本协定和谅解备忘录中关于附件列出的组成部分的规定而使合作国(或地区)获得的权利和义务,除非受影响的合作国(或地区)同意,否则改进性能的增加决不能将其更改。

第 15 条 资金

1. 按照谅解备忘录和实施安排的规定,每个合作国(或地区)依照本协定承担的责任的履行费用应当自己负担,包括在公平的基础上分担商定的共同系统的操作费用,或者空间站的整体操作的活动费用。

2. 每个合作国(或地区)依照本协定负担的财政义务应当遵循它的拨款程序和资金获得情况。因为意识到空间站合作的重要性,每个合作国(或地区)都同意依照各自的拨款程序,尽最大努力获得拨款的批准以履行那些义务。

3. 如果出现了可能会影响一个合作国(或地区)履行其在空间站的职责能力的资金问题,该合作国(或地区)应当通过其合作机构通知其他合作机构并与之协商。如果需要的话,所有合作国(或地区)也可以共同协商。

4. 各合作国(或地区)应当设法把空间站的运作成本降低到最低程度。尤其是,依照谅解备忘录的规定,各合作国(或地区)应当通过其合作机构制定相应程序,以便于把共同系统的运作成本和活动控制在核准的评估标准之内。

5. 各合作国(或地区)也应当把实施空间站合作中的资金交

换减少到最低程度,包括执行谅解备忘录和实施安排规定的具体运作活动,或者,如果相关合作国(或地区)同意,通过货物交换的方式进行。

第16条 相互免责

1. 此条的目标是建立一种各合作国(或地区)和相关实体之间相互免责的制度,以便于鼓励通过空间站参与外层空间的探测、开发和利用。这种相互免责的制度应当作广义解释,以实现这个目标。

2. 此条的目的

(1)一个"合作国(或地区)"包括它的合作机构。它还包括美国航天局与日本政府签订的谅解备忘录中列明的任何实体。这些实体是为了协助日本的合作机构实施谅解备忘录的规定。

(2)"相关实体"一词意为:

A. 一个合作国(或地区)任何层次上的承包商或分包商。

B. 一个合作国(或地区)在任何层次的用户或顾客;或者

C. 一个合作国(或地区)的用户或顾客在任何层次的承包商或分包商。

此项规定也适用于与合作国(或地区)拥有上述第2(2)A款至2(2)C款描述的同样的关系,或者以其他方式从事于实施下面第2款(6)定义的受保护的空间行动的某个国家,或者某个国家的部门或者机构。

"承包商"和"分包商"包括各个种类的供应商。

(3)"损害"一词意为:

A. 任何自然人的身体受伤、健康的其他损害或者生命的丧失。

B. 任何财产的损害、损失或者丧失效用。

C. 收入或利润的损失;或者

D. 其他直接的、间接的或者因果性损害。

(4)"运载火箭"一词意为用来发射,已从地球发射或者返回地球时运送有效负载或者个人或者两者兼而有之的一个物体(或其任何部分)。

(5)"有效载荷"一词意为被装载或者应用在运载火箭或者空

间站的所有财产。

(6)"受保护的空间行动"一词意为在执行本协定、谅解备忘录和实施安排的过程中,在地球上、在外层空间或者在地球与外层空间之间运输而发生的所有运载火箭活动、空间站活动和有效载荷活动。它包括,但不限于:

A. 研究、设计、开发、测试、制造、组装、集成、操作、使用发射或运输工具、空间站或有效载荷,以及相关的支援设备、设施和服务;及

B. 与地面支援、测试、培训、模拟,或指导和控制设备及相关设施或服务有关的所有活动。

"受保护的空间行动"也包括了第14条规定的与空间站改进相关的所有活动。"受保护的空间行动"不包括从空间站返回后在地球上实施的以进一步开发有效载荷产品的活动,也不包括在执行本协定时进行的与空间站相关的使用程序以外的活动。

3.

(1)各合作国(或地区)同意了相互免除赔偿责任的,因此每个合作国(或地区)也放弃了下面第3(1)A款至第3(1)C款列出的任何实体和人员因受保护的空间行动引起的损害的所有索赔。这种相互免责的适用,只有当受损害的个人、实体或财产参与了受保护的空间行动,并且受损害的个人、实体或财产是由于他们参与了受保护的空间行动而造成的损害。相互免责应当适用于任何损害赔偿索赔,而无论这种索赔针对以下各方的法律依据如何:

(A)另一个合作国(或地区);

(B)另一个合作国(或地区)的相关实体;

(C)上述第3(1)A款和第3(1)B款规定的任何实体的雇员。

(2)另外,各合作国(或地区)以协议或其他的方式,把上述第3(1)款提出的相互免责扩大到它的相关实体,要求这些实体这样做:

A. 放弃所有指控上述第3(1)A款至第3(1)C款规定的实体和个人的索赔要求。

B. 要求其相关实体放弃所有指控上述第3(1)A款至第3(1)C款规定的实体和个人的索赔要求。

(3) 为免生疑问,如果受损害的个人、实体或财产参与了受保护的空间行动,并且受损害的个人、实体或财产是由于其参与了受保护的空间行动而造成的损害,这种相互免责包括了由《责任公约》产生的一种相互免责。

(4) 除了本条款有其他规定以外,这种相互免责不适用于:

A. 一个合作国(或地区)与它的相关实体之间或者它的相关实体之间的索赔要求。

B. 自然人,他的/她的代理人,遗属或者被取代者(被取代者是一个合作国(或地区)的情况除外)对于因身体受伤,或者健康的损害,或者自然人的死亡而提出的索赔要求。

C. 由于故意的不当行为造成损害而提出的索赔要求。

D. 知识产权索赔。

E. 合作国(或地区)由于上述第3(2)款的扩大相互免责的失败而发生的损害索赔。

(5) 对于上述第3(1)A款所述,当日本政府代位索赔不是基于政府雇员事故赔偿法时,日本政府为了放弃这种代位索赔应当履行自己的义务,通过确保上第2(1)款规定的任何协助实体按照第15条第(2)款和日本适用的法律和规章得到赔偿,以补偿上述第3(1)A款至第3(1)C款规定的任何实体或个人由于这种日本政府的代位索赔而受到的损失。本条款不阻止日本政府放弃前述的代位索赔。

(6) 本条款绝不应被视为一种无端索赔或诉讼的依据。

第17条 《责任公约》

1. 除了在第16条中另有规定,各合作国(或地区)和欧洲航天局,仍应当遵守《责任公约》。

2. 如果发生由于《责任公约》而引起的索赔,各合作国(或地区)(和欧洲航天局,如果适用的话)应对任何潜在的责任,对这种责任的任何分担,和针对该索赔的辩护,进行及时协商。

3. 关于第12条第2款中的发射和回收服务规定,相关合作国(或地区)(和欧洲航天局,如果适用的话)可以针对《责任公约》中任何潜在的连带责任的分配单独签订协议。

第18条 海关和入境

1. 在符合它的法律和法规的情况下,每个合作国(或地区)应当为对于执行本协定必要的人员和货物的流动提供便利,方便他们进入和流出其境内。

2. 在符合其法律和法规的情况下,每个合作国(或地区)应当为另一个合作国(或地区)的国民和国民的家庭提供适当的入境和居留的文件,当他们进入、或退出、或居住在第一个合作国(或地区)的领土内是为了本协定的实施发挥必要的功能时。

3. 每个合作国(或地区)对于实施本协定必要的货物和软件,应当准许它们免除进口和出口的关税,而且,应当确保其免除海关机关收取的其他税款和关税。本款的实施应当不予以考虑这种必要的货物和软件的原产国。

第19条 数据和货物的交换

1. 除了本条另有规定,每个合作国(或地区),应通过其合作机构转让所有认为必要的技术数据和货物(可以由当事双方进行任何一种的转让),以履行该合作国(或地区)的合作机构根据相关的谅解备忘录和实施安排而产生的责任。每个合作国(或地区)保证尽快处理另一个合作国(或地区)的合作机构基于空间站合作目的而提出的技术数据和货物的任何要求。本条不应要求一个合作国(或地区)在违反其国家法律或法规的情况下转让任何技术数据和货物。

2. 各合作国(或地区)应当尽其最大努力尽快处理由个人或实体而不是各合作国(或地区)或其合作机构(例如,有可能发展的公司对公司的交易)提出的转让技术数据和货物的授权要求,而且,应当鼓励和促进这种依据本协定而进行的涉及空间站合作的转让。另外,这种转让并不适用本条的条件和情形。国家法律和规章应当适用这种转让。

3. 各合作国(或地区)同意根据本协定进行的技术数据和货物的转移也应当遵守本款提出的限制。为了履行各合作国(或地区)关于界面、集成和安全方面的责任而进行的技术数据转让通常不受本款限制。如果详细设计、制造和处理数据及相关的软件对于界面、集成和安全则是必要的,转让应当按照本条第 1 款所述,但数据和相关软件可以做适当的如下文所述的记号。本款并不限制的技术数据和货物应当不受限制地转让,除非国家法律或法规另有约束。

(1)提供方的合作机构应当以通知标明,或以其他方式特别确认为,因为出口管制的目的受到保护的技术数据或货物。这种通知或标志应表明这种技术数据或货物如何才可以由接受方的合作机构及其承包商和分包商使用的任何具体条件。其中包括:a. 这种技术数据和货物的使用,只有基于接受方的合作机构履行本协定和相关谅解备忘录产生的义务的目的;b. 这种技术数据或货物不得为接受方合作机构、它的承包商或分包商以外的个人或实体使用,或者基于其他目的,没有提供方合作国(或地区)通过其合作机构发布的事先书面许可。

(2)提供方的合作机构应当以通知标明技术数据受到所有权的保护。这种通知应说明关于这种技术数据如何才可以被接受方的合作机构及其承包商和分包商使用的任何具体条件。其中包括:a. 这种技术数据的使用、复制或披露,根据本协定和相关的谅解备忘录,只有基于履行接受方合作机构的义务的目的;b. 这种技术数据除了接受方的合作机构,它的承包商或分包商以外,不得被其他个人或实体使用,或者基于其他目的,没有提供方合作国(或地区)通过其合作机构颁布的事先书面许可。

(3)如果任何技术数据或货物的转让根据本协定是机密的,提供方合作机构应以通知标明,或以其他方式特别确认为这种技术数据或货物。被请求的合作国(或地区)可以要求任何此种转让应当根据一项信息安全协议或安排,其中提出了转移和保护这种技术数据或货物的条件。如果接受方合作国(或地区)不提供包含机密信息的或者包含国家安全性秘密的专利申请的秘密保护,就不必指导这种转移。

除非双方同意转让,非机密的技术数据或货物才可以根据本协定进行转移。

4. 每个合作国(或地区)应采取一切必要的步骤,以确保根据上述第3(1)款、3(2)款,或3(3)款接受的技术数据或货物,能够被接受国,其合作机构,和其他个人和实体(包括承包商及分包商)以如下方式予以处理,其中技术数据或货物的随后转移按照通知或确认的相关条款。每个合作国(或地区)应采取一切合理的必要的步骤,其中包括在其合同和分包合同中保证适当的合同条件,以防止未经授权的使用,泄露或再转让,或未经授权获取技术数据或物品。对于根据上述第3(3)款所述接受的技术数据或货物,接收国或合作机构应对于这样的技术数据或货物提供保护,保护水平至少相当于提供国或合作机构提供保护的级别。

5. 根据本协定或有关的谅解备忘录,接受者超越符合本条款规定条件的技术数据或货物的使用权,披露权,或再转让权以外的任何权利,不是各合作国(或地区)授权的意向。

6. 如果有一个合作国(或地区)退出本协定,不得影响退出之前根据本协定进行转让的技术数据和物品在保护方面的权利或义务,除非按照第28条,当事人在退出协定中另有约定。

7. 基于本条款的目的,由一个合作机构向欧洲航天局进行的任何技术数据和物品的转让,应被视为是向欧洲航天局,向所有的欧洲合作国(或地区),以及欧洲航天局指定的空间站承包商和分包商转让,除非在转让的时候另有特别规定。

8. 各合作国(或地区)应通过其合作机构制定信息安全的指导方针。

第20条 过境中数据和货物的处理

认识到对于空间站的继续运作和全面国际利用的重要性,每个合作国(或地区)应在其适用的法律和法规许可的尺度内,允许其他合作国(或地区)、他们的合作机构及其用户的数据和货物能够迅速过境。本条仅适用于从空间站运进和运出的数据和货物,包括但不限于在国家的边界和在其领土之上的发射点或降落点之间的转移,以及发射点或降落点和空间站之间的转移。

第21条 知识产权

1. 基于本协定的目的,"知识产权"的理解与1967年7月14日签署于斯德哥尔摩的《世界知识产权组织公约》第2条所规定的含义一致。

2. 根据本条的规定,为了知识产权法的目的,发生在空间站的飞行组成部分之内或之上的活动,应被视为只发生在这一组成部分登记的合作国(或地区)的领土内。例外情况是,欧洲航天局登记的组成部分可以认为其活动发生在任何欧洲合作国(或地区)的领土内。为免生疑问,由合作国(或地区)、其合作机构或其相关实体参与的任何其他合作国(或地区)的空间站飞行组成部分的活动,它本身不会影响或改变在前一句提及的此类活动的管辖权。

3. 关于在任何空间站飞行组成部分之内或之上取得的一项发明,而发明者不是它的国民或居民,则该合作国(或地区)并不适用其有关发明保密的法律以防止发明者在任何其他合作国(或地区)提交专利申请(例如,强加一个延误期限或需要事先授权),而其他国家(或地区)对于专利申请的秘密会提供保护,因为该专利申请包含的信息是机密的或为了国家安全目的而以其他方式受到保护。这一规定并不影响:a.专利申请第一次提交的任一合作国(或地区)的关于控制专利申请保密或限制其进一步提出申请的权利;b.申请随后提交的任何其他合作国(或地区)根据任何国际义务,拥有限制分发同一份申请的权利。

4. 如果一个人或一个实体拥有的知识产权在不止一个欧洲合作国(或地区)受到保护,对于发生在欧洲航天局登记的组成部分之内或之上的该类知识产权同种权利的同一侵权行为,该个人或实体可能无法在一个以上的国家胜诉。如果欧洲航天局登记的组成部分之内或之上发生的同一侵权行为,由于不止一个欧洲合作国(或地区)认为该行为发生在其境内时而引起的不同的知识产权所有者提起诉讼,法院在先前提交的诉讼有结果之前可以对稍后提交的诉讼实行临时中止程序。当提起不止一个诉讼时,在已做出判决的任何赔偿损失诉讼中得到了令人满意结果的,应防止从基于同一侵权行为而提出的任何悬而未决的或未来提出的侵权诉讼中得到更多的损害赔偿。

5. 对于在欧洲航天局登记的组成部分之内或之上发生的活动,如果任何关于知识产权权利行使的许可证根据任一欧洲合作国(或地区)的法律都是可实施的,则欧洲合作国(或地区)不应拒绝承认该许可证,并遵守此类许可的规定,也应禁止在任何欧洲合作国(或地区)要求侵权索赔。

6. 暂时驻留在一个合作国(或地区)境内的任何物品,包括飞行要素组成部分,在地球上任何地方和任何另一个合作国(或地区)或欧洲航天局登记的空间站飞行要素之间的转移过程中,其本身并不构成在第一个合作国(或地区)提起的任何专利侵权诉讼的依据。

第22条 刑事管辖权

鉴于这种特别的在外层空间的国际合作的唯一的、空前的特性:

1. 加拿大、欧洲合作国(或地区)、日本、俄罗斯和美国对于属于他们各自国家的任何在飞行要素之内或之上的人员,可以行使刑事管辖权。

2. 涉及在轨道上的不当行为的情况:a. 侵犯到另一个合作国(或地区)的国民的生命或安全,或 b. 对另一个合作国(或地区)的飞行组成部分产生或造成损害,被指控为犯罪人的所属合作国(或地区),应任何受影响的合作国(或地区)的要求,与该国就各自起诉的利益进行协商。受影响的合作国(或地区)可以在协商之后,在这种协商结束日期后的90天内或在共同商定的其他期限内,对被指控的犯罪人行使刑事管辖权,而被指控为犯罪人的所属合作国(或地区):

(1)同意如此行使刑事管辖权;

(2)没有提供将该案提交给其主管机关以便起诉的保证。

3. 如果一个合作国(或地区)现有的某项条约规定了引渡条件,对于另一个与该国并无引渡条约的合作国(或地区)的引渡请求,它可做出自己的选择考虑将这个协定作为关于所指控的轨道上不正当行为的引渡的法律依据。引渡应遵守程序性规定,以及被提出请求的合作国(或地区)的法律规定的其他条件。

4. 每个合作国(或地区)应在符合其国内法律和规章的情况下,向其他合作国(或地区)就被指控的轨道上不正当行为方面提供协助。

5. 本条的目的并非意在限制维持空间站秩序和空间站上人员行为的职权和程序,根据第 11 条对于这些的管理规定在《行为规范》中,而《行为规范》并不打算限制本条款的适用。

第 23 条　协商

1. 各合作国(或地区),通过其合作机构,可以对空间站的合作所提出的任何问题进行相互协商。各合作国(或地区),按照谅解备忘录中规定的程序,应通过各合作机构之间的协商,尽其最大努力来解决这些问题。

2. 任何合作国(或地区),对于空间站的合作所提出的任何问题可以请求与另一合作国(或地区)在政府层面上进行协商。被请求的合作国(或地区)应尽快同意这样的要求。如果请求合作国(或地区)通知美国,这种协商的议题是适合所有合作国(或地区)共同思考的,则美国应在可行的最早时间内邀请所有的合作国(或地区),进行多边协商。

3. 任何合作国(或地区),打算进行重大的飞行组成部分设计的变更,而该变更可能会影响到其他合作国(或地区),应当尽快找机会通知其他合作国(或地区)。被通知的合作国(或地区)可以按照本条上述第 1 款和第 2 款,要求将此事进行协商。

4. 如果问题通过协商不能解决,但需要对其加以解决,则有关合作国(或地区)可以以商定的解决纠纷的形式解决该问题,如和解、调解或仲裁。

第 24 条　空间站合作的审查

鉴于按照本协定进行的长期的、复杂的和不断变化的合作,各合作国(或地区)应保持互相通报可能会影响这方面合作的事态发展。从 1999 年开始,此后每 3 年合作国(或地区)应聚在一起以处理涉及他们合作的问题,并审查和促进空间站上的合作。

第 25 条 生效

1. 本协定应继续开放,以供协定序言中列出的国家签署。
2. 本协定须经过批准、接受、核准或加入。每个国家应根据其宪法程序进行批准,接受,核准或加入。批准书,接受书,核准书或加入书应存放于美国政府,因此美国被指定为保管国。
3.
(1) 本协定自日本、俄罗斯和美国的最后一件批准书,接受书或核准书交存之日起开始生效。保管国应通知所有签署国本协定已生效。

(2) 本协定在对欧洲合作国(或地区)生效之前不应对任一欧洲合作国(或地区)生效。在保管国收到来自至少欧洲四个签署国或缔约方的批准书、接受书、核准书或加入书之后,而且,此外还需要欧洲航天局理事会主席的一份正式通知之后,本协定才可对欧洲合作国(或地区)生效。

(3) 本协定对于欧洲的合作国(或地区)开始生效之后,它对于在序言中列出的还没有交存批准书,接受书或核准书等此种交存文书的任何欧洲国家来说已经有效。欧洲航天局的任何一个未列出在序言中的成员国(或地区),可通过向保管国交存加入书来加入本协定。

4. 本协定生效后,1988 年协定应终止其效力。
5. 如果一个合作国(或地区)在签署协定两年内本协定对于其还没有生效的,美国可以召开一次协定签署国的会议,商讨采取对这一情况必要的措施,包括任何协定的修改。

第 26 条 某些缔约方之间的实施影响

尽管有第 25 条第 3 款第 1 项的规定,本协定应从美国和俄罗斯以交存批准书、接受书或核准书的形式都表示同意受其约束之日起才可以开始实施。依照本条规定,如果本协定在美国和俄罗斯之间开始有效实施,保管国应通知所有签署国。

第27条 修订

本协定,包括其附件,可以由本协定已经对其生效的各合作国(或地区)政府通过书面协议的形式进行修订。本协定的修正,除了那些专为附件进行的修订,在符合各自的宪法程序的情况下,均须经过那些国家的批准、接受,核准或加入程序。专为附件进行的修订,应仅需要本协定已经对其生效的合作国(或地区)政府的一份书面协议。

第28条 退出

1. 任何合作国(或地区)在给保管国至少一年的事先书面通知之后,可以在任何时候退出本协定。一个欧洲合作国(或地区)的退出不应影响欧洲合伙方根据本协定获得的权利和义务。
2. 如果一个合作国(或地区)通知退出本协定,为了确保整体计划的持续进行,各合作国(或地区)应在该合作国(或地区)的退出生效前努力达成关于退出条款及条件的协议。
3.
（1）因为加拿大的贡献对于空间站是一个不可或缺的部分,而对于它的退出,加拿大应确保美国对加拿大列于附件的组成部分能够有效地使用和操作。为此,加拿大应尽快提供硬件、图纸、文档、软件、零部件、模具、特殊实验设备,及/或任何其他美国要求的必要事项。
（2）对于加拿大无论以任何理由发出的退出通知,美国和加拿大应尽快协商出一份退出协议。假定为了整体计划的持续进行,这种协议规定把那些组成部分移交给美国,美国应同时为此转让而给予加拿大适当的补偿。
4. 如果一个合作国(或地区)发出退出本协定的通知,其合作机构应被视为已退出其与美国航天局之间的相应的谅解备忘录,自它退出本协定之日生效。
5. 任何合作国(或地区)的退出,不得影响该合作国(或地区)根据第16条、17条和第19条获得的持续的权利和义务,除非按照上述本条第 2 款或第 3 款制定的退出协议中另有约定。

由以下签字证明,各自政府正式授权签署了本协定。

1998 年 1 月 29 日签署于华盛顿。本协定的英语、法语、德语、意大利语、日语和俄语的版本应具有同等效力。每种语言的原版本应保存在美国政府的档案室。保管国应将证明无误的副本转发给所有签署国。本协定一经生效,保管国应当依据联合国宪章第 102 条的规定予以登记。

附件

由各合作国(或地区)提供的空间站上的组成部分

由各合作国(或地区)提供的空间站上的组成部分归纳如下,并在备忘录有进一步的阐述:

1. 加拿大政府通过加拿大航天局,应提供:

(1)空间站的基础设施组成部分,流动服务中心。

(2)额外的飞行组成部分,专用灵巧机械臂。

(3)除了上述飞行组成部分,还有空间站独特的地面组成部分。

2. 欧洲各国政府通过欧洲航天局,应提供:

(1)一个用户组成部分,欧洲加压实验室(包括基本功能的装备)。

(2)其他供应和助推空间站的飞行组成部分。

(3)除了上述飞行组成部分,还有空间站独特的地面组成部分。

3. 日本政府应提供:

(1)一个用户组成部分,日本试验舱(包括基本功能的装备,以及舱外设施和实验后勤模块)。

(2)其他供应太空站的飞行组成部分。

(3)除了上述飞行组成部分,还有空间站独特的地面组成部分。

4. 俄罗斯政府通过俄罗斯航天局,应提供:

(1)空间站的基础设施组成部分,包括服务和其他模块。

(2)用户组成部分,研究模块(包括基本功能的装备),并随附有效载荷的住宿设备。

（3）其他供应和助推空间站的飞行组成部分。

（4）除了上述飞行组成部分，还有空间站独特的地面组成部分。

5. 美国政府通过美国航天局，应提供：

（1）空间站的基础设施组成部分，包括一个生活舱。

（2）用户组成部分，实验室模块（包括基本功能的装备），并随附有效载荷的住宿设备。

（3）其他供应空间站的飞行组成部分。

（4）除了上述飞行组成部分，还有空间站独特的地面组成部分。

Agreement among the Government of Canada, Governments of the Member States of the European Space Agency, the Government of Japan, the Government of the Russian Federation, and the Government of the United States of America Concerning Cooperation on the Civil International Space Station

The Government of Canada (hereinafter also "Canada").

The Governments of the Kingdom of Belgium, the Kingdom of Denmark, the French Republic, the Federal Republic of Germany, the Italian Republic, the Kingdom of the Netherlands, the Kingdom of Norway, the Kingdom of Spain, the Kingdom of Sweden, the Swiss Confederation, and the United Kingdom of Great Britain and Northern Ireland, being Governments of Member States of the European Space Agency (hereinafter collectively "the European Governments" or "the European Partner").

The Government of Japan (hereinafter also "Japan").

The Government of the Russian Federation (hereinafter also "Russia"), and

The Government of the United States of America (hereinafter "the Government of the United States" or "the United States").

Recalling that in January 1984 the President of the United States directed the National Aeronautics and Space Administration (NASA) to develop and place into orbit a permanently manned Space Station and invited friends and allies of the United States to participate in its development and use and to share in the benefits thereof.

Recalling the acceptance of the aforementioned invitation by the Prime Minister of Canada at the March 1985 Quebec Summit meeting with the President of the United States and the mutual confirmation of interest on cooperation at the March 1986 Washington, D. C. Summit meeting.

Recalling the terms of the relevant Resolutions adopted on 31 January 1985 and 20 October 1995 by the European Space Agency (ESA) Council meeting at the ministerial level, and that, within the framework of ESA, and in accordance with its purpose as defined in Article II of the Convention establishing it, the Columbus programme and the European participation in the international Space Station development programme have been undertaken to develop and will develop elements of the civil international Space Station.

Recalling Japan's interest in the Space Station program manifested during the NASA Administrator's visits to Japan in 1984 and 1985 and Japan's participation in the U. S. space program through the First Materials Processing Test.

Recalling ESA's and Canada's participation in the U. S. Space Transportation System through the European development of the first manned space laboratory, Spacelab, and the Canadian development of the Remote Manipulator System.

Recalling the partnership created by the Agreement Among the Government of the United States of America, Governments of Member States of the European Space Agency, the Government of Japan, and the Government of Canada on Cooperation in the Detailed Design, Development, Operation, and Utilization of the Permanently Manned Civil Space Station (hereinafter "the 1988 Agreement"), done at Washington on 29

September 1988 and related Memoranda of Understanding between NASA and the Ministry of State for Science and Technology (MOSST) of Canada, NASA and ESA, and NASA and the Government of Japan.

Recognizing that the 1988 Agreement entered into force on 30 January 1992 between the United States and Japan.

Recalling that NASA, ESA, the Government of Japan and MOSST have been implementing cooperative activities to realize the partnership in the Space Station program in accordance with the 1988 Agreement and the related Memoranda of Understanding, and recognizing that upon its establishment on 1 March 1989, the Canadian Space Agency (CSA) assumed responsibility for the execution of the Canadian Space Station Program from MOSST.

Convinced that, in view of the Russian Federation's unique experience and accomplishments in the area of human space flight and long-duration missions, including the successful long-term operation of the Russian Mir Space Station, its participation in the partnership will considerably enhance the capabilities of the Space Station to the benefit of all the Partners.

Recalling the invitation extended on 6 December 1993 by the Government of Canada, the European Governments, the Government of Japan, and the Government of the United States to the Government of the Russian Federation to become a Partner in the detailed design, development, operation and utilization of the Space Station within the framework established by the Space Station Agreements, and the positive response of the Government of the Russian Federation on 17 December 1993 to that invitation.

Recalling the arrangements between the Chairman of the Government of the Russian Federation and the Vice President of the United States to promote cooperation on important human spaceflight activities, including the Russian-U.S. Mir-Shuttle program, to prepare for building the International Space Station.

Recalling the Treaty on Principles Governing the Activities of States in the Exploration and Use of Outer Space, including the Moon and Other Celestial Bodies (hereinafter "the Outer Space Treaty"), which entered into force on 10 October 1967.

Recalling the Agreement on the Rescue of Astronauts, the Return of Astronauts, and the Return of Objects Launched into Outer Space (hereinafter "the Rescue Agreement"), which entered into force on 3 December 1968.

Recalling the Convention on International Liability for Damage Caused by Space Objects (hereinafter "the Liability Convention"), which entered into force on 1 September 1972.

Recalling the Convention on Registration of Objects Launched into Outer Space (hereinafter "the Registration Convention"), which entered into force on 15 September 1976.

Convinced that working together on the civil international Space Station will further expand cooperation through the establishment of a long-term and mutually beneficial relationship, and will further promote cooperation in the exploration and peaceful use of outer space.

Recognizing that NASA and CSA, NASA and ESA, NASA and the Government of Japan, and NASA and the Russian Space Agency (RSA) have prepared Memoranda of Understanding (hereinafter "the MOUs") in conjunction with their Governments' negotiation of this Agreement, and that the MOUs provide detailed provisions in implementation of this Agreement.

Recognizing, in light of the foregoing, that it is desirable to establish among the Government of Canada, the European Governments, the Government of Japan, the Government of the Russian Federation, and the Government of the United States a framework for the design, development, operation, and utilization of the Space Station.

Have agreed as follows:

Article 1
Object and Scope

1. The object of this Agreement is to establish a long-term international cooperative framework among the Partners, on the basis of genuine partnership, for the detailed design, development, operation, and utilization of a permanently inhabited civil international Space Station for peaceful purposes, in accordance with international law. This civil international Space Station will enhance the scientific, technological, and commercial use of outer space. This Agreement specifically defines the civil international Space Station program and the nature of this partnership, including the respective rights and obligations of the Partners in this cooperation. This Agreement further provides for mechanisms and arrangements designed to ensure that its object is fulfilled.

2. The Partners will join their efforts, under the lead role of the United States for overall management and coordination, to create an integrated international Space Station. The United States and Russia, drawing on their extensive experience in human space flight, will produce elements which serve as the foundation for the international Space Station. The European Partner and Japan will produce elements that will significantly enhance the Space Station's capabilities. Canada's contribution will be an essential part of the Space Station. This Agreement lists in the Annex the elements to be provided by the Partners to form the international Space Station.

3. The permanently inhabited civil international Space Station (hereinafter "the Space Station") will be a multi-use facility in low-earth orbit, with flight elements and Space Station-unique ground elements provided by all the Partners. By providing Space Station flight elements, each Partner acquires certain rights to use the Space Station and participates in its management in accordance with this Agreement, the

MOUs, and implementing arrangements.

4. The Space Station is conceived as having an evolutionary character. The Partner States' rights and obligations regarding evolution shall be subject to specific provisions in accordance with Article 14.

Article 2
International Rights and Obligations

1. The Space Station shall be developed, operated, and utilized in accordance with international law, including the Outer Space Treaty, the Rescue Agreement, the Liability Convention, and the Registration Convention.

2. Nothing in this Agreement shall be interpreted as:

(a) modifying the rights and obligations of the Partner States found in the treaties listed in paragraph 1 above, either toward each other or toward other States, except as otherwise provided in Article 16;

(b) affecting the rights and obligations of the Partner States when exploring or using outer space, whether individually or in cooperation with other States, in activities unrelated to the Space Station; or

(c) constituting a basis for asserting a claim to national appropriation over outer space or over any portion of outer space.

Article 3
Definitions

For the purposes of this Agreement, the following definitions shall apply:

(a) "this Agreement":
the present Agreement, including the Annex;

(b) "the Partners" (or, where appropriate, "each Partner"):

the Government of Canada; the European Governments listed in the Preamble which become parties to this Agreement, as well as any other European Government that may accede to this Agreement in accordance with Article 25(3), acting collectively as one Partner; the Government of Japan; the Government of the Russian Federation; and the Government of the United States;

(c) "Partner State":

each Contracting Party for which this Agreement has entered into force, in accordance with Article 25.

Article 4
Cooperating Agencies

1. The Partners agree that the Canadian Space Agency (hereinafter "CSA") for the Government of Canada, the European Space Agency (hereinafter "ESA") for the European Governments, the Russian Space Agency (hereinafter "RSA") for Russia, and the National Aeronautics and Space Administration (hereinafter "NASA") for the United States shall be the Cooperating Agencies responsible for implementing Space Station cooperation. The Government of Japan's Cooperating Agency designation for implementing Space Station cooperation shall be made in the Memorandum of Understanding between NASA and the Government of Japan referred to in paragraph 2 below.

2. The Cooperating Agencies shall implement Space Station cooperation in accordance with the relevant provisions of this Agreement, the respective Memoranda of Understanding (MOUs) between NASA and CSA, NASA and ESA, NASA and the Government of Japan, and NASA and RSA concerning cooperation on the civil international Space Station, and arrangements between or among NASA and the other Cooperating Agencies implementing the MOUs (implementing arrange-

ments). The MOUs shall be subject to this Agreement, and the implementing arrangements shall be consistent with and subject to the MOUs.

3. Where a provision of an MOU sets forth rights or obligations accepted by a Cooperating Agency (or, in the case of Japan, the Government of Japan) not a party to that MOU, such provision may not be amended without the written consent of that Cooperating Agency (or, in the case of Japan, the Government of Japan).

Article 5
Registration, Jurisdiction and Control

1. In accordance with Article II of the Registration Convention, each Partner shall register as space objects the flight elements listed in the Annex which it provides, the European Partner having delegated this responsibility to ESA, acting in its name and on its behalf.

2. Pursuant to Article VIII of the Outer Space Treaty and Article II of the Registration Convention, each Partner shall retain jurisdiction and control over the elements it registers in accordance with paragraph 1 above and over personnel in or on the Space Station who are its nationals. The exercise of such jurisdiction and control shall be subject to any relevant provisions of this Agreement, the MOUs, and implementing arrangements, including relevant procedural mechanisms established therein.

Article 6
Ownership of Elements and Equipment

1. Canada, the European Partner, Russia, and the United States, through their respective Cooperating Agencies, and an entity designated

by Japan at the time of the deposit of its instrument under Article 25 (2), shall own the elements listed in the Annex that they respectively provide, except as otherwise provided for in this Agreement. The Partners, acting through their Cooperating Agencies, shall notify each other regarding the ownership of any equipment in or on the Space Station.

2. The European Partner shall entrust ESA, acting in its name and on its behalf, with ownership over the elements it provides, as well as over any other equipment developed and funded under an ESA programme as a contribution to the Space Station, its operation or utilization.

3. The transfer of ownership of the elements listed in the Annex or of equipment in or on the Space Station shall not affect the rights and obligations of the Partners under this Agreement, the MOUs, or implementing arrangements.

4. Equipment in or on the Space Station shall not be owned by, and ownership of elements listed in the Annex shall not be transferred to, any non-Partner or private entity under the jurisdiction of a non-Partner without the prior concurrence of the other Partners. Any transfer of ownership of any element listed in the Annex shall require prior notification of the other Partners.

5. The ownership of equipment or material provided by a user shall not be affected by the mere presence of such equipment or material in or on the Space Station.

6. The ownership or registration of elements or the ownership of equipment shall in no way be deemed to be an indication of ownership of material or data resulting from the conduct of activities in or on the Space Station.

7. The exercise of ownership of elements and equipment shall be subject to any relevant provisions of this Agreement, the MOUs, and implementing arrangements, including relevant procedural mechanisms established therein.

Article 7
Management

1. Management of the Space Station will be established on a multilateral basis and the Partners, acting through their Cooperating Agencies, will participate and discharge responsibilities in management bodies established in accordance with the MOUs and implementing arrangements as provided below. These management bodies shall plan and coordinate activities affecting the design and development of the Space Station and its safe, efficient, and effective operation and utilization, as provided in this Agreement and the MOUs. In these management bodies, decision-making by consensus shall be the goal. Mechanisms for decision-making within these management bodies where it is not possible for the Cooperating Agencies to reach consensus are specified in the MOUs. Decision-making responsibilities which the Partners and their Cooperating Agencies have with respect to the elements they provide are specified in this Agreement and the MOUs.

2. The United States, acting through NASA, and in accordance with the MOUs and implementing arrangements, shall be responsible for management of its own program, including its utilization activities. The United States, acting through NASA, and in accordance with the MOUs and implementing arrangements, shall also be responsible for: overall program management and coordination of the Space Station, except as otherwise provided in this Article and in the MOUs; overall system engineering and integration; establishment of overall safety requirements and plans; and overall planning for and coordination of the execution of the overall integrated operation of the Space Station.

3. Canada, the European Partner, Japan and Russia, acting through their Cooperating Agencies, and in accordance with the MOUs and im-

plementing arrangements, shall each be responsible for: management of their own programs, including their utilization activities; system engineering and integration of the elements they provide; development and implementation of detailed safety requirements and plans for the elements they provide; and, consistent with paragraph 2 above, supporting the United States in the performance of its overall responsibilities, including participating in planning for and coordination of the execution of the integrated operation of the Space Station.

4. To the extent that a design and development matter concerns only a Space Station element provided by Canada, the European Partner, Japan, or Russia and is not covered in the agreed program documentation provided for in the MOUs, that Partner, acting through its Cooperating Agency, may make decisions related to that element.

Article 8
Detailed Design and Development

In accordance with Article 7 and other relevant provisions of this Agreement, and in accordance with the MOUs and implementing arrangements, each Partner, acting through its Cooperating Agency, shall design and develop the elements which it provides, including Space Station-unique ground elements adequate to support the continuing operation and full international utilization of the flight elements, and shall interact with the other Partners, through their Cooperating Agencies, to reach solutions on design and development of their respective elements.

Article 9
Utilization

1. Utilization rights are derived from Partner provision of user ele-

ments, infrastructure elements, or both. Any Partner that provides Space Station user elements shall retain use of those elements, except as otherwise provided in this paragraph. Partners which provide resources to operate and use the Space Station, which are derived from their Space Station infrastructure elements, shall receive in exchange a fixed share of the use of certain user elements. Partners' specific allocations of Space Station user elements and of resources derived from Space Station infrastructure are set forth in the MOUs and implementing arrangements.

2. The Partners shall have the right to barter or sell any portion of their respective allocations. The terms and conditions of any barter or sale shall be determined on a case-by-case basis by the parties to the transaction.

3. Each Partner may use and select users for its allocations for any purpose consistent with the object of this Agreement and provisions set forth in the MOUs and implementing arrangements, except that:

(a) any proposed use of a user element by a non-Partner or private entity under the jurisdiction of a non-Partner shall require the prior notification to and timely consensus among all Partners through their Cooperating Agencies; and

(b) the Partner providing an element shall determine whether a contemplated use of that element is for peaceful purposes, except that this subparagraph shall not be invoked to prevent any Partner from using resources derived from the Space Station infrastructure.

4. In its use of the Space Station, each Partner, through its Cooperating Agency, shall seek through the mechanisms established in the MOUs to avoid causing serious adverse effects on the use of the Space Station by the other Partners.

5. Each Partner shall assure access to and use of its Space Station elements to the other Partners in accordance with their respective allocations.

6. For purposes of this Article, an ESA Member State shall not be con-

sidered a "non-Partner".

Article 10
Operation

The Partners, acting through their Cooperating Agencies, shall have responsibilities in the operation of the elements they respectively provide, in accordance with Article 7 and other relevant provisions of this Agreement, and in accordance with the MOUs and implementing arrangements. The Partners, acting through their Cooperating Agencies, shall develop and implement procedures for operating the Space Station in a manner that is safe, efficient, and effective for Space Station users and operators, in accordance with the MOUs and implementing arrangements. Further, each Partner, acting through its Cooperating Agency, shall be responsible for sustaining the functional performance of the elements it provides.

Article 11
Crew

1. Each Partner has the right to provide qualified personnel to serve on an equitable basis as Space Station crew members. Selections and decisions regarding the flight assignments of a Partner's crew members shall be made in accordance with procedures provided in the MOUs and implementing arrangements.
2. The Code of Conduct for the Space Station crew will be developed and approved by all the Partners in accordance with the individual Partner's internal procedures, and in accordance with the MOUs. A Partner must have approved the Code of Conduct before it provides Space Station crew. Each Partner, in exercising its right to provide

crew, shall ensure that its crew members observe the Code of Conduct.

Article 12
Transportation

1. Each of the Partners shall have the right of access to the Space Station using its respective government and private sector space transportation systems, if they are compatible with the Space Station. The United States, Russia, the European Partner, and Japan, through their respective Cooperating Agencies, shall make available launch and return transportation services for the Space Station (using such space transportation systems as the U. S. Space Shuttle, the Russian Proton and Soyuz, the European Ariane − 5, and the Japanese H − II). Initially, the U. S. and Russian space transportation systems will be used to provide launch and return transportation services for the Space Station and, in addition, the other space transportation systems will be used as those systems become available. Access and launch and return transportation services shall be in accordance with the provisions of the relevant MOUs and implementing arrangements.
2. Those Partners providing launch and return transportation services to other Partners and their respective users on a reimbursable or other basis shall provide such services consistent with conditions specified in the relevant MOUs and implementing arrangements. Those Partners providing launch and return transportation services on a reimbursable basis shall provide such services to another Partner or the users of that Partner, in comparable circumstances, on the same basis they provide such services to any other Partner or the users of such other Partner. Partners shall use their best efforts to accommodate proposed requirements and flight schedules of the other Partners.
3. The United States, through NASA, working with the other Partners'

Cooperating Agencies in management bodies, shall plan and coordinate launch and return transportation services for the Space Station in accordance with the integrated traffic planning process, as provided in the MOUs and implementing arrangements.

4. Each Partner shall respect the proprietary rights in and the confidentiality of appropriately marked data and goods to be transported on its space transportation system.

Article 13
Communications

1. The United States and Russia, through their Cooperating Agencies, shall provide the two primary data relay satellite system space and ground communications networks for command, control, and operations of Space Station elements and payloads, and other Space Station communication purposes. Other Partners may provide data relay satellite system space and ground communication networks, if they are compatible with the Space Station and with Space Station use of the two primary networks. The provision of Space Station communications shall be in accordance with provisions in the relevant MOUs and implementing arrangements.

2. On a reimbursable basis, the Cooperating Agencies shall use their best efforts to accommodate, with their respective communication systems, specific Space Station-related requirements of one another, consistent with conditions specified in the relevant MOUs and implementing arrangements.

3. The United States, through NASA, working with the other Partners' Cooperating Agencies in management bodies, shall plan and coordinate space and ground communications services for the Space Station in accordance with relevant program documentation, as provided in the

MOUs and implementing arrangements.

4. Measures to ensure the confidentiality of utilization data passing through the Space Station Information System and other communication systems being used in connection with the Space Station may be implemented, as provided in the MOUs. Each Partner shall respect the proprietary rights in, and the confidentiality of, the utilization data passing through its communication systems, including its ground network and the communication systems of its contractors, when providing communication services to another Partner.

Article 14
Evolution

1. The Partners intend that the Space Station shall evolve through the addition of capability and shall strive to maximize the likelihood that such evolution will be effected through contributions from all the Partners. To this end, it shall be the object of each Partner to provide, where appropriate, the opportunity to the other Partners to cooperate in its proposals for additions of evolutionary capability. The Space Station together with its additions of evolutionary capability shall remain a civil station, and its operation and utilization shall be for peaceful purposes, in accordance with international law.

2. This Agreement sets forth rights and obligations concerning only the elements listed in the Annex, except that this Article and Article 16 shall apply to any additions of evolutionary capability. This Agreement does not commit any Partner State to participate in, or otherwise grant any Partner rights in, the addition of evolutionary capability.

3. Procedures for the coordination of the Partners' respective evolution studies and for the review of specific proposals for the addition of evolutionary capability are provided in the MOUs.

4. Cooperation between or among Partners regarding the sharing of addition(s) of evolutionary capability shall require, following the coordination and review provided for in paragraph 3 above, either the amendment of this Agreement, or a separate agreement to which the United States, to ensure that any addition is consistent with the overall program, and any other Partner providing a Space Station element or space transportation system on which there is an operational or technical impact, shall be parties.

5. Following the coordination and review provided for in paragraph 3 above, the addition of evolutionary capability by one Partner shall require prior notification of the other Partners, and an agreement with the United States to ensure that any addition is consistent with the overall program, and with any other Partner providing a Space Station element or space transportation system on which there is an operational or technical impact.

6. A Partner which may be affected by the addition of evolutionary capability under paragraph 4 or 5 above may request consultations with the other Partners in accordance with Article 23.

7. The addition of evolutionary capability shall in no event modify the rights and obligations of any Partner State under this Agreement and the MOUs concerning the elements listed in the Annex, unless the affected Partner State otherwise agrees.

Article 15
Funding

1. Each Partner shall bear the costs of fulfilling its respective responsibilities under this Agreement, including sharing on an equitable basis the agreed common system operations costs or activities attributed to the operation of the Space Station as a whole, as provided in the MOUs and

implementing arrangements.

2. Financial obligations of each Partner pursuant to this Agreement are subject to its funding procedures and the availability of appropriated funds. Recognizing the importance of Space Station cooperation, each Partner undertakes to make its best efforts to obtain approval for funds to meet those obligations, consistent with its respective funding procedures.

3. In the event that funding problems arise that may affect a Partner's ability to fulfill its responsibilities in Space Station cooperation, that Partner, acting through its Cooperating Agency, shall notify and consult with the other Cooperating Agencies. If necessary, the Partners may also consult.

4. The Partners shall seek to minimize operations costs for the Space Station. In particular, the Partners, through their Cooperating Agencies, in accordance with the provisions of the MOUs, shall develop procedures intended to contain the common system operations costs and activities within approved estimated levels.

5. The Partners shall also seek to minimize the exchange of funds in the implementation of Space Station cooperation, including through the performance of specific operations activities as provided in the MOUs and implementing arrangements or, if the concerned Partners agree, through the use of barter.

Article 16
Cross-Waiver of Liability

1. The objective of this Article is to establish a cross-waiver of liability by the Partner States and related entities in the interest of encouraging participation in the exploration, exploitation, and use of outer space through the Space Station. This cross-waiver of liability shall be

broadly construed to achieve this objective.

2. For the purposes of this Article:

(a) A "Partner State" includes its Cooperating Agency. It also includes any entity specified in the MOU between NASA and the Government of Japan to assist the Government of Japan's Cooperating Agency in the implementation of that MOU.

(b) The term "related entity" means:

(1) a contractor or subcontractor of a Partner State at any tier;

(2) a user or customer of a Partner State at any tier;

(3) a contractor or subcontractor of a user or customer of a Partner State at any tier.

This subparagraph may also apply to a State, or an agency or institution of a State, having the same relationship to a Partner State as described in subparagraphs 2(b)(1) through 2(b)(3) above or otherwise engaged in the implementation of Protected Space Operations as defined in subparagraph 2(f) below.

"Contractors" and "subcontractors" include suppliers of any kind.

(c) The term "damage" means:

(1) bodily injury to, or other impairment of health of, or death of, any person;

(2) damage to, loss of, or loss of use of any property;

(3) loss of revenue or profits; or

(4) other direct, indirect or consequential damage.

(d) The term "launch vehicle" means an object (or any part thereof) intended for launch, launched from Earth, or returning to Earth which carries payloads or persons, or both.

(e) The term "payload" means all property to be flown or used on or in a launch vehicle or the Space Station.

(f) The term "Protected Space Operations" means all launch vehicle activities, Space Station activities, and payload activities on Earth, in outer space, or in transit between Earth and outer space in implementation of this Agreement, the MOUs, and implementing arrangements. It includes, but is not limited to:

(1) research, design, development, test, manufacture, assembly, integration, operation, or use of launch or transfer vehicles, the Space Station, or a payload, as well as related support equipment and facilities and services; and

(2) all activities related to ground support, test, training, simulation, or guidance and control equipment and related facilities or services.

"Protected Space Operations" also includes all activities related to evolution of the Space Station, as provided for in Article 14. "Protected Space Operations" excludes activities on Earth which are conducted on return from the Space Station to develop further a payload's product or process for use other than for Space Station related activities in implementation of this Agreement.

3. (a) Each Partner State agrees to a cross-waiver of liability pursuant to which each Partner State waives all claims against any of the entities or persons listed in subparagraphs 3(a)(1) through 3(a)(3) below based on damage arising out of Protected Space Operations. This cross-waiver shall apply only if the person, entity, or property causing the damage is involved in Protected Space Operations and the person, entity, or property damaged is damaged by virtue of its involvement in Protected Space Operations. The cross-waiver shall apply to any claims for damage, whatever the legal basis for such claims against:

(1) another Partner State;

(2) a related entity of another Partner State;

(3) the employees of any of the entities identified in subparagraphs 3(a)(1) and 3(a)(2) above.

(b) In addition, each Partner State shall, by contract or otherwise, extend the cross-waiver of liability as set forth in subparagraph 3(a) above to its related entities by requiring them to:

(1) waive all claims against the entities or persons identified in sub-

paragraphs 3(a)(1) through 3(a)(3) above; and

(2) require that their related entities waive all claims against the entities or persons identified in subparagraphs 3(a)(1) through 3(a)(3) above.

(c) For avoidance of doubt, this cross-waiver of liability includes a cross-waiver of liability arising from the Liability Convention where the person, entity, or property causing the damage is involved in Protected Space Operations and the person, entity, or property damaged is damaged by virtue of its involvement in Protected Space Operations.

(d) Notwithstanding the other provisions of this Article, this cross-waiver of liability shall not be applicable to:

(1) claims between a Partner State and its related entity or between its own related entities;

(2) claims made by a natural person, his/her estate, survivors or subrogees (except when a subrogee is a Partner State) for bodily injury to, or other impairment of health of, or death of such natural person;

(3) claims for damage caused by willful misconduct;

(4) intellectual property claims;

(5) claims for damage resulting from a failure of a Partner State to extend the cross-waiver of liability to its related entities, pursuant to subparagraph 3(b) above.

(e) With respect to subparagraph 3(d)(2) above, in the event that a subrogated claim of the Government of Japan is not based upon government employee accident compensation law, the Government of Japan shall fulfill its obligation to waive such subrogated claim by ensuring that any assisting entity specified pursuant to subparagraph 2(a) above indemnifies, in a manner consistent with Article 15(2) and in accordance with applicable laws and regulations of Japan, any entity or person identified in subparagraphs 3(a)(1) through 3(a)(3) above against liability arising from such subrogated claim by the Government of Japan. Nothing in this Article shall preclude the Government of Japan

from waiving the foregoing subrogated claims.
(f) Nothing in this Article shall be construed to create the basis for a claim or suit where none would otherwise exist.

Article 17
Liability Convention

1. Except as otherwise provided in Article 16, the Partner States, as well as ESA, shall remain liable in accordance with the Liability Convention.
2. In the event of a claim arising out of the Liability Convention, the Partners (and ESA, if appropriate) shall consult promptly on any potential liability, on any apportionment of such liability, and on the defense of such claim.
3. Regarding the provision of launch and return services provided for in Article 12(2), the Partners concerned (and ESA, if appropriate) may conclude separate agreements regarding the apportionment of any potential joint and several liability arising out of the Liability Convention.

Article 18
Customs and Immigration

1. Each Partner State shall facilitate the movement of persons and goods necessary to implement this Agreement into and out of its territory, subject to its laws and regulations.
2. Subject to its laws and regulations, each Partner State shall facilitate provision of the appropriate entry and residence documentation for nationals and families of nationals of another Partner State who enter or exit or reside within the territory of the first Partner State in order to carry out functions necessary for the implementation of this Agreement.

3. Each Partner State shall grant permission for duty-free importation and exportation to and from its territory of goods and software which are necessary for implementation of this Agreement and shall ensure their exemption from any other taxes and duties collected by the customs authorities. This paragraph shall be implemented without regard to the country of origin of such necessary goods and software.

Article 19
Exchange of Data and Goods

1. Except as otherwise provided in this paragraph, each Partner, acting through its Cooperating Agency shall transfer all technical data and goods considered to be necessary (by both parties to any transfer) to fulfill the responsibilities of that Partner's Cooperating Agency under the relevant MOUs and implementing arrangements. Each Partner undertakes to handle expeditiously any request for technical data or goods presented by the Cooperating Agency of another Partner for the purposes of Space Station cooperation. This Article shall not require a Partner State to transfer any technical data and goods in contravention of its national laws or regulations.

2. The Partners shall make their best efforts to handle expeditiously requests for authorization of transfers of technical data and goods by persons or entities other than the Partners or their Cooperating Agencies (for example, company-to-company exchanges which are likely to develop), and they shall encourage and facilitate such transfers in connection with the Space Station cooperation under this Agreement. Otherwise, such transfers are not covered by the terms and conditions of this Article. National laws and regulations shall apply to such transfers.

3. The Partners agree that transfers of technical data and goods under

this Agreement shall be subject to the restrictions set forth in this paragraph. The transfer of technical data for the purposes of discharging the Partners' responsibilities with regard to interface, integration and safety shall normally be made without the restrictions set forth in this paragraph. If detailed design, manufacturing, and processing data and associated software is necessary for interface, integration or safety purposes, the transfer shall be made in accordance with paragraph 1 above, but the data and associated software may be appropriately marked as set out below. Technical data and goods not covered by the restrictions set forth in this paragraph shall be transferred without restriction, except as otherwise restricted by national laws or regulations.

(a) The furnishing Cooperating Agency shall mark with a notice, or otherwise specifically identify, the technical data or goods that are to be protected for export control purposes. Such a notice or identification shall indicate any specific conditions regarding how such technical data or goods may be used by the receiving Cooperating Agency and its contractors and subcontractors, including (1) that such technical data or goods shall be used only for the purposes of fulfilling the receiving Cooperating Agency's responsibilities under this Agreement and the relevant MOUs, and (2) that such technical data or goods shall not be used by persons or entities other than the receiving Cooperating Agency, its contractors or subcontractors, or for any other purposes, without the prior written permission of the furnishing Partner State, acting through its Cooperating Agency.

(b) The furnishing Cooperating Agency shall mark with a notice the technical data that are to be protected for proprietary rights purposes. Such notice shall indicate any specific conditions regarding how such technical data may be used by the receiving Cooperating Agency and its contractors and subcontractors, including (1) that such technical data shall be used, duplicated, or disclosed only for the purposes of fulfilling the receiving Cooperating Agency's responsibilities under this Agreement and the relevant MOUs, and (2) that such technical data shall not be used by persons or entities other than the receiving Cooperating Agency, its contractors or subcontractors, or for any other purposes, without the prior written permission of the furnishing Partner State, acting through its Cooperating Agency.

(c) In the event that any technical data or goods transferred under this Agreement are classified, the furnishing Cooperating Agency shall mark with a notice, or otherwise specifically identify, such technical data or goods. The requested Partner State may require that any such transfer shall be pursuant to a security of information agreement or arrangement which sets forth the conditions for transferring and protecting such technical data or goods. A transfer need not be conducted if the receiving Partner State does not provide for the protection of the secrecy of patent applications containing information that is classified or otherwise held in secrecy for national security purposes.

No classified technical data or goods shall be transferred under this Agreement unless both parties agree to the transfer.

4. Each Partner State shall take all necessary steps to ensure that technical data or goods received by it under subparagraphs 3(a), 3(b), or 3(c) above shall be treated by the receiving Partner State, its Cooperating Agency, and other persons and entities (including contractors and subcontractors) to which the technical data or goods are subsequently transferred in accordance with the terms of the notice or identification. Each Partner State and Cooperating Agency shall take all reasonably necessary steps, including ensuring appropriate contractual conditions in their contracts and subcontracts, to prevent unauthorized use, disclosure, or retransfer of, or unauthorized access to, such technical data or goods. In the case of technical data or goods received under subparagraph 3(c) above, the receiving Partner State or Cooperating Agency shall accord such technical data or goods a level of protection at least equivalent to the level of protection accorded by the fur-

nishing Partner State or Cooperating Agency.

5. It is not the intent of the Partners to grant, through this Agreement or the relevant MOUs, any rights to a recipient beyond the right to use, disclose, or retransfer received technical data or goods consistent with conditions imposed under this Article.

6. Withdrawal from this Agreement by a Partner State shall not affect rights or obligations regarding the protection of technical data and goods transferred under this Agreement prior to such withdrawal, unless otherwise agreed in a withdrawal agreement pursuant to Article 28.

7. For the purposes of this Article, any transfer of technical data and goods by a Cooperating Agency to ESA shall be deemed to be destined to ESA, to all of the European Partner States, and to ESA's designated Space Station contractors and subcontractors, unless otherwise specifically provided for at the time of transfer.

8. The Partners, through their Cooperating Agencies, will establish guidelines for security of information.

Article 20
Treatment of Data and Goods in Transit

Recognizing the importance of the continuing operation and full international utilization of the Space Station, each Partner State shall, to the extent its applicable laws and regulations permit, allow the expeditious transit of data and goods of the other Partners, their Cooperating Agencies, and their users. This Article shall only apply to data and goods transiting to and from the Space Station, including but not limited to transit between its national border and a launch or landing site within its territory, and between a launch or landing site and the Space Station.

Article 21
Intellectual Property

1. For the purposes of this Agreement, "intellectual property" is understood to have the meaning of Article 2 of the Convention Establishing the World Intellectual Property Organization, done at Stockholm on 14 July 1967.

2. Subject to the provisions of this Article, for purposes of intellectual property law, an activity occurring in or on a Space Station flight element shall be deemed to have occurred only in the territory of the Partner State of that element's registry, except that for ESA-registered elements any European Partner State may deem the activity to have occurred within its territory. For avoidance of doubt, participation by a Partner State, its Cooperating Agency, or its related entities in an activity occurring in or on any other Partner's Space Station flight element shall not in and of itself alter or affect the jurisdiction over such activity provided for in the previous sentence.

3. In respect of an invention made in or on any Space Station flight element by a person who is not its national or resident, a Partner State shall not apply its laws concerning secrecy of inventions so as to prevent the filing of a patent application (for example, by imposing a delay or requiring prior authorization) in any other Partner State that provides for the protection of the secrecy of patent applications containing information that is classified or otherwise protected for national security purposes. This provision does not prejudice (a) the right of any Partner State in which a patent application is first filed to control the secrecy of such patent application or restrict its further filing; or (b) the right of any other Partner State in which an application is subsequently filed to restrict, pursuant to any international obligation, the dissemination of

an application.

4. Where a person or entity owns intellectual property which is protected in more than one European Partner State, that person or entity may not recover in more than one such State for the same act of infringement of the same rights in such intellectual property which occurs in or on an ESA-registered element. Where the same act of infringement in or on an ESA-registered element gives rise to actions by different intellectual property owners by virtue of more than one European Partner State's deeming the activity to have occurred in its territory, a court may grant a temporary stay of proceeding in a later-filed action pending the outcome of an earlier-filed action. Where more than one action is brought, satisfaction of a judgment rendered for damages in any of the actions shall bar further recovery of damages in any pending or future action for infringement based upon the same act of infringement.

5. With respect to an activity occurring in or on an ESA registered element, no European Partner State shall refuse to recognize a license for the exercise of any intellectual property right if that license is enforceable under the laws of any European Partner State, and compliance with the provisions of such license shall also bar recovery for infringement in any European Partner State.

6. The temporary presence in the territory of a Partner State of any articles, including the components of a flight element, in transit between any place on Earth and any flight element of the Space Station registered by another Partner State or ESA shall not in itself form the basis for any proceedings in the first Partner State for patent infringement.

Article 22
Criminal Jurisdiction

In view of the unique and unprecedented nature of this particular international cooperation in space:

1. Canada, the European Partner States, Japan, Russia, and the United States may exercise criminal jurisdiction over personnel in or on any flight element who are their respective nationals.

2. In a case involving misconduct on orbit that: (a) affects the life or safety of a national of another Partner State or (b) occurs in or on or causes damage to the flight element of another Partner State, the Partner State whose national is the alleged perpetrator shall, at the request of any affected Partner State, consult with such State concerning their respective prosecutorial interests. An affected Partner State may, following such consultation, exercise criminal jurisdiction over the alleged perpetrator provided that, within 90 days of the date of such consultation or within such other period as may be mutually agreed, the Partner State whose national is the alleged perpetrator either:

(1) concurs in such exercise of criminal jurisdiction, or

(2) fails to provide assurances that it will submit the case to its competent authorities for the purpose of prosecution.

3. If a Partner State which makes extradition conditional on the existence of a treaty receives a request for extradition from another Partner State with which it has no extradition treaty, it may at its option consider this Agreement as the legal basis for extradition in respect of the alleged misconduct on orbit. Extradition shall be subject to the procedural provisions and the other conditions of the law of the requested Partner State.

4. Each Partner State shall, subject to its national laws and regulations, afford the other Partners assistance in connection with alleged misconduct on orbit.

5. This Article is not intended to limit the authorities and procedures for the maintenance of order and the conduct of crew activities in or on the Space Station which shall be established in the Code of Conduct pursuant to Article 11, and the Code of Conduct is not intended to limit

the application of this Article.

Article 23
Consultations

1. The Partners, acting through their Cooperating Agencies, may consult with each other on any matter arising out of Space Station cooperation. The Partners shall exert their best efforts to settle such matters through consultation between or among their Cooperating Agencies in accordance with procedures provided in the MOUs.
2. Any Partner may request that government-level consultations be held with another Partner on any matter arising out of Space Station cooperation. The requested Partner shall accede to such request promptly. If the requesting Partner notifies the United States that the subject of such consultations is appropriate for consideration by all the Partners, the United States shall convene multilateral consultations at the earliest practicable time, to which it shall invite all the Partners.
3. Any Partner which intends to proceed with significant flight element design changes which may have an impact on the other Partners shall notify the other Partners accordingly at the earliest opportunity. A Partner so notified may request that the matter be submitted to consultations in accordance with paragraphs 1 and 2 above.
4. If an issue not resolved through consultations still needs to be resolved, the concerned Partners may submit that issue to an agreed form of dispute resolution such as conciliation, mediation, or arbitration.

Article 24
Space Station Cooperation Review

In view of the long-term, complex, and evolving character of their cooperation under this Agreement, the Partners shall keep each other informed of developments which might affect this cooperation. Beginning in 1999, and every three years thereafter, the Partners shall meet to deal with matters involved in their cooperation and to review and promote Space Station cooperation.

Article 25
Entry into Force

1. This Agreement shall remain open for signature by the States listed in the Preamble of this Agreement.
2. This Agreement is subject to ratification, acceptance, approval, or accession. Ratification, acceptance, approval, or accession shall be effected by each State in accordance with its constitutional processes. Instruments of ratification, acceptance, approval, or accession shall be deposited with the Government of the United States, hereby designated as the Depositary.
3. (a) This Agreement shall enter into force on the date on which the last instrument of ratification, acceptance, or approval of Japan, Russia and the United States has been deposited. The Depositary shall notify all signatory States of this Agreement's entry into force.
(b) This Agreement shall not enter into force for a European Partner State before it enters into force for the European Partner. It shall enter into force for the European Partner after the Depositary receives instruments of ratification, acceptance, approval, or accession from at least four European signatory or acceding States, and, in addition, a formal notification by the Chairman of the ESA Council.
(c) Following entry into force of this Agreement for the European Partner, it shall enter into force for any European State listed in the Preamble that has not deposited its instrument of ratification, acceptance or

approval upon deposit of such instrument. Any ESA Member State not listed in the Preamble may accede to this Agreement by depositing its instrument of accession with the Depositary.

4. Upon entry into force of this Agreement, the 1988 Agreement shall cease to be in force.

5. If this Agreement has not entered into force for a Partner within a period of two years after its signature, the United States may convene a conference of the signatories to this Agreement to consider what steps, including any modifications to this Agreement, are necessary to take account of that circumstance.

Article 26
Operative Effect as Between Certain Parties

Notwithstanding Article 25 (3) (a) above, this Agreement shall become operative as between the United States and Russia on the date they have expressed their consent to be bound by depositing their instruments of ratification, acceptance or approval. The Depositary shall notify all signatory States if this Agreement becomes operative between the United States and Russia pursuant to this Article.

Article 27
Amendments

This Agreement, including its Annex, may be amended by written agreement of the Governments of the Partner States for which this Agreement has entered into force. Amendments to this Agreement, except for those made exclusively to the Annex, shall be subject to ratification, acceptance, approval, or accession by those States in accordance with their respective constitutional processes. Amendments made exclusively to the Annex shall require only a written agreement of the Governments of the Partner States for which this Agreement has entered into force.

Article 28
Withdrawal

1. Any Partner State may withdraw from this Agreement at any time by giving to the Depositary at least one year's prior written notice. Withdrawal by a European Partner State shall not affect the rights and obligations of the European Partner under this Agreement.

2. If a Partner gives notice of withdrawal from this Agreement, with a view toward ensuring the continuation of the overall program, the Partners shall endeavor to reach agreement concerning the terms and conditions of that Partner's withdrawal before the effective date of withdrawal.

3. (a) Because Canada's contribution is an essential part of the Space Station, upon its withdrawal, Canada shall ensure the effective use and operation by the United States of the Canadian elements listed in the Annex. To this end, Canada shall expeditiously provide hardware, drawings, documentation, software, spares, tooling, special test equipment, and/or any other necessary items requested by the United States.

(b) Upon Canada's notice of withdrawal for any reason, the United States and Canada shall expeditiously negotiate a withdrawal agreement. Assuming that such agreement provides for the transfer to the United States of those elements required for the continuation of the overall program, it shall also provide for the United States to give Canada adequate compensation for such transfer.

4. If a Partner gives notice of withdrawal from this Agreement, its Cooperating Agency shall be deemed to have withdrawn from its corre-

sponding MOU with NASA, effective from the same date as its withdrawal from this Agreement.

5. Withdrawal by any Partner State shall not affect that Partner State's continuing rights and obligations under Articles 16, 17, and 19, unless otherwise agreed in a withdrawal agreement pursuant to paragraph 2 or 3 above.

IN WITNESS WHEREOF the undersigned, being duly authorized thereto by their respective Governments, have signed this Agreement.

DONE at Washington, this 29th day of January, 1998. The texts of this Agreement in the English, French, German, Italian, Japanese, and Russian languages shall be equally authentic. A single original text in each language shall be deposited in the archives of the Government of the United States. The Depositary shall transmit certified copies to all signatory States. Upon entry into force of this Agreement, the Depositary shall register it pursuant to Article 102 of the Charter of the United Nations.

ANNEX
Space Station Elements to be Provided by the Parnters

The Space Station elements to be provided by the Partners are summarized below and are further elaborated in the MOUs:

1. The Government of Canada, through CSA, shall provide:

· as a Space Station infrastructure element, the Mobile Servicing Center (MSC);

· as an additional flight element, the Special Purpose Dexterous Manipulator; and

· in addition to the flight elements above, Space Station – unique ground elements.

2. The European Governments, through ESA, shall provide:

· as a user element, the European pressurized laboratory (including basic functional outfitting);

· other flight elements to supply and to reboost the Space Station; and

· in addition to the flight elements above, Space Station – unique ground elements.

3. The Government of Japan shall provide:

· as a user element, the Japanese Experiment Module (including basic functional outfitting, as well as the Exposed Facility and the Experiment Logistics Modules);

· other flight elements to supply the Space Station; and

· in addition to the flight elements above, Space Station—unique ground elements.

4. The Government of Russia, through RSA, shall provide:

· Space Station infrastructure elements, including service and other modules;

· as user elements, research modules (including basic functional outfitting) and attached payload accommodation equipment;

· other flight elements to supply and to reboost the Space Station; and

· in addition to the flight elements above, Space Station—unique ground elements.

5. The Government of the United States, through NASA, shall provide:

· Space Station infrastructure elements, including a habitation module;

· as user elements, laboratory modules (including basic functional outfitting), and attached payload accommodation equipment;

· other flight elements to supply the Space Station; and

· in addition to the flight elements above, Space Station – unique ground elements.

美国国家航天政策(2006)①(中、英文)

晓 宇译

总统于 2006 年 8 月 31 日批准了一项新的国家航天政策,确立了用于管理美国航天活动行为的总体国家政策。这一政策取代 1996 年 9 月 14 日颁布的《国家航天政策》(《总统决策指令/NSC-49/NSTC-8》)。

1. 背景

50 年来,美国在空间探索与利用领域一直处于世界领先地位,并建立了牢固的民用、商业和国家安全空间基础。航天活动改善了美国和全球的生活,增强了安全,保护了生命与环境,加快了信息流动,成为经济增长的引擎,并使人们对其在世界上和在宇宙中所处地位的看法发生了革命性的改变。空间已成为越来越多地被众多国家、财团、公司和企业家利用的一个对象。新的世纪里,谁能有效地利用空间,谁就将获得到更大的繁荣和安全,而且将会比那些不具备这种能力者拥有显著的优势。空间行动自由对美国的重要性不亚于空中力量和海上力量。为了增加知识、促进经济繁荣,加强国家安全,美国必须具有健全、有效和高效的空间能力。

2. 原则

美国航天计划和活动的开展应被作为重中之重,并应在下述

---

① 中文本来自《中国航天》2006 年第 11 期第 21~25 页。感谢《中国航天》张会庭总编的支持。

原则指导下进行:

- 美国致力于由所有国家为和平目的,并为造福全人类来开展外层空间的探索与利用。遵从于这一原则,"和平目的"允许美国为寻求国家利益而开展与防御和情报相关的活动。

- 美国反对任何国家对外层空间或天体或其任何部分的任何主权要求,并反对对美国在空间开展操作或从空间获取数据的基本权利施加任何限制。

- 美国将寻求在外层空间和平利用方面与其他国家(或地区)开展合作,以扩展空间效益,加强空间探索,并保护和促进全球自由。

- 美国认为空间系统有权不受干扰地通过空间和在空间运行。遵从于这一原则,美国将把对其空间系统的有意干扰视为对其权利的侵犯。

- 美国认为空间能力——包括地面和空间段及保障环节——对其国家利益至关重要。遵从于这一政策,美国将保留其在空间的权利、能力和行动自由;劝阻或吓阻他方不要妨碍那些权利或发展旨在进行这种妨碍的能力;采取必要行动来保护其空间能力;对干扰做出反应;并在必要时阻止敌方利用与美国国家利益相抵触的空间能力。

- 美国将反对制定新的法律制度或其他限制措施来寻求禁止或限制美国进入或利用空间。拟议中的军备控制协议或限制措施不得损害美国为其国家利益在空间开展研究、研制、试验和运行或其他活动;以及

- 美国致力于鼓励和支持形成一个日益增长和企业性的美国商业航天产业。为此目的,并服从于国家安全,美国政府将在最大现实程度上利用美国的商业空间能力。

3. 美国航天政策的宗旨

本政策的基本宗旨是:

- 巩固国家的航天领先地位,并保证空间能力能及时提供使用,以促进美国国家安全、国土安全和外交政策目标。

・使美国能不受阻碍地在空间或通过空间开展操作,以保护美国的空间利益。

・实施并维持一项创新性的载人和不载人探索计划,目的是扩展人类在整个太阳系中的存在。

・提高民用探索、科学发现和环境活动的效益。

・形成一个活跃、具有全球竞争力的国家商业航天产业,以推动产业创新,巩固美国的领先地位,并保护国家、国土和经济安全。

・形成一个健全的科学技术基础,保障国家安全、国土安全和民用航天活动。

・鼓励在航天活动领域与外国和/或财团开展互利性和能促进空间和平探索与利用以及能促进国家安全、国土安全和外交政策目标的国际合作。

4. 总体方针

为实现本政策之宗旨,美国政府应:

・培养航天专业人员。在与航天相关的科学、工程、采办和运行学科具有持续的专长对美国空间能力之未来至关重要。开展航天相关活动的部门和机构应制订标准,并开展活动,以在其工作队伍中培养和保持高度熟练、经验高度丰富和具有高度积极性的航天专业人员。

・改善空间系统研制与采购工作。美国的空间系统向广泛的民用、商业和国家安全用户提供关键的能力。空间系统研制与采购的主要目标必须是保证任务成功完成。实现这一目标要依靠行之有效的研究、研制、采办、管理、实施、监管和运行。为此目的,部门和机构应营造一个能使任务取得成功的环境,包括但不限于就现实而稳定的要求与运行方案达成共识;明确地确定和管理风险,包括系统安全;设立并维持现实而稳定的经费;及时并按照预算提供空间能力;并为采办管理部门提供实现这一目标所需的工具、职责、预算灵活性和权限。

・增进并加强机构间合作。应对 21 世纪的挑战需要开展重点突出而且专一的团结协作。机构间合作可为共同确定所需的效果、能力和战略带来机遇。部门和机构应利用好开展活跃合作的机遇——不论是通过协作、信息共享、结盟,还是通过融合。

· 巩固并保持美国与航天相关的科学、技术和工业基础。健全的科学、技术和工业基础对美国的空间能力至关重要。部门和机构应:鼓励在空间科学和新的技术应用领域取得新发现;使未来空间系统能达到新的更高的能力,包括激励实现高风险高回报和转型空间能力。此外,部门和机构应:开展能提高能力和降低成本的基础和应用研究;鼓励形成一个创新性的商业航天产业,包括采用有奖竞赛方式;保证用于支持关键政府职能的航天相关工业能力的可用性。

5. 国家安全航天方针

美国国家安全对空间能力具有至关重要的依赖性,且这种依赖性还会增加。国防部长和国家情报局长在与国务卿以及其他部门和机构负责人进行适当磋商后,并按照修订的《1947年国家安全法案》《美国法典》第10篇和《美国法典》第50篇、《2004年国家安全情报改革法案》和其他适用法律所规定的其各自的职责。应:

· 支持总统和副总统履行行政职能,支持高级行政部门国家安全、国土安全和外交政策决策人员;其他相应联邦官员;以及经常的宪法政府运作和基础设施。

· 在和平、危机时期和在所有各级别冲突过程中支持并实现防御和情报要求及运作。

· 发展并部署能保持美国优势和支持防御及情报转型的空间能力。

· 采取能形成保障国家和国土安全所需的作战兵力结构和优化的空间能力的适当的规划、计划和预算活动,机构设置及战略。

为实现本政策之宗旨,国防部长应:

· 保持执行空间支援、兵力增强、空间控制和兵力运用任务所需的能力。

· 制订可利用战术、作战或国家级情报搜集能力加以满足的具体情报要求。

・作为防御和情报部门的发射代理,提供服务于国家安全目的的可靠、经济和及时的空间进入能力。

・提供空间能力来保障连续、全球性的战略和战术预警以及多层和一体化的导弹防御。

・建立能力、规划和选项来保证空间行动自由,并在得到指示时阻止敌方获得此等行动自由;

・负责空间态势感知;按照这一职能,国防部长应支持国家情报局长的空间态势感知要求,并为下列目的开展空间态势感知:美国政府;用于国家和国土安全目的的美国商业空间能力和服务;民用空间能力及运行,特别是载人航天飞行活动;适当的商业和国外航天实体。

・制订并实施政策和办法来保护有关航天相关防御活动的管制、分发和解密的敏感信息。

为实现本政策之宗旨,国家情报局长应:

・为情报部门制定目标、情报要求、工作重点和指导方针,以保证能及时而有效地采集、处理、分析和分发国家情报。

・保证能用及时的信息和数据来支持外交、防御和经济政策;外交活动;指征和报警;危机管理;履约核查;适当的民用、国土安全和执法用户;开展与这些职能相关的研究与开发工作。

・作为重大情报任务支持军事规划并满足作战要求。

・提供航天相关能力的情报搜集与分析,以及为以下目的支持空间态势感知:美国政府;用于国家和国土安全目的的美国商业空间能力和服务;民用空间能力及运行,特别是载人航天飞行活动;相应的商业和国外航天实体。

・提供健全的国外航天情报搜集与分析能力,以便提供及时的信息和数据,保障国家和国土安全。

・协调由美国政府部门或机构开展的任何空间无线电频率勘测,并在适当情况下审批由私营部门、州或地方政府开展的任何空间无线电频率勘测。

・制订并实施政策和办法,以便:对所采集的可归属的航天相关信息和情报活动运作细节实行保密;保护敏感活动;在局长认定不再需要这种保护时对此等信息予以解密和公布。

6. 民用航天方针

美国应提高民用探索、科学发现和运行环境监测活动的效益。为此目的,国家航空与航天局局长应:实施一项持续而经济的载人和不载人空间探索计划,并研制、采购和利用民用空间系统来增长对我们的地球系统、太阳系和宇宙的基本科学知识。

商业部长应通过国家海洋与大气局局长,并同国家航空与航天局局长协调,按以下要求负责业务型民用环境天基遥感系统以及对相关要求和采购过程进行管理:

・商务部长将通过国家海洋与大气局,并通过空军部长与国防部长合作,和国家航空与航天局局长一道继续依照现行政策指示整合民用和军用极轨业务环境遥感系统;

・商务部长应通过国家海洋与大气局,并在国家航空与航天局的支持下,继续开展一项民用静地业务环境卫星计划;以及

・商务部长应通过国家海洋与大气局,和国家航空与航天局局长一道保证尽最大可能使民用航天采购过程和能力不出现重复。

内务部长应通过美国地质调查局局长采集、归档、处理和向美国政府及其他用户分发陆地表面数据,并确定陆地表面数据的使用要求。

美国将从空间研究地球系统,并发展新的天基和相关能力,以加深科学认识和加强民用天基对地观测。特别是:

・国家航空与航天局局长应开展一项研究计划,以通过天基观测和开发并部署使能通过技术来增长有关地球的科学知识;以及

・商务部长和国家航空与航天局局长以及其他相应部门和机构应将成熟的研究与开发能力过渡到适当的长期运行,以支持长期使用要求。

美国将在可行的情况下利用政府和商业天基与相关能力来加强灾害预警、监测和反应活动;并在国际论坛上发挥领导作用,以

建立起一项长期计划来协调一个一体化的全球对地观测系统,并推动便于在平等条件下全面而公开地获取政府环境数据的政策得到国际上的采纳。

7. 商业航天方针

培育美国商业空间能力在全球的利用和形成一个活跃的国家商业航天产业符合美国的利益。为此目的,部门和机构应:

- 在最大现实程度上利用美国商业空间能力和服务;采购商业能力和服务,前提是这种能力和服务已出现在商业市场上并满足美国政府的要求;对可通过商业渠道获得的能力和服务进行改造来满足美国政府的要求,前提是这种改造具有高效费比。
- 在符合国家利益且没有合适的、高效费比的美国商业或适当的国外商业服务或系统可供使用或可在未来需要时提供使用的情况下研制这些系统。
- 继续让美国私营部门参与美国政府空间系统和基础设施的设计和研制,并提高这种参与的程度。
- 除非出于国家安全或公共安全之需要,避免开展会妨碍、阻止美国商业航天活动或与美国商业航天活动相抵触的活动。
- 在服从于国家安全的前提下,在最大现实程度上保证美国政府的航天活动、技术和基础设施可在有偿和不产生干扰的基础上供私人使用。
- 在符合商务部和运输部以及联邦通信委员会主席的监管和其他权限的前提下,保持一个及时且反应迅速的商业航天活动许可证发放监管环境,并在不利用联邦政府直接补贴的条件下追求商业航天目标。

8. 国际航天合作

美国政府将在适当情况下,并在符合美国国家安全利益的前提下,寻求在航天活动领域与外国和/或财团开发互利性和能促进空间和平探索与利用以及能促进国家安全、国土安全和外交政策目标的国际合作。潜在国际合作领域包括但不限于:

- 空间探索;提供符合安全要求和美国国家安全及外交政策

利益的空间监视信息;研制并运行对地观测系统。

国务卿应在与相应部门和机构负责人磋商后开展适当的外交和公共外交努力,以建立对美国国家航天政策和计划的理解和支持,并鼓励友方和盟友利用美国的空间能力和系统。

9. 空间核动力

在空间核动力系统能安全地实现或明显地增强空间探索或运行能力的领域,美国应研制和利用这些系统。空间核动力系统的利用应符合美国国家和国土安全以及外交政策利益,并应考虑潜在风险。有鉴于此:

· 依照现行的机构间评审程序,采用有临界可能或超出最低放射性阈值的核动力源的美国政府和非政府航天器的发射和使用应需得到总统或其指定人员的批准。

· 为此目的,能源部长应:开展核安全分析,由一个特别的机构间核安全评审委员会进行评定,包括评定与发射和在空间内使用相关的风险;帮助运输部长进行空间运输许可证办理;提供核安全监测,以保证空间运行符合所做的安全评定;维持研制和在美国政府的空间系统上装备核动力系统所需的能力和基础设施;以及:

· 对于政府航天器来说,主管部门或机构的负责人应请求得到发射许可,并应负责该航天器在空间的安全运行。

· 对于采用核动力源的非政府航天器来说,运营者将负责该航天器,包括核动力源,在空间的安全运行。为此目的:

· 美国政府应指定一个进入点并制订采用空间核动力系统的非政府任务的评审办法。

· 运输部长应根据上述要求,承担包含核材料的美国商业发射活动的许可证办理权限,包括有效载荷的确认。

· 核监管委员会将在包含不归能源部所有的利用设施和核材料的发射进行前为相关活动办理许可证。

· 美国政府将在法律允许的限度内以收取服务费的方式开展安全性分析、评定和核安全监测,运营者将为所提供的服务向该美国政府实体支付全部费用。

・能源部长应制订并实施政策和办法来保护有关航天相关核活动的管制、分发和解密的敏感信息。

10. 无线电频谱和轨道管理与干扰防护

服务于国家和国土安全、民用、科学和商业目的的空间利用依赖于可靠地取得并利用无线电频谱和轨道分配。为保证基于这些目的的空间利用的连续性,美国政府应:

・寻求获取并保护美国全方位地获得保障美国政府和商业用户空间利用所需的无线电频谱和轨道分配的权利。

・在批准采办新的空间能力之前明确阐明对无线电频谱和轨道分配的需求。

・在符合现行办法的条件下,在最大现实程度上保证美国国家安全、国土安全、民用和商业空间能力和服务以及对美国政府有益的外国空间能力和服务不受有害干扰的影响;以及

・按照管理资质所赋予的商业运行并按照卫星服务的分配资质,为由美国政府所有和运作的、通过商业卫星来运行的地球站寻求美国国内法规之下的频谱管理资质。

11. 轨道碎片

轨道碎片对天基服务和运行的连续可靠使用以及对空间和地面的人员和财产安全构成威胁。美国应寻求最大限度地减少政府和非政府空间运行所产生的轨道碎片,以为后人保护空间环境。为此目的:

・部门和机构应依照任务要求和高效费比原则,在采购和运行航天器、发射服务和在空间开展试验和实验的过程中,继续遵守《美国政府轨道碎片减缓标准办法》。

・商务部长和运输部长应与联邦通信委员会主席协调,继续通过其各自的许可证办理办法解决轨道碎片问题;以及

・美国应在国际论坛上取得领导地位,以鼓励外国和国际机构采取旨在最大限度地减少碎片的政策和办法,并应在有关碎片研究和更好的碎片减缓办法的确定的信息交流上开展合作。

12. 有效的出口政策

作为一项方针，国际市场上目前已有或行将出现的航天相关出口将得到优先考虑。

敏感或先进技术数据、系统、技术和组件的出口只在个别情况下才应批准，并以采取一事一议的方式。这些项目包括系统工程和系统集成能力以及技术或能力明显优于现行或近期国外系统可达到的水平的使能组件或技术。

13. 与航天相关的安全保密

与情报和防御相关的航天活动的设计、研制、运行和产品应依照第12958号行政令（E.O.）、第12951号行政令和修订后的适用法律及规则，并根据保护敏感技术、来源和方法以及运行的需要进行保密。

·国防部长和国家情报局长应制订并实施政策和办法来保护、分发与本政策中规定的其各自职责相关的活动和信息，并适当地予以保密和解密。适当情况下，他们应协调其各自的保密指导方针。

下述事实是不保密的：

·美国政府开展：包含近实时能力的卫星照相侦察；过顶信号情报搜集；过顶测量和特征情报搜集；以及

·美国政府的照相侦察用于：

·搜集情报；监测军备控制协议的遵守情况；搜集用于保障防御和其他与测绘相关活动的测绘、制图和测地数据；搜集科学和环境数据以及有关自然或人为灾害的数据；上述各类信息可提供给经授权的联邦机构；

·提供用于指征和预警以及用于规划和开展军事行动的信息；以及

·依照适用法律，为包括但不限于国土安全的目的，对美国及其领土和属地进行成像。

U. S. National Space Policy

August 31, 2006 (Unclassified)

The President authorized a new national space policy on August 31, 2006 that establishes overarching national policy that governs the conduct of U. S. space activities. This policy supersedes Presidential Decision Directive/NSC – 49/NSTC – 8, National Space Policy, dated September 14, 1996.

1. Background
2. Principles
3. United States Space Policy Goals
4. General Guidelines
5. National Security Space Guidelines
6. Civil Space Guidelines
7. Commercial Space Guidelines
8. International Space Cooperation
9. Space Nuclear Power
10. Radio Frequency Spectrum and Orbit Management and Interference Protection
11. Orbital Debris
12. Effective Export Policies 13. Space-Related Security Classification

1. Background

For five decades, the United States has led the world in space exploration and use and has developed a solid civil, commercial, and national security space foundation. Space activities have improved life in the United States and around the world, enhancing security, protecting lives and the environment, speeding information flow, serving as an engine for economic growth, and revolutionizing the way people view their place in the world and the cosmos. Space has become a place that is increasingly used by a host of nations, consortia, businesses, and entrepreneurs.

In this new century, those who effectively utilize space will enjoy added prosperity and security and will hold a substantial advantage over those who do not. Freedom of action in space is as important to the United States as air power and sea power. In order to increase knowledge, discovery, economic prosperity, and to enhance the national security, the United States must have robust, effective, and efficient space capabilities.

2. Principles

The conduct of U.S. space programs and activities shall be a top priority, guided by the following principles:

• The United States is committed to the exploration and use of outer space by all nations for peaceful purposes, and for the benefit of all humanity. Consistent with this principle, "peaceful purposes" allow U.S. defense and intelligence-related activities in pursuit of national interests;

• The United States rejects any claims to sovereignty by any nation over outer space or celestial bodies, or any portion thereof, and rejects any limitations on the fundamental right of the United States to operate in and acquire data from space;

· The United States will seek to cooperate with other nations in the peaceful use of outer space to extend the benefits of space, enhance space exploration, and to protect and promote freedom around the world;

· The United States considers space systems to have the rights of passage through and operations in space without interference. Consistent with this principle, the United States will view purposeful interference with its space systems as an infringement on its rights;

· The United States considers space capabilities—including the ground and space segments and supporting links—vital to its national interests. Consistent with this policy, the United States will: preserve its rights, capabilities, and freedom of action in space; dissuade or deter others from either impeding those rights or developing capabilities intended to do so; take those actions necessary to protect its space capabilities; respond to interference; and deny, if necessary, adversaries the use of space capabilities hostile to U. S. national interests;

· The United States will oppose the development of new legal regimes or other restrictions that seek to prohibit or limit U. S. access to or use of space. Proposed arms control agreements or restrictions must not impair the rights of the United States to conduct research, development, testing, and operations or other activities in space for U. S. national interests; and

· The United States is committed to encouraging and facilitating a growing and entrepreneurial U. S. commercial space sector. Toward that end, the United States Government will use U. S. commercial space capabilities to the maximum practical extent, consistent with national security.

3. United States Space Policy Goals

The fundamental goals of this policy are to:
• Strengthen the nation's space leadership and ensure that space capabilities are available in time to further U. S. national security, homeland security, and foreign policy objectives;
• Enable unhindered U. S. operations in and through space to defend our interests there;
• Implement and sustain an innovative human and robotic exploration program with the objective of extending human presence across the solar system;
• Increase the benefits of civil exploration, scientific discovery, and environmental activities;
• Enable a dynamic, globally competitive domestic commercial space sector in order to promote innovation, strengthen U. S. leadership, and protect national, homeland, and economic security;
• Enable a robust science and technology base supporting national security, homeland security, and civil space activities; and
• Encourage international cooperation with foreign nations and/or consortia on space activities that are of mutual benefit and that further the peaceful exploration and use of space, as well as to advance national security, homeland security, and foreign policy objectives.

4. General Guidelines

In order to achieve the goals of this policy, the United States Government shall:
• Develop Space Professionals. Sustained excellence in space-related science, engineering, acquisition, and operational disciplines is vital to the future of U. S. space capabilities. Departments and agencies that

conduct space related activities shall establish standards and implement activities to develop and maintain highly skilled, experienced, and motivated space professionals within their workforce.

• Improve Space System Development and Procurement. United States space systems provide critical capabilities to a wide range of civil, commercial, and national security users. The primary goal of space system development and procurement must be mission success. Achieving this goal depends on effective research, development, acquisition, management, execution, oversight, and operations. Toward that end, departments and agencies shall create an environment that enables mission success, including, but not limited to, creating a common understanding of realistic and stable requirements and operational concepts; clearly identifying and managing risks, including system safety; setting and maintaining realistic and stable funding; delivering space capabilities on time and on budget; and providing acquisition managers with the tools, responsibility, budget flexibility, and authority to achieve this goal.

• Increase and Strengthen Interagency Partnerships. The challenges of the 21st century require a focused and dedicated unity of effort. Interagency partnerships provide opportunities to jointly identify desired effects, capabilities, and strategies. Departments and agencies shall capitalize on opportunities for dynamic partnerships—whether through collaboration, information sharing, alignment, or integration.

• Strengthen and Maintain the U. S. Space-Related Science, Technology, and Industrial Base. A robust science, technology, and industrial base is critical for U. S. space capabilities. Departments and agencies shall: encourage new discoveries in space science and new applications of technology; and enable future space systems to achieve new and improved capabilities, including incentives for high-risk/high-payoff and transformational space capabilities. Additionally, departments and agencies shall: conduct the basic and applied research that increases capability and decreases cost; encourage an innovative commercial space sector, including the use of prize competitions; and ensure the availability of space related industrial capabilities in support of critical government functions.

5. National Security Space Guidelines

United States national security is critically dependent upon space capabilities, and this dependence will grow. The Secretary of Defense and the Director of National Intelligence, after consulting, as appropriate, the Secretary of State and other heads of departments and agencies, and consistent with their respective responsibilities as set forth in the National Security Act of 1947, as amended, Title 10, U.S.C. and Title 50 U.S.C., the National Security Intelligence Reform Act of 2004, and other applicable law, shall:

• Support the President and the Vice President in the performance of Executive functions, and senior Executive Branch national security, homeland security, and foreign policy decisionmakers; other Federal officials, as appropriate; and the enduring constitutional government operations and infrastructure;

• Support and enable defense and intelligence requirements and operations during times of peace, crisis, and through all levels of conflict;

• Develop and deploy space capabilities that sustain U.S. advantage and support defense and intelligence transformation; and

• Employ appropriate planning, programming, and budgeting activities, organizational arrangements, and strategies that result in an operational force structure and optimized space capabilities that support the national and homeland security;

To achieve the goals of this policy, the Secretary of Defense shall:

• Maintain the capabilities to execute the space support, force enhancement, space control, and force application missions;

· Establish specific intelligence requirements that can be met by tactical, operational, or national-level intelligence gathering capabilities;

· Provide, as launch agent for both the defense and intelligence sectors, reliable, affordable, and timely space access for national security purposes;

· Provide space capabilities to support continuous, global strategic and tactical warning as well as multi layered and integrated missile defenses;

· Develop capabilities, plans, and options to ensure freedom of action in space, and, if directed, deny such freedom of action to adversaries;

· Have responsibility for space situational awareness; in this capacity, the Secretary of Defense shall support the space situational awareness requirements of the Director of National Intelligence and conduct space situational awareness for: the United States Government; U. S. commercial space capabilities and services used for national and homeland security purposes; civil space capabilities and operations, particularly human space flight activities; and, as appropriate, commercial and foreign space entities; and

· Establish and implement policies and procedures to protect sensitive information regarding the control, dissemination, and declassification of defense activities related to space.

To achieve the goals of this policy, the Director of National Intelligence shall:

· Establish objectives, intelligence requirements, priorities and guidance for the intelligence community to ensure timely and effective collection, processing, analysis and dissemination of national intelligence;

· Ensure that timely information and data support foreign, defense, and economic policies; diplomatic activities; indications and warning;

crisis management; treaty compliance verification; appropriate civil, homeland security, and law enforcement users; and perform research and development related to these functions;

· Support military planning and satisfy operational requirements as a major intelligence mission;

· Provide intelligence collection and analysis of space related capabilities to support space situational awareness for: the United States Government; U.S. commercial space capabilities and services used for national and homeland security purposes; civil space capabilities and operations, particularly human space flight activities; and, as appropriate, commercial and foreign space entities;

· Provide a robust foreign space intelligence collection and analysis capability that provides timely information and data to support national and homeland security;

· Coordinate on any radio frequency surveys from space conducted by United States Government departments or agencies and review, as appropriate, and approve any radio frequency surveys from space conducted by the private sector, State, or local governments; and

· Establish and implement policies and procedures to: classify attributable collected information and operational details of intelligence activities related to space; protect sensitive activities; and declassify and release such information when the Director determines that protection is no longer needed.

6. Civil Space Guidelines

The United States shall increase the benefits of civil exploration, scientific discovery, and operational environmental monitoring activities. To that end, the Administrator, National Aeronautics and Space Administration shall: execute a sustained and affordable human and robotic program of space exploration and develop, acquire, and use civil space systems to advance fundamental scientific knowledge of our Earth system, solar system, and universe.

The Secretary of Commerce, through the Administrator of the National Oceanic and Atmospheric Administration, shall in coordination with the Administrator, National Aeronautics and Space Administration, be responsible for operational civil environmental space-based remote sensing systems and management of the associated requirements and acquisition process as follows:

• The Secretary of Commerce, through the National Oceanic and Atmospheric Administration, in collaboration with the Secretary of Defense through the Secretary of the Air Force, and the Administrator, National Aeronautics and Space Administration will continue to consolidate civil and military polar-orbiting operational environmental sensing systems in accordance with current policy direction;

• The Secretary of Commerce, through the National Oceanic and Atmospheric Administration, shall continue a program of civil geostationary operational environmental satellites with support from the National Aeronautics and Space Administration; and

• The Secretary of Commerce, through the National Oceanic and Atmospheric Administration, and the Administrator, National Aeronautics and Space Administration shall ensure to the maximum extent possible that civil space acquisition processes and capabilities are not duplicated.

The Secretary of the Interior, through the Director of the U. S. Geological Survey, shall collect, archive, process, and distribute land surface data to the United States Government and other users and determine operational requirements for land surface data.

The United States will study the Earth system from space and develop new space-based and related capabilities to advance scientific understanding and enhance civil space-based Earth observation. In particular:

• The Administrator, National Aeronautics and Space Administration shall conduct a program of research to advance scientific knowledge of the Earth through space-based observation and development and deployment of enabling technologies; and

• The Secretary of Commerce and the Administrator, National Aeronautics and Space Administration, and other departments and agencies as appropriate, in support of long-term operational requirements, shall transition mature research and development capabilities to long-term operations, as appropriate.

The United States will utilize government and commercial space – based and related capabilities wherever feasible to enhance disaster warning, monitoring, and response activities; and take a leadership role in international fora to establish a long-term plan for coordination of an integrated global Earth observation system and promote the adoption of policies internationally that facilitate full and open access to government environmental data on equitable terms.

7. Commercial Space Guidelines

It is in the interest of the United States to foster the use of U. S. commercial space capabilities around the globe and to enable a dynamic, domestic commercial space sector. To this end, departments and agencies shall:

• Use U. S. commercial space capabilities and services to the maximum practical extent; purchase commercial capabilities and services when they are available in the commercial marketplace and meet United States Government requirements; and modify commercially available capabilities and services to meet those United States Government requirements when the modification is cost effective;

• Develop systems when it is in the national interest and there is no suitable, cost effective U. S. commercial or, as appropriate, foreign commercial service or system that is or will be available when required;

· Continue to include and increase U. S. private sector participation in the design and development of United States Government space systems and infrastructures;

· Refrain from conducting activities that preclude, deter, or compete with U. S. commercial space activities, unless required by national security or public safety;

· Ensure that United States Government space activities, technology, and infrastructure are made available for private use on a reimbursable, non-interference basis to the maximum practical extent, consistent with national security; and

· Maintain a timely and responsive regulatory environment for licensing commercial space activities and pursue commercial space objectives without the use of direct Federal subsidies, consistent with the regulatory and other authorities of the Secretaries of Commerce and Transportation and the Chairman of the Federal Communications Commission.

8. International Space Cooperation

The United States Government will pursue, as appropriate, and consistent with U. S. national security interests, international cooperation with foreign nations and/or consortia on space activities that are of mutual benefit and that further the peaceful exploration and use of space, as well as to advance national security, homeland security, and foreign policy objectives. Areas for potential international cooperation include, but are not limited to:

· Space exploration; providing space surveillance information consistent with security requirements and U. S. national security and foreign policy interests; developing and operating Earth-observation-systems.

The Secretary of State, after consultation with the heads of appropriate

Departments and Agencies, shall carry out diplomatic and public diplomacy efforts, as appropriate, to build an understanding of and support for U. S. national space policies and programs and to encourage the use of U. S. space capabilities and systems by friends and allies.

9. Space Nuclear Power

Where space nuclear power systems safely enable or significantly enhance space exploration or operational capabilities, the United States shall develop and use these systems. The use of space nuclear power systems shall be consistent with U. S. national and homeland security, and foreign policy interests, and take into account the potential risks. In that regard:

• Approval by the President or his designee shall be required to launch and use United States Government and non-government spacecraft utilizing nuclear power sources with a potential for criticality or above a minimum threshold of radioactivity, in accordance with the existing interagency review process;

• To that end, the Secretary of Energy shall: conduct a nuclear safety analysis for evaluation by an ad hoc Interagency Nuclear Safety Review Panel which will evaluate the risks associated with launch and in-space operations; assist the Secretary of Transportation in the licensing of space transportation; provide nuclear safety monitoring to ensure that operations in space are consistent with the safety evaluation performed; and maintain the capability and infrastructure to develop and furnish nuclear power systems for use in United States Government space systems; and

• For government spacecraft, the head of the sponsoring Department or Agency shall request launch approval and be responsible for the safe operation of the spacecraft in space.

• For the launch and use of non-government spacecraft utilizing nuclear power sources, the operator will be responsible for the safe operation of the spacecraft in space, including nuclear power sources. To that end:

· The United States Government shall designate a point of entry and develop procedures for reviewing non-governmental missions that use space nuclear power systems;

· The Secretary of Transportation shall be the licensing authority for U. S. commercial launch activities involving nuclear materials, including a payload determination, subject to the requirements described above;

· The Nuclear Regulatory Commission will license activities prior to launch that involve utilization facilities and nuclear materials not owned by the Department of Energy;

· The United States Government will conduct safety analysis, evaluation, and nuclear safety monitoring on a fee-for-service basis, to the extent allowed by law, where the operator will fully reimburse the United States Government entity for services provided; and

· The Secretary of Energy shall establish and implement policies and procedures to protect sensitive information regarding the control, dissemination, and declassification of space-related nuclear activities.

10. Radio Frequency Spectrum And Orbit Management And Interference Protection

The use of space for national and homeland security, civil, scientific, and commercial purposes depends on the reliable access to and use of radio frequency spectrum and orbital assignments. To ensure the continued use of space for these purposes, the United States Government shall:

· Seek to obtain and protect U. S. global access to the radio frequency spectrum and orbital assignments required to support the use of space by the United States Government and commercial users;

• Explicitly address requirements for radio frequency spectrum and orbit assignments prior to approving acquisition of new space capabilities;

• Consistent with current approaches, assure, to the maximum practical extent, that U. S. national security, homeland security, civil, and commercial space capabilities and services and foreign space capabilities and services of interest to the United States Government are not affected by harmful interference; and

• Seek spectrum regulatory status under U. S. domestic regulations for United States Government owned and operated earth stations operating through commercial satellites, consistent with the regulatory status afforded commercial operations and with the allocation status of the satellite service.

11. Orbital Debris

Orbital debris poses a risk to continued reliable use of space-based services and operations and to the safety of persons and property in space and on Earth. The United States shall seek to minimize the creation of orbital debris by government and non-government operations in space in order to preserve the space environment for future generations. Toward that end:

• Departments and agencies shall continue to follow the United States Government Orbital Debris Mitigation Standard Practices, consistent with mission requirements and cost effectiveness, in the procurement and operation of spacecraft, launch services, and the operation of tests and experiments in space;

• The Secretaries of Commerce and Transportation, in coordination with the Chairman of the Federal Communications Commission, shall continue to address orbital debris issues through their respective licensing procedures; and

• The United States shall take a leadership role in international fora to encourage foreign nations and international organizations to adopt policies and practices aimed at debris minimization and shall cooperate in the exchange of information on debris research and the identification of improved debris mitigation practices.

12. Effective Export Policies

As a guideline, space-related exports that are currently available or are planned to be available in the global marketplace shall be considered favorably.

Exports of sensitive or advanced technical data, systems, technologies, and components, shall be approved only rarely, on a case-by-case basis. These items include systems engineering and systems integration capabilities and techniques or enabling components or technologies with capabilities significantly better than those achievable by current or near – term foreign systems.

13. Space-Related Security Classification

The design, development, acquisition, operations, and products of intelligence and defense – related space activities shall be classified as necessary to protect sensitive technologies, sources and methods, and operations, consistent with E. O. 12958, E. O. 12951, and applicable law and regulation as amended.

• The Secretary of Defense and the Director of National Intelligence shall establish and implement policies and procedures to protect, disseminate, and appropriately classify and declassify activities and information related to their respective responsibilities outlined in this policy. Where appropriate, they shall coordinate their respective classification guidance.

The following facts are unclassified:
· The United States Government conducts: satellite photoreconnaissance that includes a near real-time capability; overhead signals intelligence collection; and overhead measurement and signature intelligence collection; and
· United States Government photoreconnaissance is used to:
  · Collect intelligence; monitor compliance with arms control agreements; collect mapping, charting, and geodetic data that is used to support defense and other mapping-related activities; collect scientific and environmental data and data on natural or man-made disasters; and the foregoing categories of information can be provided to authorized federal agencies;
  · Provide information for indications and warning and the planning and conduct of military operations; and
Image the United States and its territories and possessions, consistent with applicable laws, for purposes including, but not limited to, homeland security.

美国国家航天政策(2010)①(中、英文)

航天时代始于两个超级大国为安全和威望而展开的一场竞赛,它带来的机遇是没有界线的。随后几十年里我们的日常生活方式出现了根本性转变,而这在很大程度上要归功于空间的利用。空间系统已把我们带往其他天体,并把人类的视野拉回到宇宙诞生的最初时刻和扩展到遥远的星系。卫星帮助各国提高了相互之间的透明性和稳定性,并为避免潜在冲突带来一种非常重要的沟通途径。空间系统丰富了我们众多科学领域的知识,因此也大大改善了地球上的生活。

空间的利用造就了新的市场,通过提供自然灾害预警、加快搜救行动速度及使恢复重建工作得以更快和更有效地进行,帮助拯救了生命,提高了农业和自然资源管理的效率和可持续性,拓展了我们的边疆,并使全球各地都能享受到先进的医疗、天气预报、地理空间信息、财务运行、宽带和其他通信以及众多其他服务。空间系统使全球各地的民众和政府部门能够清晰地观察、确切地交流、准确地导航和可靠地运行。

航天以往的成功及其转变也带来了新的挑战。航天时代之初,有机会利用空间的还只限于少数几个国家,不负责任或无意行

---

① 中文本来自《中国航天》2010年第7期第13~20页。感谢《中国航天》张会庭总编的支持。

为所造成的后果也很有限。而现在,我们发现,在自己身处的世界里,空间效益已渗透到我们生活的几乎每个侧面。全球经济的增长和发展已使越来越多的国家和组织开始利用空间。航天能力目前已无处不在并相互关联,加之全球对这些能力的日益依赖,意味着不负责任的空间行为会给各方都带来破坏性的后果。例如,数十年的空间活动在地球轨道上遗撒下了碎片,而随着全球各航天国家空间活动的继续增加,发生碰撞的概率也在增大。

作为处于领先地位的航天国家,美国致力于应对这些挑战。但这不应只是美国一个国家的义务。所有各国均有权利用和探测空间,但伴随着这项权利的还有义务。因此,美国呼吁各国共同努力,采取开展负责任的空间活动的理念,为子孙后代的利益来保护这项权利。

自人类进入空间之初起,美国就宣布将致力于通过与他国合作来维护空间自由,从而改善人类福祉。

美国特此重申其开展合作的承诺,相信通过加强国际合作和重振美国的领导地位,各国及其民众———包括航天国家和航天受益者———都会看到其视野将得到扩大,知识将得到丰富,生活将得到极大改善。

原则

依照这一合作精神,美国将遵守并建议其他国家(或地区)也认识到并遵守的以下原则:

采取负责任的空间行动来帮助防范事故、误判和猜疑符合各国的共同利益。美国认为,空间的可持续性和稳定性及自由出入和利用对其国家利益至关重要。空间行动应以强调开放和透明的方式开展,以改善公众对政府活动的了解,并使他方能共享空间利用所带来的效益。

一个强健而有竞争力的商业航天行业对航天的持续进步至关重要。美国致力于鼓励和支持美国商业航天行业的成长,使之能保障美国所需,具备全球竞争力,并提升美国在造就新市场和靠创新来驱动的创业方面的领导地位。

各国均有权出于和平目的并为全人类的利益,依照国际法来探测和利用空间。遵照这一原则,"和平目的"允许将空间用于国家和国土安全活动。

正如国际法中所确立的,各国均不应对外层空间或任何天体提出主权要求。美国认为,各国的空间系统均有权不受干扰地通过空间和在空间运行。有意干扰空间系统,包括干扰配套基础设施,将被认为是对一国权利的侵犯。

美国将动用各种措施来帮助确保所有负责任各方的空间利用,并依照固有的自卫权吓阻他方不要从事干扰和攻击行为,保卫我们的空间系统并帮助保卫盟国的空间系统,并在吓阻失败的情况下挫败对这些空间系统的攻击行为。

目标

依照这些原则,美国将寻求在其国家航天计划下实现以下目标:

——振兴有竞争力的国内工业界,使之能参与全球市场,并推动发展卫星制造、星基服务、航天发射、地面应用和更多的创业。

——在互利航天活动方面扩大国际合作,以拓展和普及空间效益,深化空间的和平利用,并加强源自空间的信息的采集工作及在此类信息共享方面的合作。

——通过以下措施来加强空间的稳定性:采取国内和国际措施来推动实现安全和负责任的空间运行;改善空间物体避撞信息的采集与共享;保护关键空间系统及配套基础设施,尤其要关注空间与信息系统至关重要的相互依赖性;加强轨道碎片减缓措施。

——提高由商业、民用、科学和国家安全航天器来保障的任务基础功能的可靠性和耐受力,避免其出现中断、性能下降和解体,无论是出于环境、机械、电子还是敌对原因。

——寻求开展载人和无人计划来发展创新型技术,扶持新兴行业,加强国际伙伴关系,激励我国和世界,加深人类对地球的认识,加强科学发现,并探测我们的太阳系及更遥远的宇宙。

——改善开展科学研究、预报地面和近地空间天气、监测气候和全球变化、管理自然资源以及支持灾害反应与恢复所需的天基地球和太阳观测能力。

各部门和机构为落实这一指令而采取的所有行动均须在总统赋予的总体资源和政策方针之内进行。符合美国法律和规则、美国作为签约方的条约和其他协议、其他适用国际法、美国国家和国土安全要求、美国对外政策和国家利益,并遵守《总统透明与开放政府备忘录》。

跨行业方针

为寻求实现本指令的目标,各部门和机构均须执行以下方针:

基础活动的能力。增强美国在天基科学、技术和工业基础方面的领导地位。各部门和机构应:开展政府所大力支持的能提高能力并降低成本的基础和应用研究;鼓励发展具有创新性和创业性的商业航天部门,并帮助确保用于保障关键政府职能的航天相关工业能力的可用性。

增强确保进入空间的能力。美国的空间进入能力首先要取决于发射能力。除非获得国家安全顾问和总统科技助理兼科技政策办公室主任依照既定标准和协调方针而做出的特许,美国政府的有效载荷均须由在美国制造的运载工具发射。在适用于其职责的情况下,各部门和机构应:

——联合采办可靠、进度符合美国政府需求且具有高效费比的航天发射服务和搭乘有效载荷安排;

——通过投资进行航天发射基础设施的现代化改造来增强运行效率,提高运载能力,并降低发射成本;

——在尚无充足的美国商业能力与服务可用的情况下,同美国工业界合作,发展确保和保持未来可靠而高效地进入空间的能力所需的运载系统和技术。

维护和加强天基定位、导航与授时系统。美国必须保持其在全球导航卫星系统(GNSS)的服务、供应和使用方面的领导地位。为此目的,美国须：

——使全球都能为和平的民用目的而持续地使用"全球定位系统"(GPS)及其由政府提供的增值服务,且免收直接用户费用。

——与国外 GNSS 供应方接触,以鼓励实现兼容性和通用性,提高民用服务供应的透明性,并为美国工业界带来市场准入。

——运行并维护 GPS 星座,以依照所发布的性能标准和干扰指标来满足民用和国家安全需求。国外的定位、导航与授时(PNT)服务可用于提高和加强 GPS 的耐受能力。

——投资发展国内能力,并支持开展国际性活动,以探测和减缓对 GPS 的有害干扰且提高对此类干扰的耐受能力,并找出且在必要和适当情况下落实针对关键基础设施、关键资源和任务基础功能的冗余和备份系统或方法。

培养并保持航天专业人才。航天专业人员培养和保持工作的主要目标是:在航天运行与采购方面实现任务的成功;刺激创新,以提高商业、民用和国家安全航天能力;推动科学、探测和发现。为此目的,各部门和机构须与工业界和学术界合作,制订标准,寻求为现有航天队伍创造机遇,并采取措施来培养、维持和保持政府和商业队伍中的熟练航天专业人员,包括工程和科研人员以及富有经验的航天系统研制和操作人员。各部门和机构还须促进和扩展公私合营关系,以在有针对性的相关计划投资的支持下,提高科学、技术、工程与数学(STEM)课程的教学成绩。

改善航天系统研制与采办工作。各部门和机构须:

——通过加强成本估算、技术风险与成熟度和工业基础能力方面的工作来改善航天系统的及时采购与部署工作。

——通过改进需求管理并通过利用高效费比的机遇来在空间或相关环境下试验高风险部件、有效载荷和技术来降低计划的风险;

——支持创新,以培育和保持具有创业性的美国研发环境;

——与工业伙伴接触,以改善办法,并有效地管理供应链。

加强跨部门伙伴关系。各部门和机构须通过合作、协作、信息共享和/或理顺共同的需求来改善其伙伴关系。各部门和机构需相互提供各自的能力和专长,以增强我们实现国家目标、确定所期望的成果、充分利用美国能力和制订实施与反应战略的能力。

国际合作

巩固美国的航天领导地位。各部门和机构须同国务卿协调,开展以下工作:

·展现美国在航天相关领域和活动方面的领导地位,以便:再度向盟国保证美国致力于集体自卫,找出共同感兴趣和互利的领域,并推行美国的商业航天规则和鼓励与这些规则的通用性。

·在增强空间安全与稳定和加强负责任空间行为方面起领导作用。

·帮助美国商业航天能力和服务寻找新的市场机遇,涉及依赖于由政府提供的空间系统的商业上可行的地面应用。

·推动国际上采取有助于全面、公开和及时获取政府环境数据的政策。

·推动在加入国际伙伴关系的国家之间实现成本和风险共担。

·通过充分利用盟国和航天伙伴现有和计划中的航天能力来提升美国的能力。找出潜在的国际合作领域。各部门和机构须找出潜在的国际合作领域,可能包括但不限于:空间科学;空间探测,包括载人航天飞行活动;用于支持空间科学和探测的空间核动力;航天运输;以碎片监测与感知为目的的空间监视;导弹预警;地球科学与观测;环境监测;卫星通信;GNSS;地理空间信息产品与服务;减灾救灾;搜索与救援;利用空间进行海域感知;针对人类活动与利用的空间环境长期保护。

·国务卿须在同相应部门和机构负责人磋商后,采取外交和公共外交努力,以增加对美国国家航天政策和计划的认识和支持,并鼓励国外利用美国的航天能力、系统和服务。

- 制订透明与信任建立措施。美国将寻求采取双边和多边的透明与信任建立措施,以鼓励采取负责任的空间行动和对空间加以和平利用。美国将对相关的军备控制措施建议和方案加以考虑,只要这些建议和方案公平、可有效核查,且能增强美国及其盟国的国家安全。

保护空间环境及负责任的空间利用保护空间环境。为最大限度地减少碎片和保护空间环境,以供所有用户负责任、和平和安全地加以利用,美国须:

领导继续制订和采纳旨在最大限度地减少碎片的国际和行业标准及政策,比如《联合国空间碎片减缓准则》。

建立、维护和使用来自商业、民用和国家安全渠道的空间态势感知(SSA)信息,用以探测、识别和归咎与空间环境负责任利用和长期可持续性相背离的空间行动。

按照任务要求和效费比,在航天器采购与运行、发射服务和空间试验与实验的开展方面继续遵守《美国政府轨道碎片减缓标准办法》。

通过国家航空航天局(NASA)局长和国防部长,寻求研究和开发技术和方法,以减缓和清除在轨碎片,减少危害,并增进对现有和未来碎片环境的认识。

请求主管部门或机构负责人特许免于遵守《美国政府轨道碎片减缓标准办法》,并向国务卿通报。扶持发展空间碰撞预警措施。国防部长经同国家情报主任、NASA局长及其他部门和机构磋商,可同工业界和外国协作,以维护和改进空间物体数据库,寻求制订共同的国际数据标准和数据完好性措施,并向商业和国际实体提供服务和分发轨道跟踪信息,包括空间物体交会预报。

有效的出口政策

依照美国出口管制评审报告,各部门和机构应寻求在满足国家安全需求的同时增强美国航天工业基础的竞争力。

美国将致力于遏止先进航天技术流向未经授权的各方。各部门和机构有义务在其各项计划的实施过程中防止出现有害的技术转移。

美国政府将按一事一议的方式，依照和根据《国际武器交易规则》《出口管理规则》以及其他适用法律、条约和规则来办理航天相关出口许可证的发放。按照上述法规，被认定为已在全球市场上普遍可得的航天相关物项应得到优先考虑，原因在于此类出口通常符合美国的国家利益。

敏感或先进航天器的相关出口可能需要有政府与政府间的协议或其他可接受的安排。

空间核动力

在空间核动力系统可安全地实现或显著地增强空间探测或运行能力的情况下，美国应发展和使用此类系统。

依照现行的跨部门审核办法，发射和使用采用具有临界的可能或超过最低放射性阀值的核动力系统的美国政府航天器须经总统或其指定人员批准。为明智地做出这一决策，能源部长须开展一项核安全分析，由一个特别的跨部门核安全评审委员会对与发射和空间运行相关的风险进行评估。

能源部长须：

——协助运输部长办理涉及带有核动力系统的航天器的航天运输活动的许可。

——开展核安全监测，以保证空间运行符合所开展的任何安全性评估。

——维护研制和供应给美国政府空间系统使用的核动力系统的能源和基础设施。

无线电频谱与干扰防护

美国政府须：

——寻求保护美国全面获取和使用支持美国政府、其盟国及美国商业用户空间利用工作所需的无线电频谱及相关轨位分配的能力；

——在批准采购航天能力之前明确地阐明对无线电频谱和轨位分配的要求；

——寻求确保必要的国内和国际监管框架在系统的寿命期内仍将继续有效；

——在为商业、联邦或共同使用而重新分配频谱之前确定会给政府空间系统带来的影响；

——与民用、商业和国外伙伴合作，增强对无线电频率干扰源进行识别、定位和归咎的能力和技术，并采取必要措施来维护有美国关键空间系统从中运行的射频环境；

——依照发放给类似商业地球站的监管部门批准手续，寻求根据美国国内规则为借助商用卫星来运行的美国政府各地球站取得相应的监管部门批准。任务基础功能的保证和耐受力，美国须：

——通过建立保持业务连续性所需的技术、措施、关系和能力来保证依托于航天的任务基础功能。

——此等工作可能包括加强个别航天器和配套基础设施的保护和耐受力。

——为保持任务基础功能而发展并落实在恶化、遭破坏或遭阻止空间环境内或通过此等环境运行的能力和规划。

——在未来空间能力及配套基础设施的采购中解决任务保证要求和空间系统耐受力问题。

行业方针

美国航天活动在三个截然不同但又相互依存的行业内进行：商业行业、民用行业和国家安全行业。

商业航天方针

在本政策文件中，"商业"一词系指由私营部门企业提供的航天产品或服务或开展的活动。这些企业承担相当一部分投资风险和活动责任，按照典型的基于市场的成本控制和投资回报优化激励因素来运营，并具有向现有或潜在非政府用户提供这些产品或服务的法人资质。为推动建设一个健全的国内商业航天工业，各部门和机构须：

——在市场上存在商业航天能力和服务且满足政府要求的情

况下,最大限度地采购和使用此等能力和服务。

——在商业航天能力和服务尚不能完全满足政府要求但通过潜在改造可为政府带来高效费比和更为及时的一条采购途径的情况下,对商业能力和服务进行改造,使之满足政府要求。

——积极探索采用有创造力的、非传统的安排来采购商业航天产品和服务,以满足美国政府的要求,包括公私合营、在商业航天器上搭乘政府能力和从商业卫星运营商那里购买科学或业务数据产品来支持政府任务等措施。

——只有在符合国家利益且没有或不会有适宜的、高效费比的美国商业服务或系统或适当的国外商业服务或系统可用的情况下,才去发展政府的航天系统。

——除非出于国家安全或公共安全之需,不开展会妨碍或不利于美国商业航天活动或与之产生竞争的美国政府航天活动。

——在有益和可取得高效费比的情况下,为把例行的业务应用型航天职能转交给商业航天行业寻求潜在的机遇,除非政府法律、安保或安全上的需求不允许进行商业化。

——通过利用奖励和竞赛等激励机制,在商业航天行业内培育更多的技术创新和创业项目。

——确保美国政府的航天技术和基础设施能最大限度地以可补偿、无干扰和公平的方式供商业使用。

——最大限度地减少商业航天活动的监管负担,并保证航天活动许可证监管环境的及时性和反应速度。

——通过推行在听取美国工业界意见的条件下制订出来的适宜的标准和规则来扶持公平而开放的全球贸易与商业。

——鼓励按照国际合作安排来采购和使用美国的商业航天服务和能力。

——依照美国的技术转移和防扩散目标,积极推动美国通过商业方式开发和供应的航天产品和服务的出口,包括由中小企业开发的产品和服务,以供国外市场使用。

美国贸易代表办公室(US-TR)是联邦政府内主管美国作为

签约方的各种国际贸易安排的主要负责机构。美国贸易代表办公室将与其他相关部门和机构磋商，牵头开展管理航天相关产品与服务贸易的贸易规则的所有谈判和实施相关工作。

民用航天方针

空间科学、探测与发现

NASA 局长须：

——设定长远的探测工作节点要求。2025 年前启动月球以远的载人探测任务，包括送人前往一颗小行星。30 年代中期前送人绕火星做轨道飞行，并使其安全返回地球。

——与其他国际伙伴合作，继续运行国际空间站（ISS），可能运行到 2020 年或更晚，并扩展以下工作：将国际空间站用于科学、技术、商业、外交和教育目的；支持需要利用人类在空间中的特有属性的活动；将国际空间站作为人员在地球轨道上持续居留的一个场所；支持载人空间探测领域的未来目标。

——寻求与私营部门建立伙伴关系，以实现针对国际空间站人员与货物往返运输的安全、可靠和高效费比的商业航天飞行能力和服务。

——实施一项新的航天技术开发与试验计划，同工业界、学术界和国际伙伴一道建立飞行和试验几项能提高能力、降低成本并拓展未来空间活动机遇的关键技术。

——开展能支持下一代运载系统的研发工作，包括新的美国火箭发动机技术。

——保持在太阳系内的持续无人探测，以对其他行星体开展科学研究，验证新技术，并对未来载人探测任务的地点进行侦察。

——继续开展一项强有力的空间科学计划，以对太阳、太阳系和宇宙进行观测、研究和分析，从而丰富宇宙知识，深化我们对基础性自然和物理科学的认识，认识可能支持生命发展的条件，并在绕其他恒星运行的轨道上寻找行星体和类地行星。

——与其他部门、机构和商业伙伴合作，寻求对近地天体进行探测、跟踪、编目和表征的能力，以降低因其意外撞击地球而危害人类的风险,并找出可能含有丰富资源的行星类天体。

与环境相关的对地观测和天气

继续开展和完善范围广泛的天基地球陆地、海洋与大气观测、研究和分析计划:

NASA局长须与其他相应部门和机构协调,开展一项计划,以加强美国的全球气候变化研究和持续监测能力;通过加速研制新型对地观测卫星来深化地球科学知识研究,并发展和试验供其他民用部门和机构用于业务目的的能力。

商务部长须根据业务要求,通过国家海洋与大气局局长,并与NASA局长和其他相应部门和机构协调,开展以下工作:

——将成熟的研发型对地观测卫星转入长期业务运行。

——利用国际伙伴关系来帮助保持和加强天气、气候、海洋和海岸带观测工作。

——负责民用业务环境卫星的技术要求、经费、采购和运行,以支持天气预报、气候监测、海洋与海岸带观测和空间天气预报。NOAA将主要利用NASA作为这些活动和计划所需的业务环境卫星的采购代理。

商务部长(通过NOAA局长)、国防部长(通过空军部长)和NASA局长须共同努力,并与其国际伙伴一道,确保不间断的、业务应用型的极轨环境卫星观测。国防部长须负责上午轨道,而商务部长须负责下午轨道。这些部门须继续在研制和部署共同的地面系统方面开展合作,经协调的计划由NOAA负责运行。此外,这些部门须保证来自所有系统的数据得到持续的全面共享。

陆地遥感

内务部长须通过美国地质调查局(USGS)局长开展以下工作:

——对自然和人为造成的地球陆地、土地覆盖和内陆地表水的变化进行研究,并管理一座全球陆地表面数据国家档案库及其分发。

——确定陆地表面数据采集、处理、归档及其向美国政府和其他用户分发的运行要求。

——负责与国防部长、国土安全部长和国家情报主任协调,向其他民用政府机构提供由国家安全空间系统获取的与环境和灾害相关的遥感信息。

——为保障这些关键需求,内务部长(通过美国地质调查局局长)和 NASA 局长须共同努力,维护一项业务型陆地遥感观测计划。

NASA 和 NOAA 局长和美国地质调查局局长须:

——确保民用航天采购办法和能力不出现不必要的重复设置。

——继续开发基于由对地观测卫星采集的数据的民用应用和信息工具。这些民用能力将最大限度地利用已知的标准和开放工具来开发,其成果将提供给公众使用。

——商务部长须通过 NOAA 局长对商业部门遥感系统的运行进行监管和许可证审批。

国家安全航天方针

国防部长和国家情报主任须同其他相应部门和机构负责人磋商,开展以下工作:

——研制、采购和运行空间系统及配套的信息系统和网络,以在和平、危机和冲突时期保障美国国家安全并使国防和情报行动得以进行;

——保证包括配套信息系统和网络在内的空间能力具备高效费比的生存能力,并与其计划中的应用、能力损毁或下降的后果、威胁和能完成该任务的其他手段的可用性相匹配。

——通过推动技术开发、提升工业界实力和保持保障我们最关键的国家安全利益所必需的一个强健的供应商群体来重振美国的领导地位。

——建立并落实保证依托于国家安全航天的关键任务所必需的规划、程序、办法和能力。任务保证选项可能包括空间资产的迅速恢复及充分利用盟国、外国和/或商业航天及非航天能力来帮助完成任务。

——维护并整合空间监视、情报和其他信息,以建立精确而及时的空间态势感知能力。空间态势感知信息须用于支持国家和国土安全、民用航天机构(尤其是载人航天飞行活动)以及商业和国外空间行动;

——同相关部门和机构及商业和国外实体合作,改进、发展和验证对关系美国利益的空间系统所受的自然和人为干扰进行快速探测、预警、表征和归咎的能力。

发展和应用能对威胁环境的变化做出反应的先进技术和能力。

国防部长须:

——在国家情报主任的支持下,负责空间态势感知能力的发展、采购、运行、维护和现代化。

——建立能力、规划和选项,以吓阻、防御及在必要时挫败干扰或攻击美国或盟国空间系统的行为。

——维护实施空间支援、力量增强、空间控制和力量运用任务的能力。

——作为国防和情报部门的发射代理,为国家安全目的提供可靠、经济上可承受和及时的空间进入能力。

国家情报主任须:

——加强基础性情报采集以及单源和全源情报分析工作。

——发展、获取和运行空间能力,以支持战略目标、情报工作重点和所分配的任务。

——对国外空间和配套信息系统活动的信息进行强有力、及时和有效的采集、处理、分析和分发。

——开发和增强创新型的分析工具和方法,以利用和共享来自传统和非传统渠道的信息,用以掌握国外的航天相关活动。

——对美国空间任务所面临的现时和未来威胁进行识别和表征,以实现有效的保护、威慑和防御。

——对国外航天能力和意图的全源情报同空间监视信息进行整合,以生成能支持空间态势感知的更强有力的情报产品。

——作为一项重大情报任务，支持国防和国土安全规划，并满足使用要求。

——支持透明与信任建立措施以及适用情况下军备控制协议的监督、遵守和核查。

——协调由美国政府部门或机构在空间开展的任何射频测量工作，并在适当情况下审核由获得许可的私营部门运营商或由各州和地方政府从空间进行的任何射频测量工作。

U. S. National Space Policy

June 28, 2010

Table of Contents

Introduction
Principles
Goals
Intersector Guidelines
Sector Guidelines

Introduction

The space age began as a race for security and prestige between two superpowers. The opportunities were boundless, and the decades that followed have seen a radical transformation in the way we live our daily lives, in large part due to our use of space. Space systems have taken us to other celestial bodies and extended humankind's horizons back in time to the very first moments of the universe and out to the galaxies at its far reaches. Satellites contribute to increased transparency and stability among nations and provide a vital communications path for avoiding potential conflicts. Space systems increase our knowledge in many scientific fields, and life on Earth is far better as a result.

The utilization of space has created new markets; helped save lives by warning us of natural disasters, expediting search and rescue operations, and making recovery efforts faster and more effective; made agriculture and natural resource management more efficient and sustainable; expanded our frontiers; and provided global access to advanced medicine, weather forecasting, geospatial information, financial operations, broadband and other communications, and scores of other activities worldwide. Space systems allow people and governments around the world to see with clarity, communicate with certainty, navigate with accuracy, and operate with assurance.

The legacy of success in space and its transformation also presents new challenges. When the space age began, the opportunities to use space were limited to only a few nations, and there were limited consequences for irresponsible or unintentional behavior. Now, we find ourselves in a world where the benefits of space permeate almost every facet of our lives. The growth and evolution of the global economy has ushered in an ever-increasing number of nations and organizations using space. The now-ubiquitous and interconnected nature of space capabilities and the world's growing dependence on them mean that irresponsible acts in space can have damaging consequences for all of us. For example, decades of space activity have littered Earth's orbit with debris; and as the world's space-faring nations continue to increase activities in space, the chance for a collision increases correspondingly.

As the leading space-faring nation, the United States is committed to addressing these challenges. But this cannot be the responsibility of the United States alone. All nations have the right to use and explore space, but with this right also comes responsibility. The United States, therefore, calls on all nations to work together to adopt approaches for responsible activity in space to preserve this right for the benefit of future generations.

From the outset of humanity's ascent into space, this Nation declared its commitment to enhance the welfare of humankind by cooperating with others to maintain the freedom of space.

The United States hereby renews its pledge of cooperation in the belief that with strengthened international collaboration and reinvigorated U. S. leadership, all nations and peoples-space-faring and space-benefiting—will find their horizons broadened, their knowledge enhanced, and their lives greatly improved.

Principles

In this spirit of cooperation, the United States will adhere to, and proposes that other nations recognize and adhere to, the following principles:

· It is the shared interest of all nations to act responsibly in space to help prevent mishaps, misperceptions, and mistrust. The United States considers the sustainability, stability, and free access to, and use of, space vital to its national interests. Space operations should be conducted in ways that emphasize openness and transparency to improve public awareness of the activities of government, and enable others to share in the benefits provided by the use of space.

· A robust and competitive commercial space sector is vital to continued progress in space. The United States is committed to encouraging and facilitating the growth of a U. S. commercial space sector that supports U. S. needs, is globally competitive, and advances U. S. leadership in the generation of new markets and innovation-driven entrepreneurship.

· All nations have the right to explore and use space for peaceful purposes, and for the benefit of all humanity, in accordance with international law. Consistent with this principle, "peaceful purposes" allows for space to be used for national and homeland security activities.

• As established in international law, there shall be no national claims of sovereignty over outer space or any celestial bodies. The United States considers the space systems of all nations to have the rights of passage through, and conduct of operations in, space without interference. Purposeful interference with space systems, including supporting infrastructure, will be considered an infringement of a nation's rights.

• The United States will employ a variety of measures to help assure the use of space for all responsible parties, and, consistent with the inherent right of self-defense, deter others from interference and attack, defend our space systems and contribute to the defense of allied space systems, and, if deterrence fails, defeat efforts to attack them.

Goals

Consistent with these principles, the United States will pursue the following goals in its national space programs:

• Energize competitive domestic industries to participate in global markets and advance the development of: satellite manufacturing; satellite-based services; space launch; terrestrial applications; and increased entrepreneurship.

• Expand international cooperation on mutually beneficial space activities to: broaden and extend the benefits of space; further the peaceful use of space; and enhance collection and partnership in sharing of space-derived information.

• Strengthen stability in space through: domestic and international measures to promote safe and responsible operations in space; improved information collection and sharing for space object collision avoidance; protection of critical space systems and supporting infrastructures, with special attention to the critical interdependence of space and information systems; and strengthening measures to mitigate orbital debris.

· Increase assurance and resilience of mission-essential functions enabled by commercial, civil, scientific, and national security spacecraft and supporting infrastructure against disruption, degradation, and destruction, whether from environmental, mechanical, electronic, or hostile causes.

· Pursue human and robotic initiatives to develop innovative technologies, foster new industries, strengthen international partnerships, inspire our Nation and the world, increase humanity's understanding of the Earth, enhance scientific discovery, and explore our solar system and the universe beyond.

· Improve space-based Earth and solar observation capabilities needed to conduct science, forecast terrestrial and near-Earth space weather, monitor climate and global change, manage natural resources, and support disaster response and recovery.

All actions undertaken by departments and agencies in implementing this directive shall be within the overall resource and policy guidance provided by the President; consistent with U. S. law and regulations, treaties and other agreements to which the United States is a party, other applicable international law, U. S. national and homeland security requirements, U. S. foreign policy, and national interests; and in accordance with the Presidential Memorandum on Transparency and Open Government.

Intersector Guidelines

In pursuit of this directive's goals, all departments and agencies shall execute the following guidance:

Foundational Activities and Capabilities

· Strengthen U. S. Leadership In Space-Related Science, Technology, and Industrial Bases. Departments and agencies shall: conduct basic and applied research that increases capabilities and decreases costs, where this research is best supported by the government; encourage an innovative and entrepreneurial commercial space sector; and help ensure the availability of space-related industrial capabilities in support of critical government functions.

· Enhance Capabilities for Assured Access To Space. United States access to space depends in the first instance on launch capabilities. United States Government payloads shall be launched on vehicles manufactured in the United States unless exempted by the National Security Advisor and the Assistant to the President for Science and Technology and Director of the Office of Science and Technology Policy, consistent with established interagency standards and coordination guidelines. Where applicable to their responsibilities departments and agencies shall:

· · Work jointly to acquire space launch services and hosted payload arrangements that are reliable, responsive to United States Government needs, and cost – effective;

· · Enhance operational efficiency, increase capacity, and reduce launch costs by investing in the modernization of space launch infrastructure; and

· · Develop launch systems and technologies necessary to assure and sustain future reliable and efficient access to space, in cooperation with U. S. industry, when sufficient U. S. commercial capabilities and services do not exist.

· Maintain and Enhance Space – based Positioning, Navigation, and Timing Systems. The United States must maintain its leadership in the service, provision, and use of global navigation satellite systems (GNSS). To this end, the United States shall:

· · Provide continuous worldwide access, for peaceful civil uses, to the Global Positioning System (GPS) and its government-provided augmentations, free of direct user charges;

· · Engage with foreign GNSS providers to encourage compatibility and interoperability, promote transparency in civil service provision, and enable market access for U. S. industry;

· · Operate and maintain the GPS constellation to satisfy civil and national security needs, consistent with published performance standards and interface specifications. Foreign positioning, navigation, and timing (PNT) services may be used to augment and strengthen the resiliency of GPS; and

· · Invest in domestic capabilities and support international activities to detect, mitigate, and increase resiliency to harmful interference to GPS, and identify and implement, as necessary and appropriate, redundant and back-up systems or approaches for critical infrastructure, key resources, and mission-essential functions.

· Develop and Retain Space Professionals. The primary goals of space professional development and retention are: achieving mission success in space operations and acquisition; stimulating innovation to improve commercial, civil, and national security space capabilities; and advancing science, exploration, and discovery. Toward these ends, departments and agencies, in cooperation with industry and academia, shall establish standards, seek to create opportunities for the current space workforce, and implement measures to develop, maintain, and retain skilled space professionals, including engineering and scientific personnel and experienced space system developers and operators, in government and commercial workforces. Departments and agencies also shall promote and expand public-private partnerships to foster educational achievement in Science, Technology, Engineering, and Mathematics (STEM) programs, supported by targeted investments in such initiatives.

· Improve Space System Development and Procurement. Departments and agencies shall:

· · Improve timely acquisition and deployment of space systems through enhancements in estimating costs, technological risk and maturity, and industrial base capabilities;

 · · Reduce programmatic risk through improved management of requirements and by taking advantage of cost-effective opportunities to test high-risk components, payloads, and technologies in space or relevant environments;

 · · Embrace innovation to cultivate and sustain an entrepreneurial U. S. research and development environment; and

 · · Engage with industrial partners to improve processes and effectively manage the supply chains.

 · Strengthen Interagency Partnerships. Departments and agencies shall improve their partnerships through cooperation, collaboration, information sharing, and/or alignment of common pursuits. Departments and agencies shall make their capabilities and expertise available to each other to strengthen our ability to achieve national goals, identify desired outcomes, leverage U. S. capabilities, and develop implementation and response strategies.

International Cooperation

Strengthen U. S. Space Leadership. Departments and agencies, in coordination with the Secretary of State, shall:

 · Demonstrate U. S. leadership in space-related fora and activities to: reassure allies of U. S. commitments to collective self-defense; identify areas of mutual interest and benefit; and promote U. S. commercial space regulations and encourage interoperability with these regulations;

 · Lead in the enhancement of security, stability, and responsible behavior in space;

 · Facilitate new market opportunities for U. S. commercial space capabilities and services, including commercially viable terrestrial applications that rely on government-provided space systems;

· Promote the adoption of policies internationally that facilitate full, open, and timely access to government environmental data;

· Promote appropriate cost-and risk-sharing among participating nations in international partnerships; and

· Augment U. S. capabilities by leveraging existing and planned space capabilities of allies and space partners.

Identify Areas for Potential International Cooperation. Departments and agencies shall identify potential areas for international cooperation that may include, but are not limited to: space science; space exploration, including human space flight activities; space nuclear power to support space science and exploration; space transportation; space surveillance for debris monitoring and awareness; missile warning; Earth science and observation; environmental monitoring; satellite communications; GNSS; geospatial information products and services; disaster mitigation and relief; search and rescue; use of space for maritime domain awareness; and long-term preservation of the space environment for human activity and use.

The Secretary of State, after consultation with the heads of appropriate departments and agencies, shall carry out diplomatic and public diplomacy efforts to strengthen understanding of, and support for, U. S. national space policies and programs and to encourage the foreign use of U. S. space capabilities, systems, and services.

Develop Transparency and Confidence-Building Measures. The United States will pursue bilateral and multilateral transparency and confidence-building measures to encourage responsible actions in, and the peaceful use of, space. The United States will consider proposals and concepts for arms control measures if they are equitable, effectively verifiable, and enhance the national security of the United States and its allies.

Preserving the Space Environment and the Responsible Use of Space
Preserve the Space Environment. For the purposes of minimizing debris and preserving the space environment for the responsible, peaceful, and safe use of all users, the United States shall:

· Lead the continued development and adoption of international and industry standards and policies to minimize debris, such as the United Nations Space Debris Mitigation Guidelines;

· Develop, maintain, and use space situational awareness (SSA) information from commercial, civil, and national security sources to detect, identify, and attribute actions in space that are contrary to responsible use and the long-term sustainability of the space environment;

· Continue to follow the United States Government Orbital Debris Mitigation Standard Practices, consistent with mission requirements and cost effectiveness, in the procurement and operation of spacecraft, launch services, and the conduct of tests and experiments in space;

· Pursue research and development of technologies and techniques, through the Administrator of the National Aeronautics and Space Administration (NASA) and the Secretary of Defense, to mitigate and remove on-orbit debris, reduce hazards, and increase understanding of the current and future debris environment; and

· Require the head of the sponsoring department or agency to approve exceptions to the United States Government Orbital Debris Mitigation Standard Practices and notify the Secretary of State.

Foster the Development of Space Collision Warning Measures. The Secretary of Defense, in consultation with the Director of National Intelligence, the Administrator of NASA, and other departments and agencies, may collaborate with industry and foreign nations to: maintain and improve space object databases; pursue common international data standards and data integrity measures; and provide services and disseminate orbital tracking information to commercial and international entities, including predictions of space object conjunction.

Effective Export Policies

Consistent with the U. S. export control review, departments and agencies should seek to enhance the competitiveness of the U. S. space industrial base while also addressing national security needs.

The United States will work to stem the flow of advanced space technology to unauthorized parties. Departments and agencies are responsible for protecting against adverse technology transfer in the conduct of their programs.

The United States Government will consider the issuance of licenses for space-related exports on a case-by-case basis, pursuant to, and in accordance with, the International Traffic in Arms Regulations, the Export Administration Regulations, and other applicable laws, treaties, and regulations. Consistent with the foregoing space-related items that are determined to be generally available in the global marketplace shall be considered favorably with a view that such exports are usually in the national interests of the United States.

Sensitive or advanced spacecraft-related exports may require a government-to-government agreement or other acceptable arrangement.

Space Nuclear Power

The United States shall develop and use space nuclear power systems where such systems safely enable or significantly enhance space exploration or operational capabilities.

Approval by the President or his designee shall be required to launch and use United States Government spacecraft utilizing nuclear power systems either with a potential for criticality or above a minimum threshold of radioactivity, in accordance with the existing interagency review process. To inform this decision, the Secretary of Energy shall conduct a nuclear safety analysis for evaluation by an ad hoc Interagency Nuclear Safety Review Panel that will evaluate the risks associated with launch and in-space operations.

The Secretary of Energy shall:

• Assist the Secretary of Transportation in the licensing of space transportation activities involving spacecraft with nuclear power systems;

• Provide nuclear safety monitoring to ensure that operations in space are consistent with any safety evaluations performed; and

• Maintain the capability and infrastructure to develop and furnish nuclear power systems for use in United States Government space systems.

Radiofrequency Spectrum and Interference Protection

The United States Government shall:

• Seek to protect U. S. global access to, and operation in, the radiofrequency spectrum and related orbital assignments required to support the use of space by the United States Government, its allies, and U. S. commercial users;

• Explicitly address requirements for radiofrequency spectrum and orbital assignments prior to approving acquisition of space capabilities;

• Seek to ensure the necessary national and international regulatory frameworks will remain in place over the lifetime of the system;

• Identify impacts to government space systems prior to reallocating spectrum for commercial, federal, or shared use;

• Enhance capabilities and techniques, in cooperation with civil, commercial, and foreign partners, to identify, locate, and attribute sources of radio frequency interference, and take necessary measures to sustain the radiofrequency environment in which critical U. S. space systems operate; and

• Seek appropriate regulatory approval under U. S. domestic regulations for United States Government earth stations operating with commercially owned satellites, consistent with the regulatory approval granted to analogous commercial earth stations.

Assurance and Resilience of Mission-Essential Functions

The United States shall:

· Assure space-enabled mission-essential functions by developing the techniques, measures, relationships, and capabilities necessary to maintain continuity of services;

Such efforts may include enhancing the protection and resilience of selected spacecraft and supporting infrastructure;

· Develop and exercise capabilities and plans for operating in and through a degraded, disrupted, or denied space environment for the purposes of maintaining mission-essential functions; and

· Address mission assurance requirements and space system resilience in the acquisition of future space capabilities and supporting infrastructure.

Sector Guidelines

United States space activities are conducted in three distinct but interdependent sectors: commercial, civil, and national security.

Commercial Space Guidelines

The term "commercial," for the purposes of this policy, refers to space goods, services, or activities provided by private sector enterprises that bear a reasonable portion of the investment risk and responsibility for the activity, operate in accordance with typical market-based incentives for controlling cost and optimizing return on investment, and have the legal capacity to offer these goods or services to existing or potential nongovernmental customers. To promote a robust domestic commercial space industry, departments and agencies shall:

· Purchase and use commercial space capabilities and services to the maximum practical extent when such capabilities and services are available in the marketplace and meet United States Government requirements;

• Modify commercial space capabilities and services to meet government requirements when existing commercial capabilities and services do not fully meet these requirements and the potential modification represents a more cost-effective and timely acquisition approach for the government;

• Actively explore the use of inventive, nontraditional arrangements for acquiring commercial space goods and services to meet United States Government requirements, including measures such as public-private partnerships, hosting government capabilities on commercial spacecraft, and purchasing scientific or operational data products from commercial satellite operators in support of government missions;

• Develop governmental space systems only when it is in the national interest and there is no suitable, cost-effective U. S. commercial or, as appropriate, foreign commercial service or system that is or will be available;

• Refrain from conducting United States Government space activities that preclude, discourage, or compete with U. S. commercial space activities, unless required by national security or public safety;

• Pursue potential opportunities for transferring routine, operational space functions to the commercial space sector where beneficial and cost-effective, except where the government has legal, security, or safety needs that would preclude commercialization;

• Cultivate increased technological innovation and entrepreneurship in the commercial space sector through the use of incentives such as prizes and competitions;

• Ensure that United States Government space technology and infrastructure are made available for commercial use on a reimbursable, noninterference, and equitable basis to the maximum practical extent;

• Minimize, as much as possible, the regulatory burden for commercial space activities and ensure that the regulatory environment for licensing space activities is timely and responsive;

• Foster fair and open global trade and commerce through the promotion of suitable standards and regulations that have been developed with input from U. S. industry;

• Encourage the purchase and use of U. S. commercial space services and capabilities in international cooperative arrangements; and

• Actively promote the export of U. S. commercially developed and available space goods and services, including those developed by small- and medium-sized enterprises, for use in foreign markets, consistent with U. S. technology transfer and nonproliferation objectives.

The United States Trade Representative (USTR) has the primary responsibility in the Federal Government for international trade agreements to which the United States is a party. USTR, in consultation with other relevant departments and agencies, will lead any efforts relating to the negotiation and implementation of trade disciplines governing trade in goods and services related to space.

Civil Space Guidelines

Space Science, Exploration, and Discovery

The Administrator of NASA shall:

• Set far-reaching exploration milestones. By 2025, begin crewed missions beyond the moon, including sending humans to an asteroid. By the mid-2030s, send humans to orbit Mars and return them safely to Earth;

• Continue the operation of the International Space Station (ISS), in cooperation with its international partners, likely to 2020 or beyond, and expand efforts to: utilize the ISS for scientific, technological, commercial, diplomatic, and educational purposes; support activities requiring the unique attributes of humans in space; serve as a continuous human presence in Earth orbit; and support future objectives in human

space exploration;
• Seek partnerships with the private sector to enable safe, reliable, and cost-effective commercial spaceflight capabilities and services for the transport of crew and cargo to and from the ISS;
• Implement a new space technology development and test program, working with industry, academia, and international partners to build, fly, and test several key technologies that can increase the capabilities, decrease the costs, and expand the opportunities for future space activities;
• Conduct research and development in support of next-generation launch systems, including new U.S. rocket engine technologies;
• Maintain a sustained robotic presence in the solar system to: conduct scientific investigations of other planetary bodies; demonstrate new technologies; and scout locations for future human missions;
• Continue a strong program of space science for observations, research, and analysis of our Sun, solar system, and universe to enhance knowledge of the cosmos, further our understanding of fundamental natural and physical sciences, understand the conditions that may support the development of life, and search for planetary bodies and Earth–like planets in orbit around other stars; and
• Pursue capabilities, in cooperation with other departments, agencies, and commercial partners, to detect, track, catalog, and characterize near-Earth objects to reduce the risk of harm to humans from an unexpected impact on our planet and to identify potentially resource-rich planetary objects.

Environmental Earth Observation and Weather

To continue and improve a broad array of programs of space-based observation, research, and analysis of the Earth's land, oceans, and atmosphere:
• The NASA Administrator, in coordination with other appropriate de-

partments and agencies, shall conduct a program to enhance U. S. global climate change research and sustained monitoring capabilities, advance research into and scientific knowledge of the Earth by accelerating the development of new Earth observing satellites, and develop and test capabilities for use by other civil departments and agencies for operational purposes.

· The Secretary of Commerce, through the National Oceanic and Atmospheric Administration (NOAA) Administrator, and in coordination with the NASA Administrator and other appropriate departments and agencies, shall, in support of operational requirements:

· · Transition mature research and development Earth observation satellites to long-term operations;

· · Use international partnerships to help sustain and enhance weather, climate, ocean, and coastal observation from space; and

· · Be responsible for the requirements, funding, acquisition, and operation of civil operational environmental satellites in support of weather forecasting, climate monitoring, ocean and coastal observations, and space weather forecasting. NOAA will primarily utilize NASA as the acquisition agent for operational environmental satellites for these activities and programs.

· The Secretary of Commerce, through the NOAA Administrator, the Secretary of Defense, through the Secretary of the Air Force, and the NASA Administrator shall work together and with their international partners to ensure uninterrupted, operational polar-orbiting environmental satellite observations. The Secretary of Defense shall be responsible for the morning orbit, and the Secretary of Commerce shall be responsible for the afternoon orbit. The departments shall continue to partner in developing and fielding a shared ground system, with the coordinated programs operated by NOAA. Further, the departments shall ensure the continued full sharing of data from all systems.

Land Remote Sensing

The Secretary of the Interior, through the Director of the United States Geological Survey (USGS), shall:

· Conduct research on natural and human-induced changes to Earth's land, land cover, and inland surface waters, and manage a global land surface data national archive and its distribution;

· Determine the operational requirements for collection, processing, archiving, and distribution of land surface data to the United States Government and other users; and

· Be responsible, in coordination with the Secretary of Defense, the Secretary of Homeland Security, and the Director of National Intelligence, for providing remote sensing information related to the environment and disasters that is acquired from national security space systems to other civil government agencies.

In support of these critical needs, the Secretary of the Interior, through the Director of the USGS, and the NASA Administrator shall work together in maintaining a program for operational land remote sensing observations.

The NASA and NOAA Administrators and the Director of the USGS shall:

· Ensure that civil space acquisition processes and capabilities are not unnecessarily duplicated; and

· Continue to develop civil applications and information tools based on data collected by Earth observation satellites. These civil capabilities will be developed, to the greatest extent possible, using known standards and open protocols, and the applications will be made available to the public;

The Secretary of Commerce, through the Administrator of NOAA, shall provide for the regulation and licensing of the operation of commercial sector remote sensing systems.

National Security Space Guidelines

The Secretary of Defense and the Director of National Intelligence, in consultation with other appropriate heads of departments and agencies, shall:

• Develop, acquire, and operate space systems and supporting information systems and networks to support U. S. national security and enable defense and intelligence operations during times of peace, crisis, and conflict;

Ensure cost-effective survivability of space capabilities, including supporting information systems and networks, commensurate with their planned use, the consequences of lost or degraded capability, the threat, and the availability of other means to perform the mission;

• Reinvigorate U. S. leadership by promoting technology development, improving industrial capacity, and maintaining a robust supplier base necessary to support our most critical national security interests;

• Develop and implement plans, procedures, techniques, and capabilities necessary to assure critical national security space-enabled missions. Options for mission assurance may include rapid restoration of space assets and leveraging allied, foreign, and/or commercial space and non-space capabilities to help perform the mission;

• Maintain and integrate space surveillance, intelligence, and other information to develop accurate and timely SSA. SSA information shall be used to support national and homeland security, civil space agencies, particularly human space flight activities, and commercial and foreign space operations;

• Improve, develop, and demonstrate, in cooperation with relevant departments and agencies and commercial and foreign entities, the ability to rapidly detect, warn, characterize, and attribute natural and man-made disturbances to space systems of U. S. interest;and

• Develop and apply advanced technologies and capabilities that respond to changes to the threat environment.

The Secretary of Defense shall:

· Be responsible, with support from the Director of National Intelligence, for the development, acquisition, operation, maintenance, and modernization of SSA capabilities;

· Develop capabilities, plans, and options to deter, defend against, and, if necessary, defeat efforts to interfere with or attack U. S. or allied space systems;

· Maintain the capabilities to execute the space support, force enhancement, space control, and force application missions; and

· Provide, as launch agent for both the defense and intelligence sectors, reliable, affordable, and timely space access for national security purposes.

The Director of National Intelligence shall:

· Enhance foundational intelligence collection and single – and all – source intelligence analysis;

Develop, obtain, and operate space capabilities to support strategic goals, intelligence priorities, and assigned tasks;

· Provide robust, timely, and effective collection, processing, analysis, and dissemination of information on foreign space and supporting information system activities;

· Develop and enhance innovative analytic tools and techniques to use and share information from traditional and nontraditional sources for understanding foreign space-related activities;

· Identify and characterize current and future threats to U. S. space missions for the purposes of enabling effective protection, deterrence, and defense;

Integrate all-source intelligence of foreign space capabilities and intentions with space surveillance information to produce enhanced intelligence products that support SSA;

· Support national defense and homeland security planning and satisfy operational requirements as a major intelligence mission;

· Support monitoring, compliance, and verification for transparency and confidence-building measures and, if applicable, arms control agreements; and

· Coordinate on any radiofrequency surveys from space conducted by United States Government departments or agencies and review, as appropriate, any radiofrequency surveys from space conducted by licensed private sector operators or by state and local governments.

外层空间法大事记(2010年)

陈丽君 马闻羲 李红

相关国家驻京大使和外交官出席亚太空间合作组织迎新之旅。据亚太空间合作组织网站发布,有关国家驻北京使馆工作的外交官于2010年1月12日应邀参观了亚太空间合作组织的设施等,并听取了简报。在听取了亚太空间合作组织活动的介绍并参观了亚太空间合作组织设施后,许多与会者表现出了作为准成员加入亚太空间合作组织的兴趣,并询问项目合作的细节。秘书长张伟先生邀请所有非成员加入亚太空间合作组织。所有参加国希望在未来继续与亚太空间合作组织进行合作。

亚太区域空间机构论坛第十六届会议召开。2010年1月26—29日在曼谷举行了亚洲太平洋区域空间机构论坛(亚太区域空间机构论坛)第十六届会议。会议的主题是"空间应用:对人的安全和安保的贡献"。论坛参加者除其他外审议了与"亚洲哨兵"步骤2阶段、亚太区域空间机构论坛亚太区域卫星技术方案、环境方面空间应用方案、全球导航卫星系统以及空间教育和提高认识有关的活动。

联合国和平利用外层空间委员会科技小组委员会第47届会议召开。据联合国外空委网站发布,2010年2月8~19日,联合国外空委科技小组委员会第 47 届会议在维也纳召开。有 57 个成员国的代表、国际原子能机构(原子能机构)、国际电信联盟(国际电联)和世界气象组织的观察员、欧空局等在委员会享有常设观察员地位的政府间组织的观察员及国际宇航联合会等在委员会享有常设观察员地位的非政府组织的观察员出席了该届会议。会议主要就联合国空间应用方案;第三次外空会议各项建议的执行情况;有关用卫星对地球进行遥感的事项,包括对发展中国家的各种应用和对地球环境的监测;空间碎片;借助空间系统的灾害管理支助;全球导航卫星系统最新发展情况;在外层空间使用核动力源;近地天体;国际空间气象举措;外层空间活动的长期可持续性等议题进行审议。中国代表团团长田玉龙在会议上做了发言。

联合国外空委法律小组委员会第 49 届会议召开。据联合国外空委网站发布,2010 年 3 月 22 日—4 月 1 日,联合国外空委法律小组委员会第 49 届会议在维也纳召开。为期两周的会议主要就联合国五项外层空间条约的现状和适用情况、外层空间的定义和划界、《移动设备国际利益公约》空间资产议定书草案、与和平探索和利用外空有关的国家立法交流等议题进行审议。中国驻维也纳联合国及其他国际组织代表胡小笛大使率由外交部、国家航天局组成的中国代表团与会,并就一般性交换意见议题做了发言。会议期间,国际空间法学会和欧洲空间法中心举行了一次题为"国家空间立法:为空间活动的增长精心打造法律引擎"的专题讨论会,专题讨论会由国际空间法学会的 Tanja Masson – Zwaan 和欧洲空间法中心的 Sergio Marchisio 主持。小组委员会在专题讨论会上听取了专题介绍。小组委员会主席和国家空间立法问题工作组主席作了闭会致辞。

人类首架空天飞机发射成功。美国 X – 37B 成功发射。据欧洲时报网报道,美国东部时间 2010 年 4 月 22 日 19 点 52 分,美国研制的人类首架空天飞机 X – 37B 成功发射升空,"阿特拉斯 5 号"火箭执行了此次发射任务。X – 37B 在战时,有能力对敌国卫星和其他航天器进行军事行动,包括控制、捕获和摧毁敌国航天器,对敌国进行军事侦察等。

X-37B 发射后进入地球轨道并在太空遨游，但在太空具体逗留时间尚未确定，X-37B 在设计上能够执行最长为期 270 天的太空任务。结束太空之旅后，X-37B 进入自动驾驶模式返回地球，最后在加州范登堡空军基地或者附近备用基地——爱德华兹空军基地着陆。

X-37B 空天飞机尺寸大约只有美国现役航天飞机的四分之一，长约 8.8 米，翼展约 4.6 米，起飞重量超过 5 吨。专家分析称，X-37B 空天飞机是 1983 年"哥伦比亚号"航天飞机爆炸之后最值得期待的太空发射之一，在近 20 年的研制中，美国政府共投入数亿美元资金。虽然 X-37B 仅是一种小型航天飞行器，但却是美军最高等军事机密之一。除了该航天器的运行性能、存在缺陷等细节都被严格保密之外，其控制中枢的方位也被列为高等军事机密。

中国成功发射第四颗北斗导航卫星。中新网西昌 6 月 3 日电，2010 年 6 月 2 日晚 23 时 53 分，中国在西昌卫星发射中心用"长征三号丙"运载火箭，将第四颗北斗导航卫星成功送入太空预定轨道，这标志着北斗卫星导航系统组网建设又迈出重要一步。第四颗北斗导航卫星及其运载火箭"长征三号丙"，分别由中国航天科技集团公司所属中国空间技术研究院和中国运载火箭技术研究院研制。本次卫星发射是中国"长征"系列运载火箭的第 124 次航天飞行。

第二届环太平洋地区空间法研讨会在美国夏威夷召开。2010 年 6 月 18—19 日，第二届环太平洋地区空间法研讨会在美国夏威夷召开。本次会议的主题是亚太地区地球观测、环境和遥感法。来自美国、中国、日本、澳大利亚、韩国、墨西哥、哥伦比亚等国的空间法学者和专家就会议主题进行了两天的密集讨论。本次会议是由美国密西西比大学国家遥感、航空和空间法中心主办的，会议由该中心主任乔安娜·葛布里诺兹教授主持。本次会议在去年召开的亚太国家空间立法峰会的基础上，对环太平洋国家的空间法律问题做了进一步的探讨和交流，加深了环太平洋国际空间法学者的相互了解和友谊。

国际空间站政策与法律问题研讨会在北京举行。2010年6月25日,由北京航空航天大学法学院主办、外层空间法研究所承办的"国际空间站政策与法律问题研讨会"在北京举行,来自美国密西西比大学、香港大学、中国政法大学、北京理工大学、北京航空航天大学、中国空间法学会、《中国航天报》等单位的共20余位代表与会。研讨会开幕式由北京航空航天大学法学院副院长孙新强教授主持。北京航空航天大学法学院外层空间法研究所所长高全喜教授和中国空间法学会秘书长戚永亮研究员分别致辞。

奥巴马发布美国太空政策,扬弃"太空军事对抗"。据中国新闻网报道,美国总统奥巴马2010年6月28日发布新版国家航天政策。与早前公布的国家安全战略如出一辙,奥巴马扬弃前任小布什"太空军事对抗"的单边主义论调,再举"和为贵"大旗,寻求加强国际航天合作。遵循"和平合作"基调,新版美国国家太空政策列出诸多国际太空合作领域,包括空间探索、地球观测、气候变化研究及环境数据共享、减灾救灾乃至监测太空垃圾等。引人关注的是,奥巴马将过去美国排斥他国介入的全球卫星导航系统(GPS)研发也纳入合作领域,表示未来美国可利用境外全球卫星导航系统服务,以此增强美国全球卫星导航系统的适应能力与兼容程度。

韩国首枚运载火箭发射升空,卫星未进入预定轨道。2010年8月25日下午,韩国首枚运载火箭"罗老"号搭载着本国生产的科学技术卫星在本土罗老宇航中心发射升空。由于星箭未能按计划分离,卫星未进入预定轨道。韩国专家认为,这次发射应视为"成功一半",因为尽管卫星未能进入预定轨道,但火箭一切功能正常。

第61届国际宇航大会暨第53届国际空间法研讨会在布拉格召开。2010年9月27日至10月1日,第61届国际宇航联合会(IAF)大会在捷克布拉格举行,来自世界各国航天界的近3 000名代表将在5天的时间内,围绕航天工业、科学和教育等方面的最新动态展开交流和对话。本届国际宇航联大会的主题是"造福人类及探索未来的航天"。包括"政府航天政策对工业界的影响"、推进全球探索战略发展下一代航天系统运行构想、国际空间站上科学实验研究等议题。除了继续关注民用空间技术,同时也将目光投向了未来空间科学探索。大会不仅包括涉及空间科学、空间技术、空间应用、空间人文等方面的技术分组和互动分组讨论会,还包括航天展览,各国航天局官员、专家学者参与的高端讲坛、青年学者计划、学生会议以及丰富多彩的民族文化活动等。会议还宣布,第64届国际宇航联大会将于2013年在中国举办。

大会期间,国际空间法学会也组织召开了第53届国际空间法年会,主题为"合作型人类空间项目的法律问题",这也是由国际宇航联合会与国际空间法学会共同举办的跨学科研讨会。此外,第19届Manfred Lachs空间法模拟法庭世界总决赛也同时举行。

中国"嫦娥二号"卫星发射成功。中新网西昌10月1日电,西昌卫星发射中心宣布,"嫦娥二号"卫星准确入轨,发射圆满成功。"嫦娥二号"卫星是中国自主研制的第2颗月球探测卫星,继2007年"嫦娥一号"一举实现中华民族千年奔月梦想之后,"嫦娥二号"的成功发射,标志着中国探月工程又向前迈出重要一步。本次发射是"长征三号丙"运载火箭首次担负月球探测卫星发射任务,也是中国"长征"系列运载火箭第131次航天飞行。

空间站伙伴国发布国际对接标准。据美国航空航天局网站2010年10月19日报道,国际空间站多边协调委员会(MCB)已经批准了《国际对接系统标准》(International Docking System Standard)。这项国际标准将为未来航天器的对接提供通用界面指导方针。适用的航天器范围从低地球轨道任务到深空探测任务的载人飞行器和自动飞行器。

多边协调委员会主席比尔·杰斯腾梅尔(Bill Gerstenmaier)表示,该标准的目标就是明确"创建标准界面"的必要条件,以确保在未来的任务和活动中,两个不同的航天器能够在太空中对接。这个标准将使新近的国际合作太空任务的开发变得简单,使国际乘员救援任务的实现成为可能。

多边协调委员会由来自NASA、俄罗斯联邦航天局、日本文教省、欧空局和加拿大航天局的高级代表组成,是空间站的高级管理委员会。它在各伙伴国之间协调空间站这个在轨实验室的运行和活动。

外层空间的新发展研讨会在泰国曼谷举行。2010年11月16日至19日,由联合国外空事务办公室、欧洲空间局、亚太空间合作组织及泰国政府举办主题为"外空活动新发展:确立责任制度及国内法律和政策框架"的联合国外空事务办公室/泰国空间法论坛在泰国曼谷举行。来自世界各地官员、学者及国际组织的官员100余人参加了该会议。联合国外空事务办公室每年将组织举办一次空间法论坛,并将会议成果予以总结,在每年3月份正式报告联合国和平利用外层空间委员会法律小组委员会会议。

全球导航卫星系统(ICG)国际委员会第五次会议在意大利都灵举行。2010年12月18—22日,全球导航卫星系统(ICG)国际委员会第五次会议在意大利都灵举行,本次活动由意大利和代表欧盟的欧洲委员会联合主办。会议讨论了全球导航卫星系统技术处于多系统接收器时代以及全球导航卫星系统的互操作性对时序和其他用户的应用影响。

南非走向"新太空时代"。南非科技部于2010年12月在南非最大城市约翰内斯堡宣布,南非将组建自己的航天机构。这一引人注目的举措将使南非成为继尼日利亚、阿尔及利亚和埃及之后,第四个成立国家航天机构的非洲国家。南非还同时发布了国家航天战略。南非科技部表示,这标志着南非进入了一个"新太空时代"。